Buddha Land
in the
Human World

The Making of the Buddha Memorial Center

Written by Pan Xuan
with Venerable Master Hsing Yun

Translated by Robert Smitheram, Ph.D
Edited by Fo Guang Shan International Translation Center

© 2013 Buddha's Light Publishing
First English edition

By Pan Xuan
Translated by Robert Smitheram Ph.D
Book and cover design for the Chinese edition by Commonwealth Publishing

Published by Buddha's Light Publishing
3456 S. Glenmark Drive
Hacienda Heights, CA 91745, U.S.A.
Tel: (626) 923-5144
Fax: (626) 923-5145
E-mail: itc@blia.org
Website: www.blpusa.com

Printed in Taiwan.

Library of Congress Cataloging-in-Publication Data

Pan, Xuan.
  [Ren jian fo guo. English]
  Buddha land in the human world : the making of the Buddha Memorial Center / written by Panxuan with Venerable Master Hsing Yun ; translated by Robert Smitheram. -- First English Edition.
      pages cm
  ISBN 978-1-932293-81-4
  1. Buddhist centers—Taiwan. 2. Fo guang shan (Kao-hsiung hsien, Taiwan). Fo tuo ji nian guan. I. Xingyun, 1927- II. Smitheram, Robert, translator. III. Title.

BQ6354.T282F613 2013
294.3'4350951249—dc23

                              2013001357

Acknowledgement

Like all of Buddha's Light Publishing's endeavors, this project benefited from the contributions of many people. We would like to thank the Chief Executive of the Fo Guang Shan International Translation Center, Venerable Tzu Jung, as well as its Director, Venerable Yi Chao. We would also like to thank Venerable Hui Chi and Venerable Hui Dong, the abbots of Hsi Lai Temple, for their support and leadership.

We would like to thank the team at Commonwealth Publishing for the richly textured design of the Chinese edition, and to the many people who allowed use of their photographs and their interviews. Robert Smitheram provided the translation for the English edition, and the translation was edited by John Gill and Jonathan Ko. The book design was adapted for the English edition by Wan Kah Ong and Xiaoyang Zhang. The manuscript was proofread and prepared for publication by Louvenia Ortega, Tom Manzo, Shujan Cheng, Amanda Ling, and Nathan Michon. Our appreciation goes to everyone who supported this project from conception to completion.

 Building Space

All Wisdom and All Conditions

A Word from the Publisher

Compassion and Wisdom

——The Buddha Memorial Center Founded by the Venerable Master
Hsing Yun

Charles H.C. Kao

Whenever a great new building appears in the world, it becomes a point of international focus. Now a new structure is about to be born that has already grabbed the attention of so many people. It is a place that radiates the light of culture and the brilliance of Buddhism. I am of course speaking of the Buddha Memorial Center of Fo Guang Shan.

The mastermind behind this magnificent complex is Venerable Master Hsing Yun. For many years now he has harbored a fervent dream deep within his heart: to make it possible for the people of the world to experience the Buddha's spirit. And in December of the hundredth year of the Republic of China's founding (2011), Venerable Master Hsing Yun realized his dream and presented it to the people of Taiwan, the Chinese world, and the international Buddhist community.

Looking back on how the building and consecration of this space began with the touring of the Buddha relic in 1998, the Buddha Memorial Center occupies one hundred hectares (247 acres) of land at Fo Guang Shan in Kaohsiung, Taiwan. It has been nine years in the making, and will be completed in

December of this year. During this lengthy process, we can well imagine the countless hardships, the countless exertions, and the countless expectations that arose along the way.

For the past few years I have celebrated the Lunar New Year at Fo Guang Shan. Every time I went to hear Venerable Master Hsing Yun speak and see the Buddha Memorial Center under construction. Every time I walked over to the construction site, I was overwhelmed by the magnificence of the memorial complex. Every time I left, I was concerned as to whether these grand buildings could really be completed on schedule.

On my most recent visit, I was strolling about the complex of towering buildings that were just about completed. Regardless of whether I was gazing up at the Main Hall, peering distantly at the Four Noble Truths Stupas, or taking a panoramic view of the eight pagodas, I enjoyed the view of the complex from every angle. This has left me with a lasting sense of admiration for Venerable Master Hsing Yun's vision and dedication.

I am not a Buddhist, but finding myself situated in this vast complex that is the Buddha Memorial Center, I became suddenly struck by three compelling feelings:

First, the Scope of the Center is Expansive

The Buddha relic enshrined in the Buddha Memorial Center returns us to the Buddha's teachings twenty-six hundred years ago. But not only does the center trace itself back to the Buddha's mind of the ancient past, but it also looks forward thousands of years into the future. One example is the forward-looking design of the "Underground Palaces."

The "Underground Palaces" beneath the Buddha Memorial Center store cultural items that are both contemporary and commemorative in nature, which will enable future generations to better understand the history of their predecessors. In the future, one Underground Palace will be opened every one hundred years, with all forty-eight being unearthed only after forty-eight hundred years—an immense amount of time.

In February of 2011, I participated in a Dharma Service to consign the cultural treasures to the Underground Palaces. I was fortunate enough to have the positive karmic connections which allowed me to be the one to place a "five-grain brick," a precious cultural artifact from the Buddha's homeland, into the Underground Palace with my own hands. When it is unearthed again in the future, I suspect several hundred years will have elapsed. On that occasion I realized that humanity continues on over generations, for indeed, each generation is a link to the next.

Second, the Space of the Center is Vibrant

For more than half a century now, Venerable Master Hsing Yun has taken the profound principles of Buddhism and recorded them in books and articles, presented them as easily understandable stories, edited them into clear and sonorous songs, and choreographed them into moving plays. Now, by constructing the Buddha Memorial Center, he has taken the profound principles of Buddhism and mapped them into a space that is welcoming and accessible to everyone.

For those who like to worship the Buddha or practice meditation, the center has Buddha shrines and small caves to practice mediation. For those who like art and literature, the center has art galleries. For those who like the secluded serenity of a garden, there is a recreation of the "Jetavana Grove" from the sutras, where luxurious flowers and trees are nestled amid the stones and hills. For those who like food and drink, the center has the Water Drop teahouses, with their graceful, beauteous design, kept in pristine condition.

Be they adults, children, or seniors, everyone can find a comfortable, suitable location at the Buddha Memorial Center. This demonstrates how Fo Guang Shan excels in its understanding of people's hearts: All these locations leave a vivid, lasting impression upon everyone, due to the fact that all of this is built with a sense of devotion and a commitment to good works.

Third, the Center has a Human Quality

I have never forgotten the Venerable Master Hsing Yun's explanation of Humanistic Buddhism:

"What the Buddha taught, what is needed by the people, what is pure, what is good and beautiful—all such teachings that can help enhance human happiness constitute Humanistic Buddhism."

This reasonable and easily understandable explanation is physically embodied in the "eight pagodas."

The second to seventh floors in each of the eight pagodas serve as museum spaces for enshrining Buddhist cultural artifacts, fulfilling "what the Buddha taught." The ground floor of each pagoda is built for youth activities, and the facilities are specifically designed to appeal to young people. There are social services provided by the Public Education Trust Fund, as well as reception areas that provide visitors with tea and other services, focusing on "what is needed by the people."

The scope, the place, and the human quality of the Buddha Memorial Center fuses history with religion, faith with culture, and life with practice. These are all drawn together to make the Buddha Memorial Center truly substantial.

Venerable Master Hsing Yun is the leader of the "Humanistic Buddhism" movement, as well as an active participant in the rapid economic development dubbed the "Taiwan Miracle," the "Quiet Revolution" of Taiwan's democratization, and the growing sense of "Taiwan Pride." In his life, he has reformed religion, improved people's hearts, and changed the world.

Standing tall in southern Taiwan, the Buddha Memorial Center represents the innovative spirit of Fo Guang Shan. More importantly, it is also a new spiritual landmark which Venerable Master Hsing Yun has dedicated his life to construct, one that opens the way for all people to pursue compassion and wisdom.

October 18th, 2011

Charles H.C. Kao
Founder
Commonwealth Publishing
Global Views Educational Foundation

Preface

Hsing Yun

Forty years ago, I made my first trip to India on a pilgrimage to the sacred sites of Buddhism. Since then, I have made six more trips to India. I have walked through the Uruvilva Forest where the Buddha practiced asceticism. I have climbed to the top of Vulture Peak where the Buddha preached the Dharma. I have bowed before the seat under the *bodhi* tree where the Buddha attained awakening, and I have also knelt outside Kusinagara where the Buddha passed into final *nirvana*. I have tried hard to commit such moments to memory and have carefully made my search: oh Buddha, where are you?

Later on, I wandered around the world teaching. I have walked through the Red Square in Moscow. I have seen the Temple of Venus and Roma with its pantheon of statues. I once paced before the murals at Dunhuang, and have stood transfixed before the great Buddha statutes at the Yungang and Longmen grottoes. Even as I exclaimed in wonderment at the magnificent adornments, I still thought this: Where is the sacred Buddhist site that is dedicated to the hearts and minds of modern people?

I recalled how in February of 1998 a true relic of the Buddha, given by Kunga Dorje Rinpoche and attested to by a signed statement from twelve other rinpoches, was welcomed to Taiwan after its flight from India through Thailand. The excitement of that grand occasion was unprecedented, and the crowds were joyously enthusiastic. Such was the incomparable influence it had upon society that we decided to start planning for the construction of the Buddha Memorial Center. Then, we went from site selection to construction, and now thirteen years have passed in a flash.

During this period, there were quite a few difficulties with harried personnel, as well as many project meetings that entailed construction changes, all of which had to be coordinated with the government's various rules and regulations. But thanks to the intercession of the Buddha's light and joint effort of positive connections from all directions, we were fortunately able to overcome each and every difficulty. With the hope and blessings of people around the world, the Buddha Memorial Center was officially completed and opened to the public on December 25th, 2011.

People ask me: "Why build a Buddha Memorial Center?" Actually, it holds the same importance as the construction of the Taipei Metro or the Taiwan High Speed Rail. What makes them different is that the metro or high speed rail was built for worldly needs, while the Buddha Memorial Center was built for posterity and for the hearts and minds of humanity. That is why I said, "One who is able to understand 'non-self,' is one who is able to build the Buddha Memorial Center."

The completed Buddha Memorial Center includes a Front Hall which provides various services. Then there are the three main shrines and eight exhibition halls, for worship and sight-seeing. This is followed by the eight pagodas, with the 108-meter tall Buddha statute towering straight above, the statues of the founders of the Eight Schools of Chinese Buddhism, and the eighteen arhats, with their compassionate features. It is our hope that everyone who comes here can make a heartfelt connection with the Buddha, light the lamp of the human spirit, and learn from the Buddha's compassion and wisdom. Once one's spirit is purified and one's character is refined, we can then create a Buddha Land in the human world that is blessed with happiness. We can come to understand that the Pure Land is right before us, and that the Buddha is in the heart of everyone.

Once completed, the Buddha Memorial Center will belong to everyone, everywhere: As long as there is someone who needs it, that person can come to it. It is both cultural and educational; everyone can join here in fellowship, be they individuals, families, school groups, or organizations. They can all come together and learn here. It is our hope that those who come here will be able to experience what the collective power of everyone's vows can accomplish. We also wish that everyone will be inspired by the beauty and goodness of positive connections in the world.

Here I would like to thank those individuals everywhere who at one time or another participated and supported the construction of this center. In particular, it was under the leadership of Professor Charles H.C. Kao, the founder of the Commonwealth Publishing Group, that Miss Pan Xuan wrote this volume, entitled: *Buddha Land in the Human World*. Many of her colleagues also contributed to the editing. This book gives everyone an understanding of the Buddha Memorial Center as well as the story behind its construction. I would like to thank them for all their effort and devotion.

On this fortuitous moment marking the one hundredth year of the Republic of China's establishment, I pray that the completion of the Buddha Memorial Center and its opening to the public, as well as the publishing of *Buddha Land in the Human World*, will bring harmony to society and peace to humankind. I pray for the blessings of the Triple Gem, peace in the world, and a permanent end to war. May all your wishes be fulfilled and may you find peace and happiness.

——Founder's Hall at Fo Guang Shan, October of 2011

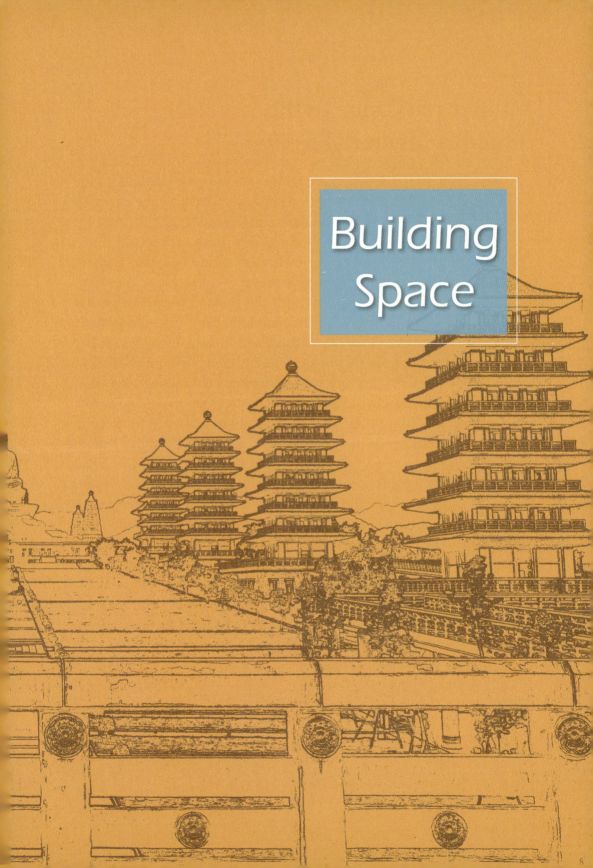

Building
Space

When You Come to the
Buddha Memorial Center

"Wow, the Buddha Memorial Center is really huge!"

Nearly everyone who finds their way here says such words. The magnificent buildings that greet their eyes far exceed what many would imagine a "reliquary pagoda" to be.

Venerable Master Hsing Yun built the Buddha Memorial Center due to the extraordinary circumstances that led to acquiring the Buddha's tooth relic. Throughout Buddhist history, many glorious pagodas became pilgrimage sites for Buddhists to visit, pay homage to the Buddha's relics, and quietly contemplate the Dharma. Many of these ancient pagodas were built of wood, stone, or brick. Owing to the harsh effects of weather and the passage of time, they have slowly fallen into decay. Even if repaired, they would still be things from antiquity.

Aside from enabling visitors to climb its heights for the view and to worship a true relic of the Buddha in person, what then does it mean to be a twenty-first century pagoda? What can be done to ensure that the larger community can connect with the Buddha Memorial Center? What can be done to ensure that this connection grants each individual a heart filled with joy, so that they are inspired and touched, and can take the experience home with them? These questions have been the center of attention for Master Hsing Yun for many years. Many ideas and opinions were proposed and considered. The Buddha's greatness is without peer, so what is the need to build a center devoted to him? On this point, Venerable Master Hsing Yun is quite clear.

Words of Venerable Master Hsing Yun:

I wrote The Biography of Sakyamuni Buddha some years ago. In the biography, when the Buddha had reached eighty years of age, he announced the day that he will enter final nirvana. All of his disciples feared that they would lose the support of their teacher.

Ananda was crying. He asked the Buddha what they should do after he entered final nirvana. After pondering the matter, the Buddha gave the following instructions:

"After I pass into final nirvana and am cremated, gather up my relics and build a stupa¹ at the crossroads, so that those who see it can admire it and develop faith."

The Buddha does not need anyone's worship or reverence, it is living beings that need inspiration to develop wholesome thoughts and purify their minds. By worshipping a memorial, people can come to know the Buddha's Dharma body, and their feelings of admiration can be elevated into wanting to learn about the Buddha's virtues and practice them in everyday life.

The Buddha doesn't need a memorial, but living beings do. I built this pagoda with that story in mind.

---

1 Stupa is a Sanskrit word that originally refered to ancient Indian burial mounds constructed over the relics of important religious figures, like the Buddha. The practice of building monuments to honor the relics of the Buddha and other awakened beings has continued to spread to other Buddhist lands.

On That Day in 543 BCE ....

The pagoda at the center of the Buddha Memorial Center is built in the Indian style. The yellow sandstone that makes up its exterior lends it an atmosphere of remote antiquity, but on the inside the technology is completely modern. This is the way Venerable Master Hsing Yun tells his stories. He employs the architecture as a means for telling the timeless story of the Buddha.

In 543 BCE, the Buddha passed into final *nirvana* at Kusinagara. As the kings of neighboring clans heard the news, they rushed over hoping to claim the Buddha's relics as their own so they could return to their kingdoms and enshrine them in stupas. But the Malla clan of Kusinagara felt that since the Buddha had passed into final *nirvana* in their territory, there was no reason to share the relics with anyone else. This was met with disapproval by the other kingdoms, who began to send armies in preparation to take the relics by force.

Seeing that the kings were on the verge of war, one brahman spoke up and said, "For a long time now, the Buddha amassed virtue and cultivated patience. All of you have often heard the Buddha teach the Dharma. How can you send your armies to seize his relics now that he has passed into final nirvana?"

The brahman proposed that a peaceful means be employed to divide the relics into equal shares, and everyone agreed. The Buddha's relics were then divided into eight shares so that each king got what they wished: a portion of the relics to take back to their kingdom and enshrine in a stupa.

By the 3rd century BCE, King Asoka of India's Mauryan dynasty had unified the entire Indian subcontinent. In order to propagate the Dharma, he

After refinement through more than a hundred design plans, a blueprint for the Buddha Memorial Center incorporating both Chinese and Indian architecture was born.

ordered that the relics be taken out and placed in eighty-four thousand treasure boxes for distribution to locations throughout the land, where eighty-four thousand stupas were constructed. Thus, the transmission of Buddhism popularized the building of stupas.

Two thousand years later, the Buddha's tooth relic is enshrined in the Main Hall of the Buddha Memorial Center in Taiwan. In Chinese the Main Hall is called the benguan (本館), or "founder's hall," meant to evoke Sakyamuni Buddha, the founder of Buddhism. For when you view the entire complex of the Buddha Memorial Center, including the Four Noble Truths Stupas and the eight pagodas, one can see that there is no division between primary and secondary structures, but simply a perfect symmetry between left and right, and front and back.

The Buddha Memorial Center's "Main Hall" and two of the "Four Noble Truths Stupas."
"Main" refers to the founder, Sakyamuni Buddha. In its layout, the Buddha Memorial Center
has no primary or secondary structures, only symmetrically positioned buildings.

When You Worship the Buddha's Tooth Relic

There is always a deep sense of yearning in the heart of a Buddhist: If only one could have been born during the time of the Buddha and heard his teachings with one's own ears, what a wonderful thing that would be.

It has been twenty-six hundred years since the Buddha passed into final *nirvana*, and there are many places on earth where the Dharma is no longer found. Taiwan is indeed fortunate. The growth of the Dharma has ensured that many people have developed good karmic connections so that they can revere Buddhism, believe in it, and learn about it.

When the mind and body become tranquil, life is able to develop the profound nature of awakening.

In 1998, Taiwanese society experienced a spiritual movement. Hundreds of thousands of the Buddhist faithful welcomed the Buddha's tooth relic in a solemn ceremony of homage. During the process of raising funds to build the Buddha Memorial Center, Fo Guang Shan received input from many quarters.

In Venerable Master Hsing Yun's view, clear discussion is a necessary process for strengthening faith.

The reliquary holding the Buddha's tooth relic.

Words of Venerable Master Hsing Yun:

Enshrining the Buddha's tooth relic inside the Buddha Memorial Center was not meant to emphasize the supernatural. Rather, the goal of enshrining the Buddha's tooth relic was to create activities that show the Buddha's compassion and wisdom in a way that people can experience concretely.

Through their homage to the Buddha relic, people can transform their own heart into the Buddha's heart, creating a sense of compassionate solicitude toward society and the larger community. They can transform their own hands into the Buddha's hands, so that they can dedicate themselves to good works, enthusiastically assist with public welfare, and refrain from unwholesome acts. They can transform their own eyes into the Buddha's eyes so they do not discriminate against or treat others unfairly; and they can transform their own mouth into the Buddha's mouth, so that they will always speak words of praise and not harm others with vulgar language and slander. When this happens, then the meritorious qualities of the Buddha relic can truly be embodied as the perfect integration of compassion and wisdom.

The Vow Made by a Truck Driver

While the Buddha Memorial Center was being built, the Buddha's tooth relic was temporarily enshrined in the Buddha's Tooth Relic Hall on the fourth floor of the Tathagata Hall at Fo Guang Shan. It was here

The Mani pearl on top of the Main Hall.

that wholesome connections began to form.

Fo Guang Shan's receptionist monastic shares a story of what happened not long ago:

One day a truck driver named Abiao visited and asked the receptionist, "Do you have any of those Buddha protection cards left?"

The venerable did not know what the rather abrupt question was referring to, so he asked, "Can I ask what you mean?"

As it turned out, one month ago he and a group of drivers had visited the shrine to worship the Buddha's tooth relic. Before they left, a venerable gave each of them a photograph of the relic. The truck driver took it home and told his wife, "This picture of the Buddha's tooth relic was given to me by a venerable at Fo Guang Shan. He said it can give me protection when driving my truck."

His wife then respectfully attached the photograph to the windshield in front of the driver's seat.

Several days later, this truck driver was driving down the freeway when he was rear-ended by a ten-wheeler. He was hit hard from behind and crashed into the vehicle in front of him. He was petrified with fear. Just as his life hung by a thread, he felt as if someone grabbed him by the collar and tossed him onto the right shoulder of the road.

When the paramedics found him he was badly shaken. They asked him about his condition, and as he looked over his body and moved his limbs, he said, "It seems only my arms have been scratched a bit from the thorn bushes here."

He got up and walked to the freeway and discovered that the roof above the driver's seat had been crushed inward and that the picture of the Buddha's tooth relic was ripped to pieces.

"Unbelievable!" one of the paramedics blurted out.

The same paramedic pointed to the picture and asked, "What was that?"

The driver said, "That was a picture of the Buddha's tooth relic at Fo Guang Shan."

All those who were present couldn't help but feel touched, as the crowd joined their palms together in veneration. One person said to the driver, "Fo Guang Shan's Buddha really works! Your life has been saved by the Buddha: you should go to make a vow as a way of giving thanks for the Buddha's life-saving kindness."

That was when the receptionist encountered the truck driver: he had returned to Fo Guang Shan to make a vow, but while he was there he also wanted to ask if they had any more pictures of the Buddha's tooth relic so that he could give them to his colleagues. After explaining the story to the receptionist, he vowed in front of the Buddha: "Starting today, I will be a vegetarian for the rest of my life."

Perhaps that vegetarian truck driver does not know about the history of Buddhism nor understand the profound meaning of the Dharma—but the moment he made his vow he connected with the heart of the Buddha from twenty-six hundred years ago.

The Long Journey of the Buddha's Tooth Relic

How much we understand the Dharma is something that each of us can only know for ourselves. Even if we look upon the Buddha's tooth relic and see but a small, tiny thing, we should know that the history behind it is long, and extraordinarily vast.

In 543 BCE, after the Buddha passed into final *nirvana* and was cremated, it is recorded that only three Buddha's tooth relics remained in the world. One is in Sri Lanka, and one is in Mainland China. but the third tooth drifted about on a long, winding journey.

Originally, this particular Buddha's tooth relic was carefully stored in India for more than a thousand years. During the Muslim invasion of India during the 13th century, the relic was secretly taken from the great Buddhist college of Nalanda in India and brought to Tibet, where it was enshrined in the Sakya Namgyal Monastery. That monastery was destroyed in 1968 during the Cultural Revolution, and the whereabouts of the Buddha's tooth relic were unknown. But it turned out that the relic was obtained by the Tibetan Lama Kunga Dorje Rinpoche. In order to protect the Buddha's tooth relic, Kunga Dorje Rinpoche crossed over the Himalayas at great risk to his own life. After an arduous journey, he was finally able to send the Buddha's tooth relic back to India. In India, the tooth's authenticity was confirmed by the rinpoche's teacher and several other eminent Buddhist teachers from Tibet. Kunga Dorje Rinpoche would keep and protect the relic in secret for the next thirty years.

As the years went by and Kunga Dorje Rinpoche grew older, he feared that he did not have the ability to build a temple to enshrine the Buddha's tooth relic. He hoped that he might be able to find someone to whom he could entrust it. In February of 1998, Venerable Master Hsing Yun went to India to officiate at the Triple Platform Full Ordination Ceremony. Kunga Dorje Rinpoche was moved by Venerable Master Hsing Yun's efforts to promote international Buddhist dialog, and, along with a document jointly signed by twelve other rinpoches, he presented the Buddha's tooth relic to Venerable Master Hsing Yun. In April of the same year, the relic was brought to Taiwan.

The certificate signed by twelve rinpoches verifying the authenticity of the Buddha's tooth relic.

With your great compassion and wisdom, you have broadly advanced the Buddha's teachings, and therefore we extend our heartfelt greetings:

In order to advance the Buddha's teachings in the world, you established Fo Guang Shan Monastery in Kaohsiung, Taiwan, as well as Hsi Lai Temple in Los Angeles, USA. To promote harmonious development between the Prajnayana and the Vajrayana, you inaugurated the World Buddhist Forum between the Esoteric and Exoteric traditions. To promote exchange between the Chinese and Tibetan cultures, you instituted the Chinese-Tibetan Cultural Association. To promote the growth of the Dharma, you conducted fellowship conventions worldwide. You also founded the Buddha's Light International Association, which has more than eighty chapters around the world. ensuring that the light of the Buddha's teachings reach around the world and the Dharma clouds cover all the continents. We earnestly pray that your vows will be auspiciously fulfilled.

But there is much more: You built the Fo Guang Shan Tsung Lin University in order to instruct your students. Each year you travel around the world to spread the Buddha's teachings, diligently turning the Dharma wheel, hurrying here and there in the conscientious service of the Dharma for all peoples of the world. When the Chinese Communists entered Tibet, Kunga Dorje Rinpoche obtained this relic of the Buddha at the Sakya Namgyal Monastery, which he then carried to India. Now we offer it to your Fo Guang Shan Monastery, for it is our wish that all living beings will obtain such benefit and merit. (1998)

(Translated from the Tibetan into Chinese by Prof. Liu Kuo-wei, chair of the Religious Studies Dept. at Fo Guang University.)

In 1998, Taoyaun International Airport held a ceremony to welcome the Buddha's tooth relic.

In That Moment the Relic Reappeared

The Buddha's tooth relic then began a transnational journey. Venerable Tzu Jung, a senior monastic at Fo Guang Shan, remembers, "When venerable master first heard about how the rinpoche wanted to present the Buddha's tooth relic, he felt it was very unexpected."

Ven. Tzu Jung also spoke of how twelve other rinpoches had jointly signed a statement attesting to the relic's authenticity, how Venerable Master Hsing Yun felt the relic was a wholesome karmic connection for the people of Taiwan, and how he decided to do his utmost to make this project a success.

When it was decided to receive the relic in Thailand, Ven. Tzu Jung was put in charge of organizing a "Welcoming Delegation" made up of prominent Buddhist and secular leaders.

In April of 1998, Kunga Dorje Rinpoche decided to start his trip from India on the sixth, and arrive in Thailand via Nepal. Venerable Master Hsing Yun was concerned that complications might arise from political turmoil in Nepal, so he hoped that Kunga Dorje Rinpoche could begin his trip one day earlier, on the fifth of April. Venerables Tzu Jung and Tzu Chuang had already arrived in Thailand and were prepared to meet the rinpoche. Ven. Tzu Jung remembers: "Fortunately, the rinpoche left on the fifth. The next day, due to

the political crisis, the airport was closed. Such events are truly wonderful and mysterious."

After welcoming the travel weary Kunga Dorje Rinpoche, the entire group went back to the Fo Guang Shan center in Bangkok. Ven. Tzu Jung remembers when she first set eyes upon the Buddha's tooth relic:

"When I first saw Kunga Dorje Rinpoche exiting from customs at the airport, I couldn't tell from his luggage where he was keeping the relic. It was not until we arrived at our resting place and he produced the Buddha's tooth relic that we discovered he had kept it secretly hidden on his person. I immediately prepared a reliquary and respectfully placed the Buddha's tooth relic safely within. It was then enshrined in the Buddha Hall at Fo Guang Shan Bangkok Vihara."

The relic had reappeared. From that moment onward, it would change all who came before it.

On the morning of April 8, the Buddha's birthday, after bowing before the Buddha's tooth relic, Kunga Dorje Rinpoche personally handed over the relic he had protected for thirty years to Lama Tien Pi-shuang. The relic was then brought by the welcoming delegation to the headquarters of the World Fellowship of Buddhists.

The Buddha's tooth relic had been jointly documented with the signatures of twelve rinpoches of perfect moral conduct from the four major schools of

1. The Kunga Dorje Rinpoche (Center) informs Master Hsing Yun of the intention to give him the relic.
2. Venerable Master Hsing Yun travels to Thailand to welcome the Buddha relic.
3. Devotees welcome the Buddha relic as it travels southward along Taiwan.

Tibetan Buddhism, and it had been authenticated beyond any doubt by such eminent monks as H. H. Sakya Trizin and H. H. Dilgo Khyentse Rinpoche of the Nyingma School. Upon certification and reception by Venerable Somdet Phra Phutthacharn, the deputy supreme patriarch of Thailand, the relic was formally placed into the hands of Venerable Master Hsing Yun.

Afterwards, upon the invitation of Buddhist circles in Thailand, the Buddha's tooth relic was welcomed by the World Fellowship of Buddhists in the Queen's Garden, so that the people of Thailand would be able to see and worship it.

The Taiwan Tour of the Buddha's Tooth Relic

On April 9, at 2:30 pm, a chartered China Airlines plane brought the Buddha's tooth relic to Taiwan.

The relic was escorted from Taoyuan Airport to Fo Guang Shan's Taipei Vihara by police cars. With the freeway cleared, the journey went swiftly and was free of traffic jams.

"We had just gotten on the freeway when a sudden rainstorm struck," Ven. Tzu Jung remembers, "The rain was just pouring down. I was wondering how, with such heavy rain, we would manage to get the relic out of the car when we got to Taipei. I was quite worried the whole time."

But a miracle occurred as the motorcade came down from the Yuanshan interchange, as described here by Ven. Tzu Jung:

"I remember quite clearly that as soon as I stepped out of the car, I still felt a couple drops of rain, but then in an instant, it stopped! It seemed as if the downpour had been cut off with a knife; the rain stopped smooth and clean."

The heavy rain stopped instantly, as if heaven had sent the rain specifically to purify the sanctuary.

At the temporary sanctuary in front of the Songshan Train Station, devotees had prepared altar tables in advance and were kneeling in lines

along both sides of Songlong Road to welcome the Buddha's tooth relic. Ven. Tzu Jung was directing all the activities enthusiastically.

"Once when we were very busy, we heard a lot of people making a commotion. Just as it was getting dark, a beam of light shot out of the sky and flooded Songlong Road with a golden light. Dr. Chao Ning, who was broadcasting from the scene, could not help exclaiming: 'It's truly a broad avenue of shining gold!' Ven. Yi Fa who was officiating with him said right away, 'This is the Buddha's light that shines everywhere, and so this is the path of the Buddha's light!'"

This scene was reported directly as it appeared by many TV stations, including Beautiful Life Television. On this rare occasion, many viewers from various parts of the world and the devotees present there all had a shared feeling of being blessed by the Buddha's light.

Afterwards, the Buddha's tooth relic was temporarily enshrined at Fo Guang Shan's Taipei Vihara. In a short span of eight months, members of the public who went to worship there numbered as many as several hundred thousand. On December 12th, the reliquary containing the Buddha's tooth relic boarded a train especially reserved for it by the Taiwan Railway Administration for its journey south. The train made stops along the way at such stations as Changhua, Chiayi, Tainan, and Kaohsiung to provide local devotees an opportunity to view and worship the relic. By the morning of the second day, the Buddha's tooth relic had made its tour around the cities of Fengshan and Dashu, and was on its way back to Fo Guang Shan.

An Introduction to the Dharma in Three Dimensions

Venerable Master Hsing Yun recalls the process of welcoming the Buddha's tooth relic to Taiwan:

"When we were in Thailand, the supreme patriarch of Thailand, Somdet Phra Nyanasamvara, said that the Buddha's tooth relic is a sacred object small in physical size. But when it reaches Taiwan, it will require a very large area of land."

Fourteen years later, in 2011, the Buddha Memorial Center was completed and opened to the public. It occupies an immense one hundred hectares, just as the supreme patriarch of Thailand had wished.

The heart of the Buddha Memorial Center is the Buddha's tooth enshrined in the Jade Buddha Shrine within the Main Hall. All the other buildings at the Buddha Memorial Center were built because of the Buddha's tooth relic. Venerable Master Hsing Yun has taken the essential teachings of Buddhism such as the Four Noble Truths, the Noble Eightfold Path, the twelve links of dependent origination, the thirty-seven factors of enlightenment, the Mahayana bodhisattva ideal, and others, and assembled them into buildings. In this way he has formed a three-dimensional introduction to the Dharma which serves as a textbook of Buddhism on an immense scale.

When people gaze reverently upon the Buddha's tooth and worship it, when they find themselves situated within this cluster of buildings, recollecting the Buddha and contemplating the Dharma, it is as if they are hearing and practicing the Dharma directly from the Buddha himself. This was Venerable Master Hsing Yun's goal in his earnest devotion in designing the Buddha

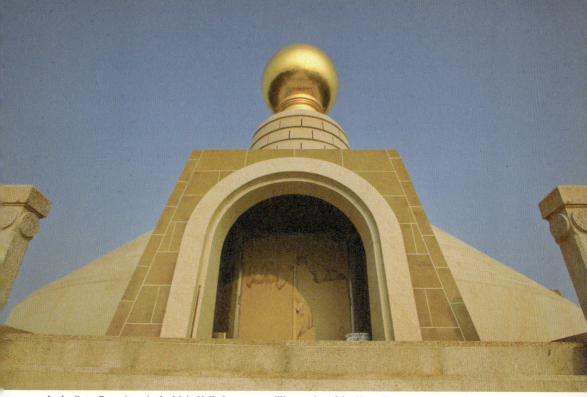

In the Sutra Repository in the Main Hall, there are a million copies of the *Heart Sutra,* representing the innumerable vows and minds tied together by these words.

Memorial Center: to allow people to bow before a true relic of the Buddha and seek refuge in the relic of the Buddha's Dharma body.

During his lifetime, the Buddha taught the Dharma for forty-nine years. He delivered such teachings as the Four Noble Truths, the Noble Eightfold Path, and the twelve links of dependent origination. The many teachings of the Buddha encompass those in the *Flower Adornment Sutra*, the *Agama Sutras*, the *Prajnaparamita Sutras*, and the *Lotus Sutra*. All these words flowed from the Buddha's mouth. It was from his mouth, through the teeth of his physical body, that the Buddha taught the meaning of life and guided living beings to strive for the higher good, recognize their inherent mind, and realize their intrinsic nature. Thus the Buddha's tooth relic has been formed through cultivation and imbued with profound merit. As the earliest Buddhist sutras state: Whoever hears about it with their ears or sees it with their eyes, or worships and praises it, or joyfully reveres it, and so on, will obtain wholesome conditions in this life, be free from difficulties, and experience peace and happiness in both mind and body.

When You Walk into
the Main Hall's Three Shrines

For Buddhists, the most important thing to do when arriving at a Buddhist temple is to enter the main shrine and bow to the Buddha. Through this devout act of worship afflictions are eliminated, karmic obstacles are repented, and a sense of humility is cultivated. The architecture of the main shrine in traditional temples is constructed around a central axis. Through its thoroughly modern and technological design, the Buddha Memorial Center that has appeared in the 21st century also implements this central axis idea with its three shrines within the Main Hall.

Upon walking straight in through the Main Hall's entrance, one will see, in this order, the "Avalokitesvara Shrine," the "Golden Buddha Shrine," and the "Jade Buddha Shrine," as well as the Sutra Repository on the fifth floor. The clear sense of sequence in this design frames the heart of faith for the Buddha Memorial Center.

The front most of the three shrines is the "Avalokitesvara Shrine," which contains thirty-three images of Avalokitesvara Bodhisattva set in a circle. Clear, bright mirrors are set on the four surrounding walls. Images are reflected on each other by the mirrors: front to back, left to right, creating an unbroken continuity with layer upon layer of images stretching far and near. In this way, a single image of Avalokitesvara Bodhisattva generates millions of compassionate reflections, creating the world as described in the *Flower Adornment Sutra,* in which everything extends into infinity.

Words of Venerable Master Hsing Yun

My conception of the Flower Adornment world is based on my understanding of a phrase from the sutra: "Mount Sumeru can store a mustard seed and a mustard seed can contain Mount Sumeru." The thousand-armed, thousand-eyed form of Avalokitesvara Bodhisattva represents the educational function of the Buddha Memorial Center, and can be seen as soon as one walks through the door. This is because Avalokitesvara Bodhisattva symbolizes loving-kindness and compassion, and her many manifestations demonstrate how the Buddha's spirit reaches everywhere.

The King of Sutras

It is said that the Buddha taught in seven locations to nine assemblies before the *Flower Adornment Sutra* was completed. Within the Buddhist teachings, the *Flower Adornment Sutra* is considered the most advanced and supreme, such that it is often called the "king of sutras." After its transmission to China, Master Dushun became the first patriarch of the *Huayan* or "Flower Adornment" School. Born during the lifetime of Emperor Wu of the Southern Chen dynasty (557-559 CE), he was a great sage who was adept at both theory and practice. According to Venerable Master Hsing Yun, many miraculous events occurred during Master Dushun's lifetime. Some of these events are recorded in the *Continuation of the Record of Eminent Monastics*, such as blind and deaf people who were able to see or hear after visiting him. Once, as he was crossing a river, it suddenly stopped flowing, and did not resume flowing until after he had reached the other shore.

From historical records, those who benefited from the great merit of reading, reciting, and practicing the *Flower Adornment Sutra* are too many to enumerate, but Venerable Master Hsing Yun did give one example:

During the Tang dynasty (618-907 CE) there was a monk named Chenghui. He had joined the monastic order at Zhenrong Temple on Mount Wutai, under the auspices of Master Dushun. His daily meals consisted only of grass and leaves, and he regularly recited the *Flower Adornment Sutra*. When he recited the sutra, five or six gentlemen wearing scholarly dress often appeared around him, sitting down and listening to his recitation. Chenghui had no idea who they were or where they came from. Some of the gentlemen presented Chenghui with offerings of flowers and fruit. While such an offering is commonplace, the flowers Chenghui received did not wither or wilt, and the fruit made one free from hunger. Chenghui thought all of this was rather strange, so he asked the gentlemen who they were.

One of the gentlemen spoke, "We are all mountain gods. The power of your recitation has made this mountain pure and peaceful, so we have made this special effort to serve and make offerings to you."

Infinite Light upon Light

The *Flower Adornment Sutra* influenced generations of Chinese patriarchs who studied and investigated the sutra, producing new systems of thought. This *huayan*, "flower adornment," philosophy became one of the most distinctive philosophical systems in Chinese Buddhist history. This traditional teaching is made manifest by the magnificent sublimity of the Avalokitesvara Shrine situated on the first floor of the Main Hall at the Buddha Memorial Center.

The ideas expressed in the *Flower Adornment Sutra* are not easy to grasp; therefore, Venerable Master Hsing Yun used a statue of the thousand-armed and thousand-eyed Avalokitesvara Bodhisattva to facilitate people's understanding. This statue of Avalokitesvara Bodhisattva is the work of Loretta Huishan Yang, whose artistic creations are made with the lost-wax process of glass casting. As a Buddhist practitioner herself, she vowed to donate this image of Avalokitesvara Bodhisattva with a thousand arms and a thousand eyes to the Buddha Memorial Hall, making a connection with all living beings. When a visitor comes to worship Avalokitesvara Bodhisattva, they will also see themselves reflected in the bright mirrors. The

The yellow shale walls of the Main Hall take visitors back to ancient times.

This "Thousand-armed and Thousand-eyed Avalokitesvara" statue is the work of Loretta Huishan Yang.

Golden Buddha statue presented by the Thai Supreme Patriarch.

The Reclining Buddha, carved from white jade from Burma.

trillions of reflected body images are endless and infinite, and are merged together with Avalokitesvara Bodhisattva.

After paying homage to Avalokitesvara Bodhisattva, one comes to the "Golden Buddha Shrine." The golden Buddha enshrined in this hall was presented by the supreme patriarch of Thailand and symbolizes the exchange and blending of the Northern and Southern traditions of Buddhism. Next, the "Jade Buddha Shrine" houses an extraordinary and magnificent image of the reclining Buddha, carved out of precious white jade from Burma. On either side of the Jade Buddha statue are magnificent relief carvings, one depicting the Pure Land of Crystal Radiance and the other depicting the Pure Land of Ultimate Bliss. Arrayed along the walls to the left and right are relief carvings of famous Buddhist stupas from around the world, etched into various aromatic woods. Together they form a veritable forest of stupas, a collection of sacred Buddhist sites.

Within the Jade Buddha Shrine is housed the treasured Buddha's tooth relic, so that the public can reverently gaze upon and worship it. We should remember that, as long as the Buddha is in one's heart, whatever we hear and see becomes the teachings and manifestation of the Buddha. When we bow to and worship the Buddha in this way, we are able to bow to our own happiness, bow to our own wisdom, and bow to our own purity, light, and health.

When You See
the Sphere atop the Main Hall

The sphere atop the Main Hall sparkles like gold under the sun. Can you imagine what kind of glorious tale is kept within this towering pinnacle? It is a story of the collective creation of a million people from Taiwanese society and from the far corners of the globe.

The "One Million Copies of the *Heart Sutra* Joining the Dharma Body" movement that was launched with the construction of the Buddha Memorial Center was a sutra copying effort that spanned the globe. One million people from countries around the world were invited to make copies of the sutra as their contribution to the building project. After the million copies of the *Heart Sutra* were gathered together, they were placed within the sphere located on the highest point of the Main Hall. An individual's life is temporary, but the copies of the *Heart Sutra* transcribed by hand will endure as long as the Buddha Memorial Center itself.

This is why it is said "one moment in a thousand years," for each and every word and sentence of the sutra makes a mind-to-mind connection with all the Buddhas of the ten directions. In this same way it is said, "A thousand years in one moment," for at the moment each sutra transcriber picks up the pen, they unlock the wisdom of their own mind and body.

Words of Venerable Master Hsing Yun

The Heart Sutra is an important Buddhist sutra for all people. If you want to know yourself, you should apply the Heart Sutra in your daily life. We have heard many principles and we possess much general knowledge, but have we ever had a deep understanding of the sutra of ourselves? Have we ever had a deep understanding of our own heart?

The heart is important. Everyone has a heart, but no one truly understands it. Everyone has a true Buddha nature, but no one knows what the true Buddha nature is really like. And so they seek the Buddha outside of their hearts and minds. Now, we too are making a connection with the Buddha on the outside, in order to discover the Buddha within.

The Miracle of Two Hundred and Sixty Characters

The *Heart Sutra* is intimately connected to each individual. One moving miracle created through the sutra was seen in the Yakushi Temple in Nara, Japan.

The ancient East Pagoda of Yakushi Temple has been described as "music frozen in time" for its beauty, and has stood on the temple grounds for thirteen hundred years. Other Yakushi Temple buildings that were constructed at the same time as the East Pagoda (during the 7th and 8th centuries), such as the Golden Hall (the main hall), the Lecture Hall, the West Pagoda, the Middle Gate, and the connecting hallways were, completed destroyed in the great fire of 1528 CE. These buildings have been lost for four hundred and forty years, leaving the East Pagoda the only witness to history. When in 1967 the abbot of Yakushi Temple, Takada Kōin, vowed to rebuild them, everything changed.

The first task in the rebuilding plan was the main hall, also called the Golden Hall. Beginning in 1968, Abbot Takada Kōin made rounds to various places in Japan to announce his intention to restore the Golden Hall. He encouraged everyone to come to the temple and transcribe the *Heart Sutra*, the short text consisting of two hundred and sixty Chinese characters.

Each copy was given, with a donation of 2,000 Japanese Yen, for "receiving the sutra and transferring merit." (At the time the plan was initiated, the typical donation given for transcribing a sutra was 1,000 Japanese Yen.) The temple used this as its building fund to carry out the reconstruction project.

In less than ten years, Japanese society reached the goal of one million transcribed copies of the *Heart Sutra*. The Golden Hall was completed in 1976, and has now returned before peoples' eyes. However, the transcription of the *Heart Sutra* continued nonstop, later reaching 7.3 million copies. Not only were the original buildings replaced, but the temple added the Xuanzang Tripitaka Hall and the Hall of Tang dynasty Murals from the Western Regions. This construction project is called the "Great Hakuho Temple

Through its ancient appearance, the building projects an air of peacefulness, radiating both majesty and tranquility.

Revival" referring to the Hakuho period (673-686 CE), when the Yakushi Temple was originally built. Yakushi Temple is now a UNESCO World Heritage Site.

Hearts from All Over the World within the Sphere

An action as small as individuals copying a sutra coalesced the vast power of a community's vow. Thus, buildings from a thousand years ago reappeared. This seemingly impossible task created a Buddhist miracle for Japan in the 20th century.

In the 21st century, Taiwan began the "One Million Copies of the *Heart Sutra* Joining the Dharma Body" movement. As soon as it started, more than a thousand monastics at Fo Guang Shan took the lead, serving as an example to others: assembled in the great hall in neat and orderly ranks, they sat straight and proper as they focused their attention and devoted themselves to transcribing the *Heart Sutra*.

At all the branches of Fo Guang Shan located throughout Taiwan, there were thousands of devotees engaged in the practice of sutra transcription under the direction of the monastics. They would gather in the main shrine in front of the Buddha statue and the whole temple practiced together. The power of such concentration was very profound. One monastic at a sister temple of Fo Guang Shan was particularly overjoyed when he heard about the sutra transcribing movement. Not only did he himself participate, he also mobilized more than one hundred devotees to support it. This particular monastic was completely illiterate. Nevertheless he copied out the characters of the *Heart Sutra* by tracing their shape, keeping up with the others as they transcribed. Now this monastic can recognize sentences of the sutra and copies out the scripture on behalf of other illiterate devotees. There are actually many senior citizens who cannot read or write. Because of this, they ask their children and grandchildren to transcribe on their behalf. They themselves sit next to the transcriber, carefully watching each and every stroke of the brush. One person is writing, but two people are cultivating.

There are people from across all five continents of the world who answered the call enthusiastically, even those of nationalities who have never written Chinese characters before. Yet their interest was undampened. There was a group of young South African people who held Chinese writing brushes in their hands and wrote Chinese characters for the first time in their lives. Their first strokes were awkwardly askew, but they learned how to draw smoothly, as their minds settled, persevering until the very last character. The Sutra Repository in the sphere of the Buddha Memorial Center contains many such hand-copied *Heart Sutras*, done in an awkward yet earnest hand. They may have come from Africa, they may have come from America, or from any other corner of the world.

Making a copy of the *Heart Sutra* creates a mind-to-mind connection in which the Buddha enters our mind and our mind enters the Buddha. If you apply yourself in taking in the view of the Buddha Memorial Center's sphere, you will be seeing hearts from all over the world gathered in a rich, varied profusion.

When You Enter
the Great Enlightenment Auditorium

Whether Buddhist or not, people open Buddhist sutras and read the first sentence:

> Thus have I heard. At one time, the Buddha was in the city of Sravasti at the Jeta Grove Monastery with a gathering of monks numbering 1,250.

Many people try to imagine what it would have been like when the Buddha taught the Dharma to his disciples twenty-six hundred years ago.

Venerable Master Hsing Yun has taken what was depicted in the words of the Buddhist sutras and realized it in three dimensions. The high-vaulted "Great Enlightenment Auditorium" on the second floor of the Main Hall combines the idea of a theater with that of a place for religious cultivation. Together these two ideas generate a design that simulates reality.

The purpose of employing high-tech multimedia is not to create an awe-inspiring spectacle. Rather, it is an attempt to recreate those aspects of the Dharma that resonate most with the human heart.

After having gazed upon the Buddha's tooth relic, one then enters the Great Enlightenment Auditorium. In that instant, it seems as if one has become one of the millions of human and heavenly beings who listened to the Buddha teach the Dharma, such that one feels he or she is in the Buddha's time and in the Buddha's presence.

Words of Venerable Master Hsing Yun

All the scenes in the Great Enlightenment Auditorium are dynamic, as if one were in the midst of the Buddha land.

The sound of the Buddha teaching actually resounds through this space, powerful, magnificent, and compassionate. Clear and distinct over the vast area, every word and syllable reaches into the heart and mind. The visitors who come here take a different feeling back home with them, a sense of peace and joy.

The three-story high Great Enlightenment
Auditorium can hold up to two thousand people.

Twenty-Six Hundred Year-Old Petals

Venerable Master Hsing Yun employs high-tech lighting and sound as a way
of transporting the audience back to the time of the Buddha.

Suspended in midair, the Buddha slowly rises upwards, his golden body,
sixteen feet in height, shimmering with brilliant light. The great bodhisattvas and great arhats surround him. The four orders of disciples (monks,
nuns, laymen, and laywomen), numbering twelve hundred and fifty in all,
are gathered together. The sound of drums begins to resonate off in the
distance along with the delicate music of pipes as the Buddha is praised in
verse.

Amid the wafting Buddhist music, heavenly beings hover about and
birds in flight sing along. At that moment, a profusion of *mandarava* flowers fall like rain from the sky. The immaculate flowers float above the Buddha's body, drifting about the bodies of the bodhisattvas, arhats, and the
four orders of disciples. Sandalwood incense slowly swirls about to perme-
ate every corner, an offering to this extraordinary assembly to which the
Buddha teaches the Dharma.

Twenty-six hundred year-old petals hover and glide about one's body;
the sound of drums wreathes around one's ears; heavenly beings flutter in
the air before one's eyes, and the sound of Dharma teachings flow into one's
heart. Within this stirring display, created by Venerable Master Hsing Yun,
there is the devout joy that removes pain and grants happiness, and there is
the bright hope that joins past with present, so that each and every visitor
participates in the great chorus, uniting life across thousands of years.

The Bodhi Wisdom Concourse in front of the Main Hall, ringed by the Eight Patriarchs and Eighteen Arhats.

When You Stop by the Four Permanent Exhibits

If you are looking forward to an expansive, fantastic spectacle, the four permanent exhibits on the first floor of the Main Hall are sure to keep you captivated. You can pass through the halls of time by entering the Underground Palaces to see the sacred artifacts of Buddhism; or return to faraway India twenty-six hundred years ago. Through the 4D display of the Buddha in the midst of explaining the Buddhist sutras and teaching the Dharma; or even go for a change of pace by enjoying the eight major annual Buddhist festivals in one go; or let your mind sprout wings and fly over to the area around the Xiannü Temple in Jiangdu, Jiangsu Province, where the venerable master was born, and witness his pioneering efforts in founding Fo Guang Shan.

Leaving behind traditional styles of exhibition, visitors are given greater freedom and a richer experience for the five senses. When you stop by the exhibition halls, the long flow of history is arrayed before your eyes. Through the juxtaposition of past and present, the overlapping of space and time through the exhibits' interactive touch interfaces, you will be able to quietly and profoundly carry on a dialogue with your own life.

Words of Venerable Master Hsing Yun

There are four permanent exhibits: The first is the "Museum of Buddhist Underground Palaces," which holds the cultural artifacts donated by the Aurora Group, collected from Buddhist archeological sites from around the world. The second is the "Museum of the Life of the Buddha," which employs 4D technology and special sound and lighting effects to recreate the life and times of the Buddha twenty-six hundred years ago. The third is the "Museum of Buddhist Festivals," which displays the Buddhist festivals celebrated during the year by means of actual objects and dioramas. The fourth is the "Historical Museum of Fo Guang Shan," which narrates the causes and conditions behind the founding of Fo Guang Shan and gives an historical account of the development of Humanistic Buddhism.

Museum of Underground Palaces Permanent Exhibit

On the first floor of the Main Hall, you will find the permanent exhibit entitled the "Museum of Underground Palaces," located in the front area on the right. Its entrance recreates the gate to the Underground Palace[1] at Famen Temple in Xi'an, China. The lighting effects and the mood setting make it seem like one is passing through time, setting you on a journey through the history of Buddhism's sacred artifacts.

The cultural artifacts include such items as the stone gate to the Underground Palace; the stone steps; the gold and silver reliquary caskets; the reliquary vase of gold, silver, and colored glass; Buddhist statuary, candlesticks, incense burners, and ritual vases—a total of one hundred and fifty exhibits, all donated by Chen Bai Yuye, the wife of Chen Yungtai, chairman of the Aurora Group. Moved by ancient people's devotion to the Buddha, Chen Bai Yuye has spent decades gathering and caring for Buddhist artifacts recovered from Underground Palaces from around the world. After construction began on the Buddha Memorial Center, the Aurora Group felt that it was the best possible place to preserve this collection of treasures, and donated the collection.

Chen Yungtai emphasizes, "We gave the entire collection, without keeping a single item, so that Buddhist groups could make use of them to spread the Dharma, ensuring that even more people would benefit, in the hope that they in turn would contribute their efforts for the sake of passing on the spirit of the Dharma."

Venerable Master Hsing Yun observed that these sacred Buddhist artifacts were made by previous generations as offerings to the bone relics of the Buddha, serving as worthy reminders of the Buddha's spirit that later generations should cherish and emulate. The Aurora Group's selfless decision to donate these sacred Buddhist artifacts is tantamount to turning them over to history and to the larger community. Such an act should be praised

---

1 In a Buddhist context, an "Underground Palace", or *digong* (地宫), is a storehouse of valuable Buddhist artifacts akin to a time capsule that has been buried underground as a way to protect and preserve the artifacts for future generations.

The Museum of Buddhist Underground Palaces takes people on a journey through history with its displays of Buddha relics.

by all of Taiwan's twenty-three million people. Special plans were made for the exhibition space in the Buddha Memorial Center. After dozens of meetings were called with specialists, it was decided to recreate a Buddhist Underground Palace to exhibit the sacred artifacts for all to see. Henceforth, anyone who wishes to gain an understanding of the many famous Underground Palaces of the past need not traverse the entire globe. The artifacts are gathered here on display, to be seen one at a time.

The permanent exhibition area for the "Museum of Buddhist Underground Palaces" is generally divided into twelve sections. Among these, the section on the "Relics Born from the Buddha's Tooth" should be the greatest focus of the visitor's attention. The Buddha's tooth relic was welcomed to Taiwan in 1998 and enshrined in the Buddha's Tooth Relic Hall at Fo Guang Shan. Over the past fourteen years, several hundred relics have been born and it is these that are on special display here, enabling visitors to view the crystallization of faith and vows born from people's devout worship.

To have the exhibit itself tell the story of the relics born from the Buddha's tooth Venerable Ru Chang, general director of the Fo Guang Yuan Art Galleries, explains:

"We used a cone-shaped art installation that consisted of eight levels from top to bottom. Each level represents one of the eight major events in the Buddha's life: the descent from Tusita Heaven, entry into the womb, birth, leaving home, subduing Mara, awakening, turning the Dharma wheel, and his final *nirvana*. The relic is a symbol of this final *nirvana,* and by means of video projectors, people can clearly see the relics reborn from the Buddha's tooth on display at the exhibit.

Wu Tanghai, a consultant on the design team for this exhibit, has spoken about a personal experience he once had. In 2000, he was planning the "Buddhism's Transmission to China over Two Thousand Years: A Special

Exhibition of Buddhist Cultural Artifacts and Underground Palace Treasures." At the time a reliquary vase of extraordinary value was being kept in the Buddha's Tooth Relic Hall at Fo Guang Shan for the night. The next day, the previously empty vase was now brimming with relics! This miracle has left Wu Tanghai with an experience he cannot forget, even after many years.

Unexplainable phenomena provide insight into faith. Buddhism emphasizes the mind, so different people who visit the Museum of Buddhist Underground Palaces will have different experiences. The scholars can come here to study; non-Buddhists can come to experience what an Underground Palace is like; and Buddhists can come here for self-reflection, and to deepen their practice.

People encounter the millennia-old sacred objects of the Underground Palaces and regard them with reverence, enjoyment, or curiosity. The Buddha Memorial Center itself has forty-eight Underground Palaces, locked away and designed to reappear hundreds of years in the future to carry on the Buddha's spirit. A countdown has been set up within the "Museum of Buddhist Underground Palaces" exhibit, informing the visitor how many days are left until the next Underground Palace is opened, with one scheduled to be opened every one hundred years. This enables the public to participate in this process of space-time, and to understand that every single person living in this moment is an element in the history of the Underground Palace, one of many causes and conditions.

Museum of the Life of the Buddha Permanent Exhibit

The "Museum of the Life of the Buddha" permanent exhibit is located in the rear area on the left of the Main Hall's first floor. The first attraction upon entering the exhibit is the "4D Movie Theater." A short, eight-minute film distills the events of the Buddha's life, exhibiting how a human being like any other subdued his own afflictions and attained enlightenment, becoming the Buddha.

Upon exiting the 4D movie theater, the scenes depicted in the movie are on display before one's eyes: murals, text, and

A design draft of the Museum of Buddhist Underground Palaces

audio-video materials, as well as interactive touch displays that transport the visitor through a step by step journey through the Buddha's mind. For example, when the Buddha was still Prince Siddhartha, he walked out of the palace precincts on four occasions, and went outside the city where he saw with his own eyes birth, sickness, old age, and death. These were how living beings suffered mentally and physically amid the vagaries of impermanence.

The atmosphere of the exhibit simulates dusk as the sun sets. Walking past a sensor that activates the projector mounted above, the visitor will see the physical aspect of an old man, projected into the area where he or she is standing, giving the visitor a momentary sense of what it means to be old. When the visitor activates the opening of a window in one of the town's houses, the painful moaning of the sick and the scene of a burial procession will appear before one's eyes. Such scene designs enable people to understand what Prince Siddhartha must have felt twenty-six hundred years ago, when he witnessed the sufferings of living beings.

In order to seek out the path of liberation from suffering, Prince Siddhartha abandoned his life of privilege and pleasure and left home. After undergoing six years of asceticism, he meditated under the *bodhi* tree with his emaciated body. In the next area, the exhibit reverberates with light and sound: the howling of the wind, the thunder of a storm. Prince Siddhartha is being tested by his internal demons and external hardships. The visitor is witnessing how Prince Siddhartha overcame the physical and mental obstacles of the demonic Mara. As he sees the bright stars at night, he attains enlightenment and becomes the Buddha.

In the scene where the Buddha preaches the Dharma to his twelve hundred and fifty disciples, the exhibition area opens up with a mural twenty meters long. The painting gives a vivid depiction of people in India from various tribes and different classes. They number more than eight hundred in total, extending to the very limits of one's vision.

Having walked through the stages of the Buddha's life from birth, upbringing, renunciation, asceticism, enlightenment, Dharma teaching, and final *nirvana*, the visitor comes to the concluding exhibit. This is an interactive installation with sound-activated image retrieval. Just as Prince Siddhartha was able to become a Buddha, each and every person can become a Buddha as well. When the visitor speaks the words "I am a Buddha" in front of the interactive installation, one's image is projected on the screen superimposed over a magnificent halo of light, congratulating the speaker on their future attainment of Buddhahood.

Having vowed to become a Buddha and having recognized oneself as a Buddha, one must then refrain from doing things that should not be done. The "Museum of the Life of the Buddha" takes the stories of the Buddha and makes them tangible, educational, and interactive, allowing people to bring home the idea that "I am a Buddha," planting a seed in their minds for safekeeping.

Museum of Buddhist Festivals Permanent Exhibit

In the right-hand area of the rear section of the Main Hall, there is the "Museum of Buddhist Festivals." The first festival one sees is Maitreya Buddha's Birthday, celebrated on the first day of the first lunar month. Maitreya Buddha beams at visitors with a broad smile on his face from the center of the exhibit. Three hundred and thirty centimeters tall (almost eleven feet), he greets people by opening his mouth and saying, "Congratulations!" Seven small novices clamber about his body, their little heads bobbing. They are positioned in a playful manner, both in form and action.

The 19th day of the second lunar month marks the celebration of Avalokitesvara Bodhisattva's Birthday. The exhibit depicts a temple pilgrimage. The temple gate, the pilgrimage route, the Great Compassion Shrine, and the pilgrims themselves are all three-dimensional models. It is as if you suddenly found yourself amidst a real pilgrimage.

The first day of the first month of the Chinese lunar calendar marks the Maitreya Buddha's birthday.

The fourth lunar month is the celebration of the Buddha's Birthday. The Buddha images, Buddha niches, Dharma instruments, flower bouquets, and other objects are arranged just as they would be in the main shrine of a temple. A Buddha bathing area has been set up in the middle, with a large statue of the prince surrounded by five smaller images on petal-shaped pedestals. In front of each of the fives smaller images there is a kneeling cushion with an infrared beam detector. When the visitor kneels before the prince, the speaker above will immediately play a musical rendition of the "Bathing the Buddha Verse," giving every visitor the chance to bathe the Buddha.

The seventh lunar month is known in folk tradition as the Ghost Month, but for Buddhism this month is the month of filial piety. This originated from the story of "Maudgalyayana saving his mother." As related in the *Ullambana Sutra*, Venerable Maudgalyayana's mother had committed evil during her lifetime and fell into the hell realm upon her death. Devastated, Maudgalyayana asked the Buddha how to save her. The Buddha told him that he had to prepare rich, sumptuous offerings of food for the monastic community on the 15th day of the seventh lunar month, the very day the summer retreat ended. Only with this infinite merit could he rescue his mother from the domain of suffering. Following his example, each year during the seventh lunar month Buddhist communities hold an Ullambana Dharma Service in which lavish offerings of incense, flowers, lamps, and fruit are presented to the Buddha and the monastic order. This is done for blessings of happiness and long life for one's parents of this lifetime, and infinite joy and happiness for one's parents from lifetimes past. When the sensor in this exhibit area detects the presence of a visitor, a spotlight will immediately illuminate a mural of the story, followed by animated figures of Maudgalyayana and his mother. This demonstrates Maudgalyayana's filial piety.

The 30th day of the ninth lunar month is the celebration of the Medicine Buddha's Birthday, when people pray above all else for "peace and well-being." In the center of this exhibit there is an "interactive lamp lighting installation:" All the visitor has to do is write their name on the "signature-signing system," and their signature will be enlarged and projected onto the center of the wall. Then, it will slowly shrink down and move into the eternal flame beside the Medicine Buddha, thus completing the process for lighting the lamp and praying for blessings.

The 8th day of the twelfth lunar month is the celebration of the Dharma Gem and of the Buddha's enlightenment. Before attaining Buddhahood, the Buddha once practiced asceticism for six years, until his body became haggard and gaunt. Fortunately, he met a shepherdess on the banks of the Nairañjana River, who offered him a bowl of milk. Only then did he slowly recover his strength. Later on he meditated under the *bodhi* tree, deep in thought, and on the 8th day of the twelfth lunar month, he became enlightened and attained Buddhahood. In order to commemorate the Buddha's enlightenment and the shepherdess' offering, every eighth day of the twelfth lunar month (*laba* in Chinese), a porridge of rice, vegetables, and the five grains is cooked and offered to the Buddha and the community. In this exhibit there is an interactive Laba porridge installation. The tableau contains little puppets eating Laba porridge with the sound of them smacking their lips at the incomparably delicious taste. Now, when the visitor touches the screen, the following question appears: "Do you know what ingredients are in the bowl of Laba porridge?" By trying to guess the ingredients, visitors come to realize that Laba porridge is cooked by combining many causes and conditions, symbolizing blessings for better health, well-being, and wisdom.

Enter this place in history and experience that moment in time firsthand.

Historical Museum of Fo Guang Shan Permanent Exhibit

Located in the front on the right side of the Main Hall's first floor, the "Historical Museum of Fo Guang Shan" employs easily-understandable video narratives and displays documents and artifacts to give a smooth and fluid presentation of the development of Venerable Master Hsing Yun's thought. The exhibit also demonstrates how Fo Guang Shan implements the down-to-earth, beneficial-to-others, and contemporary-oriented qualities of Humanistic Buddhism under its four main objectives:

- To propagate the Dharma through culture.
- To nurture talent through education.
- To benefit society through charity.
- To purify people's minds through cultivation.

Photographs and objects on exhibit depict one moving event after another. Drawings and writings along with dioramas enable people to step into the past and experience the stream of feelings behind the historical events.

History marches onward within the exhibit. In a small and narrow room, a tiny window lets in a dim glow, while a half-bowl of salted vegetables sits upon a crude table. This depicts the autumn of 1943 when Venerable Master Hsing Yun had come down with a serious case of malaria and was in critical condition. When his teacher Abbot Zhikai learned of the matter, he sent someone from a great distance away to bring Venerable Master Hsing

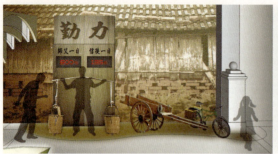

Venerable Master Hsing Yun used to carry six-hundred buckets of water a day.

In a desolate bamboo grove, a lone bus idles.

Yun this half-bowl of salted vegetables. During this time of crushing poverty, the salted vegetables were a scrumptious delicacy. Venerable Master Hsing Yun cried as he ate the food, thinking of his teacher's kindness toward him. He could not help but make a vow, even as tears streamed down his face:

"In the future, I will take up the work of spreading the Dharma for the benefit of living beings, to expand and develop Buddhism. This is how I will repay my teacher for his kindness!"

History continues onward, and we come to a squat little place under the eaves: In front of a mottled earthen wall there sits a flat-bed cart. This was the time when Venerable Master Hsing Yun first arrived in Taiwan as a wandering monk and was refused lodgings. He was nearly reduced to begging on the street. Fortunately, the old Venerable Miaoguo of Yuanguang Temple in Chungli took him in. To repay his kindness for taking him in, Venerable Master Hsing Yun worked diligently: each day, as service to the temple, he would carry six hundred buckets of water to supply the needs of the monastic community. Early in the morning he would pull the flat-bed cart to the marketplace and buy vegetables. The "interactive water buckets on a carrying pole" in the exhibit allows visitors to put their shoulders into lifting the carrying pole and experience firsthand how hard it is to carry water in this way.

History moves onward once more: A bus is parked in a remote bamboo thicket. The bus is full of devotees. It was in 1965 when Venerable Master Hsing Yun decided to build Fo Guang Shan. He had rented a bus to bring the devotees up the mountain, to what he considered the ideal spot to begin construction. To his surprise, upon seeing the mountain full of thorny bamboo and trackless stretches of wild grass, no one was willing to step out of the bus. They even said, "Not even ghosts would come to such a place as this!"

Despite this, Venerable Master Hsing Yun did not feel discouraged at all. He simply asked everyone to wait there on the bus while he spent two hours climbing the mountain all by himself. Circling back to the bus, he thought to himself, "It doesn't matter if ghosts don't come. As long as people come and the Buddha comes, then it will be fine."

Bits of emotion, life-changing moments, and with the blink of an eye, fifty years have passed. Now the Buddha's light shines throughout the three thousandfold world system and the Dharma waters flow throughout the five continents. Venerable Master Hsing Yun stresses that all this has been accomplished due to everyone's collective efforts. To represent this, an arc-shaped wall in the exhibit contains a photo collage with the myriad faces of Fo Guang members, forming a map of the world, the Fo Guang Shan logo, and the logo of the Buddha's Light International Association. Together, they serve as a commemoration to those people now linked across the globe, who participated in the Humanistic Buddhism movement.

Visitors experience the historical narrative combined with physical objects that allow them to directly experience the compassion, wisdom, vows, and practice that embody the humanistic bodhisattva. In this way, the visitor gains an appreciation of the Dharma through another person's everyday life that can prove beneficial to their own lives.

On August 23rd, 2011, leaders of Various Religions attended the Love and Peace Prayer Ceremony, praying for the happiness of all humanity (Photo by Cai Rong Feng).

When You Gaze Up at the Fo Guang Big Buddha

There are several Buddhist temples and monasteries that have grand, large-scale Buddha statues. Some are set in the main shrine, some are built on mountaintops, some are carved in caves, and some are carved on cliffsides. On the highest point of the Buddha Memorial Center, along its central axis, there sits a magnificent, colossal statue of Sakyamuni Buddha, whose compassionate eyes look downward upon all living beings.

Currently the world's largest copper-cast Buddha statue, the Fo Guang Big Buddha sits cross-legged with his hands in the lotus *mudra*. From base to tip, the Buddha statue is one hundred and eight meters tall, the equivalent of an average thirty-six story building. Its head alone is three stories tall, while a single eye is as wide as the whole floor of most other buildings.

During the process of designing the Buddha Memorial Center, Venerable Master Hsing Yun considered the Buddhist concept of "formless form," and depicting the Buddha's "Dharma body" permeating the universe: each flower and each leaf, each rock and each grain of sand are manifestations of this Dharma body appearing before living beings. What one image can touch people most directly? The traditional Buddha image. Worshipped for more than two thousand years, it creates the clearest connection with the hearts of the faithful.

Words of Venerable Master Hsing Yun

Images of the Buddha are not limited to a single appearance, for they are the original face of the individual who sees them. When people see the towering Fo Guang Big Buddha, what they are seeing is their own towering height. When they see how magnificent and grand the Fo Guang Big Buddha is, what they are seeing is their own magnificent grandeur, their own original nature. Each and every person must have faith in themselves, and must trust in themselves. Regardless of what country they hail from, what the color of their skin, or what beliefs they hold, when people come here and see the Buddha, they will feel that he is me, and that I am him. The internal and the external are one and the same, and there is no difference between the mind, the Buddha, and living beings. I wanted to take the presentation of the Dharma to such a level.

I Am a Buddha

The story goes that the sculptures at Thousand Buddha Peak on Mount Qixia near Nanjing, China, were completed by three generations of stone carvers: father, son, and grandson. As the third generation carver was carving the last statue, he counted the statues. But no matter how many times he counted them, there were only nine hundred and ninety-nine images of the Buddha. So he carved another one and counted again. It still came out as nine hundred and ninety-nine images of the Buddha. After several more tries he realized, "I am a Buddha!" Thereupon he etched himself into the stone wall, and became the one thousandth Buddha.

"No matter the veracity of this story, it touches a deep place in my heart, and has inspired me for many, many years," Venerable Master Hsing Yun sighs in admiration. "'I am a Buddha,' what a beautiful state of mind!"

But not everyone understands this state. At a certain temple, a devotee asked a Chan master, "What is the Buddha?"

At a complete loss, the Chan master looked at the devotee and said, "I can't tell you because, even if I told you, you would not believe me."

The devotee replied, "Master, how could I not believe what you say. I am asking you this very sincerely."

The Chan master nodded. "Well, if you are willing to trust me, I will tell you: You are the Buddha!"

The devotee doubted the master. "If I am the Buddha, why didn't I know that?"

The Chan master replied, "Because you're unwilling to accept it!"

The largest copper-caste statue of the Buddha in the world, seated in the lotus position.

Words That Accrue Benefits for a Whole Life

This Chan story told by Venerable Master Hsing Yun lays bare the confusion that many people share. Living beings have still not recognized their own true Buddha nature.

Venerable Master Hsing Yun built this Buddha statue so that people could recognize their own true Buddha nature. We see the Buddha fixed in space, but it symbolizes the dynamic process of developing one's own mind. Venerable Master Hsing Yun himself is a good example of this: He entered the monastic order as a young boy, and developed from the self-realization that he should be a good Buddhist, to being a messenger of the Buddha, then to being a teacher of Buddhism; later, he felt that he should aspire to enlightenment and become a bodhisattva.

Then he thought, "Why stop with just being a bodhisattva? Why not act with the mentality that 'I am a Buddha'? I should be acting as a Buddha acts, and doing what a Buddha does!"

"All living beings on this earth possess the true Buddha nature!" This was the Buddha's first sentence after he attained enlightenment twenty-six hundred years ago. The pure, intrinsic nature of ordinary people is inherently no different from that of the Buddha. It has simply been obscured by the afflictions of ignorance, so it is unable to display its clear, brilliant light.

From that point onwards, Venerable Master Hsing Yun always kept the words "I am a Buddha" in his mind. He constantly reminds himself of this, regardless of whether he is dressing, eating, or interacting with others. Even if he has suffered injury, injustice, or ridicule, he keeps this in the forefront of his mind: "I am a Buddha." Thus it is as if the Buddha's light shines into his mind, guiding him through the most turbulent times. Looking back, Venerable Master Hsing Yun has said, "My life has benefited very much indeed from the phrase 'I am a Buddha.'"

Buddha in the Heart for Self-Development

These words bring endless benefits. Venerable Master Hsing Yun uses architecture as a means of expressing "I am a Buddha," as can be seen in the Fo Guang Big Buddha at the Buddha Memorial Center.

When visitors from all around the world step into the Buddha Memorial Center, they witness the Fo Guang Big Buddha's nobility through its lofty grandeur, and the compassionate eyes that gaze upon all living beings. Venerable Master Hsing Yun has said that, "It is my hope that each and every person who comes will realize that they are Buddhas. Whether they are Catholics, Christians, or devotees of Mazu, I hope they can see how they possess the noble essence of their religion within themselves. I want to create this state of mind, so that everyone can be elevated and develop themselves by venerating and worshipping the Buddha, understand the nature of enlightenment, and be able to better face their day to day lives."

When You Start Transcribing the Heart Sutra

Transcribing Buddhist sutras brings peace to the mind and good fortune to the person. More and more people in modern society are happily participating, for it allows them to find a pure space in the hustle and bustle of their lives, a place where they can settle their spirits, achieve meditative concentration, and purify and brighten their mind.

The *Heart Sutra* encompasses all of the Buddha's teachings. It is the key that unlocks the entire canon of Buddhist sutras, and is a guide for all living beings. Transcribing sutras need not adhere to any rigid formalities, but a little preparation can allow one to more easily reach a state of tranquility and subdue the obstacles caused by afflictions. From this kind of "meditative concentration," wisdom is born.

Before starting to transcribe a sutra, one should clean up the room, put on clean clothes, wash the hands, rinse the mouth, and focus the mind and body. Then, prepare the paper, brush, ink, inkstone, and water. This process of preparation is a "ritual" of worship similar to venerating the Buddha.

When engaging in sutra transcription, one focuses on each and every stroke of the brush. The pace of writing is neither fast nor slow, as one follows the words of the sutra from beginning to end. Each and every movement in sutra transcription aims to bring peace to the mind, so that one can better contemplate oneself. By reflecting upon one's own mind in depth, one can then purify one's thoughts.

Words of Venerable Master Hsing Yun

I wish to pray for all the people who have copied the Heart Sutra, and beseech the Buddha to help us attain meditative bliss and Dharma joy, and to help us develop an open and understanding mind. We must uphold and cultivate the Buddha's teachings, and we must put into practice the Buddha's truth. I hope the Buddha can grant us healthy minds and bodies. I hope the Buddha can grant us a happy, harmonious family life. I hope the Buddha can grant us success in our work. I hope the Buddha can grant us a life blessed with joy.

Writing Until the Heart Opens Up

Granny Li Chuntao of Fengshan near Kaohsiung, Taiwan, was diagnosed with a cardiovascular disease: her three main arteries were two-thirds of the way blocked. One day, she remembered that she had not finished the special "easy-to-copy" version of the *Heart Sutra* that she had gotten from Fo Guang Shan and decided to continue transcribing the sutra in order to shift her attention away from the pain of her heart disease.

When the "Million Copies of the *Heart Sutra* Joining the Dharma Body" campaign was launched, she brought her daughter and grandchildren to the Sutra Transcribing Hall at Fo Guang Shan on three separate occasions so that they could participate. At home, she turned copying the text into her routine, never wavering from this daily practice. A few months later, she was to undergo a cardiac catheterization procedure. But when she was given a full-body MRI, the hospital miraculously discovered that the blockages in her arteries had completely disappeared. Even her chronic migraines were gone! Granny Chuntao rejoiced: "After copying the Heart Sutra so many times, my own heart has opened up!"

Religion has its origins in the contemplation of the human predicament. Facing death, Granny Chuntao was conscientious in maintaining her practice. Through this, she gained insight and understanding, and so the state of her health gradually improved.

In another instance, there was the case of the Taoyuan man named Wang that shocked the whole country. After killing his own mother in cold blood, he took his girlfriend on a trip as if nothing had happened. Even after he was arrested, questioned, and taken into custody, he had nothing to say, nonchalantly laying his head down and falling into a deep sleep while in detention. Even when his father came to talk to him, the man remained unmoved and expressionless. It was not until a prison guard brought him the *Heart Sutra*, allowing him to read and transcribe the text, that this hard-hearted murderer began shedding tears of remorse.

The merit of transcribing sutras has been celebrated since ancient times, and the results of this practice have been proven again and again in the

Venerable Master Hsing Yun uses calligraphy to connect people to the Buddha.

modern age. But spiritual miracles are not by any means the goal of religious cultivation. It takes steady cultivation over days and months to make the truth clearer and one's merit greater. Modern people often think in logical terms, so that stories of miracles are dismissed as fairy tales. But if you consider these miracles and temporarily set aside your skepticism, you will experience the spirituality of the event.

The Merit of Transcribing Sutras Is to Use the Dharma to Deal with Life

The *Diamond Sutra* contains the following passage on the merit of transcribing sutras:

> Suppose a good man or good woman were to give as many of his or her lives as there are grains of sand in the Ganges River in the morning, and give as many of his or her lives as there are grains of sand in the Ganges River at noon, and give as many of his or her lives

as there are grains of sand in the Ganges River in the afternoon, and that this giving continued for infinite hundreds of millions of billions of kalpas; if someone were to hear this sutra, believe it, and not turn his mind against it, his merit would be greater—what of the merit of one who copies, receives, upholds, reads, chants, and explains it to others?

Many touching stories came out of the "Million Copies of the *Heart Sutra* Joining the Dharma Body" campaign.

One such person who has been profoundly affected by the campaign is the laywoman Miaoying of Pumen Temple in Taipei. Now age seventy-three, she has penned forty-nine copies of the *Heart Sutra* on her own and has formed many positive karmic connections with her friends by soliciting donations and recommending that they try sutra transcription. She would often say to the elderly members of the Buddha's Light International Association that sutra transcription is not merely a practice of meditative concentration and vow-making, the copies themselves will be enshrined within the Buddha Memorial Center. This is a once in a thousand year opportunity. She feels that the most important thing she has left her descendants is not wealth, but virtuous conduct. She sees her sutra transcription as a gift she is giving to her children.

It has now been more than seventy years since the founding of Anguo Temple in Beitou, where Laywoman Meiyu serves as a receptionist. Since she must look after two grandchildren, she makes use of the time while her grandchildren are asleep to make phone calls, urging people to take up sutra transcription. Under her encouragement, her granddaughter donated the gifts of money she received from the Lunar New Year to sutra transcription.

At Anguo Temple there was an old and revered Buddhist who dared not participate in sutra transcription because she was illiterate. Meiyu encouraged her to write the sutra by tracing over the characters, thus planting a positive karmic seed in this life so as to reap the reward of literacy in the next. The dear woman committed herself to the project and produced a complete copy of the *Heart Sutra*. As Meiyu sees it, everyone wants to better themselves, so people are generally receptive when the prospect of going down the correct path is used as an encouragement for sutra transcription.

Laywoman Zhangshi Shue of Jile Temple in Keelung has been serving as a volunteer for a few decades. She tidies up the halls, sweeps the grounds, welcomes visitors, and helps with kitchen work, sparing no effort to support the temple. She has been studying Buddhism for many years, and has found that the *Heart Sutra* often helps her at home. Whenever she feels anxious or nervous, she begins wholeheartedly reciting the *Heart Sutra*, and everything is solved with much greater ease. But Shue emphasizes that she is not encouraging people to use the *Heart Sutra* with the intent of material gain. More importantly, people should use the Dharma to deal with the ups and downs of life, experiencing for themselves its incredible effects.

Laywoman Liyu of the Chan and Pure Land Center in Hsintien works in the stock market. In the stock market, every second counts. There are upticks or downturns in stock indexes every thirty seconds. To maintain a clear perspective that rises above the chaos of the markets, she copies the *Heart Sutra* after she comes home from work every day. This allows her to relax and spend time in introspection. Liyu provides the following analogy: "Transcribing sutras makes one like a tree with deep roots. The wind may blow the tree from side to side, but it will always return to balance in the center."

For her, the "Million Copies of the *Heart Sutra* Joining the Dharma Body" campaign was even more significant. "The moment I pictured my copy of the sutra being enshrined in the great reliquary of the Buddha, my heart felt an extraordinary sense of reverence."

Liyu often encounters people who say they do not know how to do calligraphy and have never held a Chinese writing brush, but she still encourages them: "Sutra transcription is not about comparing the aesthetic values of different styles of calligraphy. One should look to the mind: By focusing one's attention on each individual character, one can make a mind-to-mind connection with the Buddha."

When You Slowly Circumambulate the Four Noble Truths Stupas

The four stupas erected at the four corners of the Main Hall have a clean, simple, and well-defined design. They encircle the central stupa, symbolizing the Four Noble Truths the Buddha taught following his enlightenment: the truths of suffering (*ku*, 苦), the cause of suffering (*ji*, 集), the cessation of suffering (*mie*, 滅), and the path leading to the cessation of suffering (*dao*, 道).

The four stupas represent these four characters (*ku, ji, mie, dao*), set out under the sky. It does not matter whether the sun is shining brightly or dark clouds enshroud the stupas in gloom, for they stand tall between heaven and earth. The Four Noble Truths Stupas at the Main Hall are testaments to the Buddha's original intent.

It is as if one finds oneself within the Buddha's embrace. One can, at any time, take the stairs outside the Main Hall and approach the four stupas. With each and every step, one can circumambulate clockwise around them in reverent homage, bringing to mind the Buddha's wisdom and spiritual conduct while contemplating the truths of life.

If one merely considers suffering, its cause, its cessation, and the path to its cessation, these concepts may seem bleak. But in fact, they are quite the opposite. The Four Noble Truths are a treasury of blessings that can lead people towards happiness. This is because the framework of the Dharma is formed by these four truths: suffering, its cause, its cessation, and the path to its cessation. This framework helps us resolve our problems.

Words of Venerable Master Hsing Yun

The Four Noble Truths provide a framework similar to treating an illness: the truth of suffering identifies the disease; the truth of its cause represents the cause of the sickness; the truth of its cessation means that one has recovered from the illness; and the truth of the path is the medicine for treating the illness. Putting an end to the pain and suffering of living beings and giving them happiness is the purpose of the Buddha's compassion. It is our hope that the Buddha Memorial Center will reinvigorate everyone, so they can navigate the road of life more smoothly, and know that life is not bitter and that one can find happiness.

The Young Couple's Two Hundred Thousand

Happiness can rarely, if ever, be measured in monetary terms. Venerable Master Hsing Yun offers this telling story:

There was a chairman of the board at a large company whose income was very high. Every day, his wealth would grow, but once he got home, he felt spiritually empty, as if everything had gone wrong. He often argued with his wife, and his children were willful and unruly. Because of these circumstances, he often felt miserable and upset. Even though he lived in a magnificent mansion, he felt that his life was a living hell.

One day a friend came to visit. Seeing the state the chairman was in, he asked, "What happened today to make you feel unhappy?"

The chairman gave a long sigh, and pointed to a squat little house outside: "Look there. There is a young couple that lives in that condemned structure. They play the guitar and sing songs every day. They're so happy. Even though I am a multimillionaire, I spend my days in miserable suffering."

His friend understood. "That's why you're so annoyed and irritated? In that case, you should send them some 'suffering.'"

"What do you mean?"

His friend said, "Take out two hundred thousand dollars and give it to them."

The chairman sent the money over. Suddenly, the poor young couple had a large amount of money. They were overjoyed. But from that point on, they found themselves worrying every night. They thought about putting the money in a drawer, but the drawer had no lock. Then they thought about putting it under the bed, but they were afraid a thief would come and steal their money away. The couple looked at the money, thinking. They tried again and again to figure out what to do. They worried through the night, until the sun began to rise. They had not slept at all.

At that moment, the husband had an alarming realization.

"We've been tricked!"

The wife replied, "What?"

The husband told the wife, "We've been tricked by that rich man. He dumped his misery and pain on us. Originally, we were very happy. But ever since he gave us this two hundred thousand dollars, we can't sleep. We'd better take that miserable two hundred thousand and give it back to him. We don't want it anymore."

Suffering Cannot Be Eliminated until You See It

Just like that chairman of the board and the young couple, everyone living in this hectic society today has some sort of suffering—some more, some less. Perhaps their profession does not suit them, or maybe their relationships with others are unsatisfying, or their family life is in discord. There are also the falsehoods and betrayals from one's workplace, along with coldness and alienation in interpersonal relationships. A sense of blankness follows the never-ending pursuit of fame and fortune. Add to that the booms and busts of the economy, political tensions, global warming, and the fear that comes in the wake of typhoons, earthquakes, floods, and fires. People often find themselves struggling with painful suffering.

The existence of suffering is an undeniable facet of human life. This is why within the Four Noble Truths, the Buddha addresses suffering first.

Discord in relationship to things, discord in relationship to people, and discord in relationship to such aspects as the body, the mind, one's desires, one's understanding, and toward the natural world are all means by which people bring suffering upon themselves. This is Venerable Master Hsing Yun's analysis of "suffering." Through the building of these stupas, he hopes to guide people into contemplating the truth of suffering.

Always an advocate of taking an optimistic attitude towards life and the pursuit of happiness, Venerable Master Hsing Yun explains the positive meaning of Buddhism's emphasis on suffering: "Once you know the true nature of suffering, you can then begin to seek out ways to eliminate suffering. Understanding the existence of suffering is part of a process: eliminating suffering and attaining liberation is the final goal of Buddhism's emphasis on suffering."

Walking Towards Happiness with Every Step

To eliminate suffering, one must put an end to its cause. This is the second idea the Buddha addresses in the Four Noble Truths.

And what is the cause of suffering? Venerable Master Hsing Yun explains it as such: "We are driven by ignorance to accumulate various kinds of negative karma, incurring various kinds of painful karmic effects."

"Karma" refers to all physical, verbal, or mental actions. Karma embodies the idea that "one is responsible for one's actions." Although the accumulation of negative karma leads to painful sufferings, karmic retribution can be completely paid off. As long as one can prevent the accumulation of new painful karma, one is able to liberate oneself from the abyss of painful suffering. When one achieves this, a happy life is not far behind.

When suffering is known and the cause is removed, one can reach the third noble truth taught by the Buddha: the cessation of suffering.

"Cessation" does not mean to cease to exist, but rather refers to the cessation of afflictions and the attainment of purity. This is the ideal state, where people can obtain eternal happiness.

Venerable Master Hsing Yun tells us that the root cause of the suffering that afflicts us is our sense of self. The pursuit of fine material things to satisfy our desires is "self greed." The anger and hatred caused when things do not go the way we want is "self anger." And the insistence upon our views and ignoring reality is "self ignorance." It is because of the "self" that troublesome afflictions follow one like a shadow. To eliminate suffering, one must come to accept that there is no "self."

We do not have a "self" that exists independently of other phenomena. When we live with the understanding that we have "no independent self" it does not mean that we get rid of or abandon everything. What it means is that we consciously remove this sense of "self" so that we do not become attached to it.

Here, Venerable Master Hsing Yun tells an amusing story:

As the soccer championship for all the countries of Europe and the Americas was underway, hundreds of thousands of spectators attended every game, with the crowd jostling together in the packed stadium. One of the spectators happened to be smoking while he was watching the game—he was so completely fixated on the game, he did not notice as the ash from his cigarette accidentally burned the clothing of the gentleman sitting next to him.

The man cried out, "Ouch! That really hurts!"

The smoker was quite shocked and apologized profusely:

"I'm sorry, I'm sorry."

The man who was burned was also fixated on the game so intensely that he paid little attention. He responded, "It's not important! I'll just buy another one."

But the ash on the man's clothing was still burning, and blew over to the woman sitting next to him, setting her wig on fire.

"Ahh! My hair's on fire!"

The smoker quickly apologized again, "I'm sorry, I'm sorry!"

The young woman replied, "Who cares! I'll just buy another one!"

At that moment, there was no "self" present in the spectators. The "self" was entirely focused on the game, so the "self" that suffers was no longer of any importance. Since the "self" was completely forgotten, they did not notice the pain of being burnt. Because of this, they did not become angry or pick fights. If all the discord in life brought upon by people, the body, the mind, desires, opinions, the natural world, and other such things could be resolved by putting aside the sense of "self," then many situations could end happily and peacefully, and all would be right with the world.

Buddhism Is a Religion That Pursues Happiness

After understanding the truth of suffering, putting an end to the cause of suffering, and realizing the truth of cessation, we can practice the fourth noble truth taught by the Buddha: the "truth of the path."

In order to reach that state of happiness in which all affliction has been eliminated, the most important action is to practice according to the path. Everything, such as the four immeasurable minds, the four universal vows, the five precepts, the six perfections, the seven factors of enlightenment, the Noble Eightfold Path, the ten wholesome actions, the thirty-seven factors of enlightenment, and so on all fall within the scope of the path.

Understanding the truth of suffering, putting an end to the cause of suffering, realizing the truth of cessation, and practicing the path, are the fundamentals of the Four Noble Truths. The Four Noble Truths are a model for problem-solving. Consider the story of the young couple living in a shack: Once they obtained the two hundred thousand dollars, their suffering arrived and they had no peace for many nights. Fortunately, they clearly saw the cause of their suffering, and promptly put the unease brought about by the money into cessation. The path of resolution for the young couple was to return the money, allowing happiness to return once more.

The Four Noble Truths Stupas represent the teachings the Buddha passed on after he attained enlightenment.

When You Worship
the Four Great Bodhisattvas

When you bow before the bodhisattvas, have you considered how the four great bodhisattvas of China are represented in the Four Noble Truths Stupas?

The decision to place the four bodhisattvas within the Four Noble Truths Stupas represents a very important idea of Venerable Master Hsing Yun.

The Four Noble Truths are an outline of the entirety of the Buddha's teachings, as well as the foundation for the entire Tripitaka,[1] with its twelve divisions. However, following the development of Buddhism over time, their meaning has deepened, their connotation has expanded, and their tenets are practical and manifest. This has resulted in the formation of the four universal vows, represented by the magnificent and compassionate four great bodhisattvas: Avalokitesvara Bodhisattva, Ksitigarbha Bodhisattva, Mañjusri Bodhisattva, and Samantabhadra Bodhisattva.

---

1 Sanskrit for "three baskets." Refers to the entirety of canonical Buddhist writings, traditionally grouped into Buddhist discourses, monastic rules, and commentaries.

Words of Venerable Master Hsing Yun

The Four Noble Truths, the four universal vows, and the virtues of compassion, wisdom, vows, and practice embodied by the four great bodhisattvas form one interconnected system. This is why I employed the four stupas, creating something concrete to enshrine the four great bodhisattvas, so that the spirit of the four great bodhisattvas' compassion, wisdom, vows, and practice could be exhibited in a tangible manner.

Putting Your Life on the Line at the Advanced Age of Eighty-five

When planning where to place the four great bodhisattvas in the Four Noble Truths Stupas, Venerable Master Hsing Yun made many inspections, and contemplated the topic often. As the construction project proceeded, Venerable Master Hsing Yun rode in a wheelchair, but the elevator could only take him to the second floor. To go any further he had to take the stairs, so a few of his disciples carried him up in his wheelchair.

As one went further, however, the space became narrower, and at one point it was impossible for the wheelchair to make the turns. So Venerable Master Hsing Yun got out of the wheelchair and laboriously climbed on foot while four people assisted him. Despite his poor eyesight and eighty-five-year-old body, he climbed up step by step, stair by stair, all the way to the highest floor of the building.

One disciple said, "It was as if the master was putting his life on the line." But Venerable Master Hsing Yun put up with all these difficulties so he could evaluate the position of the four great bodhisattvas that were to be enshrined in the Four Noble Truths Stupas from the highest position in the memorial: Whether it was better to place them inside or outside the stupas.

At one point, the idea was to place them outside of the stupas, using a crane to place the bodhisattva statues on the roofs. Models were built, on-site observations made, and photos were taken for further consideration. There were weather-related concerns for the outside placement such as wind, rain, and lightning. The visual connection between the bodhisattvas and the central stupa with its golden sphere should also give the best possible impression of grandeur. All factors were weighed again and again, for Venerable Master Hsing Yun would rather be cautious in his pre-construction deliberations and thus avoid any regrets once everything was set.

Discussions went on for two months, and Venerable Master Hsing Yun put his life on the line once more to scale the stupas. Finally, the decision was made, and the four great bodhisattvas would be placed within the stupas.

The Jade Buddha Shrine contains many reliquaries made from fragrant woods.

The Power of the Four Vows to Support Humanity

Time is ever flowing. The Four Noble Truths and the four universal vows constitute four forces that support humanity:

- The truth of suffering—because living beings suffer so much, this vow is made: "Sentient beings are limitless, I vow to liberate them."
- The truth of its cause—because suffering comes from the accumulation of karma, this vow is made: "Afflictions are endless, I vow to eradicate them."
- The truth of the path to its cessation—to show living beings the Way, this vow is made: "Teachings are infinite, I vow to learn them."
- The truth of its cessation—to enable living beings to achieve enlightenment, this vow was made: "Buddhahood is supreme, I vow to attain it."

The enlightenment vows are made for the sake of living beings. As Venerable Master Hsing Yun has indicated, the four great bodhisattvas of China represent the four universal vows of Mahayana Buddhism. The bodhisattvas are listed below:

- Because of his great compassion, Avalokitesvara Bodhisattva roams the universe seeking those who cry out in pain, and fulfilling the prayers of living beings. Avalokitesvara Bodhisattva practices the great vow of "Sentient beings are limitless, I vow to liberate them."
- Because of his great vows, Ksitigarbha Bodhisattva entered the hell realm to liberate living beings from the bitter suffering that resulted from the accumulated karma of their afflictions: greed, anger, and ignorance. He liberates them from the hell realm's mountains of knives and trees of blades. This is the vow of "Afflictions are endless, I vow to eradicate them."
- Because of his great wisdom, Mañjusri Bodhisattva enables living beings to find enlightenment out of ignorance and truth from falsehood. This is the profound expression of the vow "Teachings are infinite, I vow to learn them."

Avalokitesvara Bodhisattva

Ksitigarbha Bodhisattva

• Because of his great practice, Samantabhadra Bodhisattva guides all practitioners to the Pure Land, ensuring that all living beings who have suffered pain and hardship can attain liberation. This demonstrates the compassionate mind of the vow "Buddhahood is supreme, I vow to attain it."

Humanistic Buddhism is Compassion, Wisdom, Vows, and Practice

The Four Noble Truths of India and China's Mahayana bodhisattva spirit make up one continuous tradition," says Venerable Master Hsing Yun, as he explains the Buddha Memorial Center.

"The right side of the Main Hall holds Vulture Peak, while the left side contains Jetavana Grove. There also flows the Ganges River,[1] the wide Bodhi Wisdom Concourse, and the Great Path to Buddhahood is situated in a straight line that represents how this is a Pure Buddha Land, a demonstration of Humanistic Buddhism for modern people. What is Humanistic Buddhism? In summary, it is compassion, wisdom, vows, and practice. Humanistic Buddhism is not just something to discuss, but something to put into practice."

Venerable Tzu Hui, a senior member of Fo Guang Shan, has followed Venerable Master Hsing Yun for more than half a century, remarks: "As I understand it, my teacher has taken the more than two thousand years of Buddhist history in its entirety and put it on display through the very buildings of the Buddha Memorial Center. In his lifetime of teaching, the Buddha emphasized the bodhisattva spirit of Mahayana Buddhism. A bodhisattva is

---

1 These three locations (Vulture Peak, Jetavana Grove, and Ganges River) are named after sites in India where the Buddha gave teachings.

Mañjusri Bodhisattva   Samantabhadra Bodhisattva

one who enlightens himself, and who enlightens others; who benefits both himself and others, practicing on his own while at the same time seeking the liberation of all living beings. The four great bodhisattvas manifest themselves in the human world, and three of these manifest in the form of lay members of society, indicating that the Buddha's teachings are a part of the human world. Fo Guang Shan places particular emphasis on this point."

The Sixth Patriarch Huineng, the great Chan master of China, once said: "The Dharma is within the world, apart from this world there is no awakening. Seeking *bodhi* apart from the world is like looking for a rabbit's horn."

Venerable Tzu Hui further amplifies the point: "If one attempts to find the path of enlightenment while one is separated from the human world, then it would be like trying to find horns on a rabbit's head. It is impossible. The Humanistic Buddhism advocated by Venerable Master Hsing Yun really emphasizes the source that comes from the Buddha's fundamental motivation. The structural relationship between the four stupas and the Main Hall is representative of this idea."

From a distance, the Four Noble Truths Stupas pay homage to the four great bodhisattvas. After one has reached this spot from the entrance through the "Great Path to Buddhahood," one becomes conscious of the fact that Buddhahood itself is now before one's very eyes. Surely learning of the bodhisattva's compassion, wisdom, vows, and practice is the ultimate form of practice for Humanistic Buddhism, is it not?

When You Deeply Experience the Eight Pagodas

The central axis from the entrance to the Main Hall and its stupas is a straight, broad boulevard with a sweeping vista. This is the "Great Path to Buddhahood," named after the hope that, by traveling down this avenue, people can draw closer to the Buddha's heart, and with every step, learn how to advance further towards Buddhahood.

What spiritual treasures are there along this route that can assist people in their spiritual practice, enabling them to attain realization and reach Buddhahood? The eight pagodas that stand on either side of the path can provide one with some answers.

The eight pagodas have a simple, clean design, with no fanciful interlocking beams, painted murals, or carved decorations of intricate complexity. They do not have colored glazed tiles or upturned eaves of decorative splendor. Their presence is one of towering tranquility. Venerable Master Hsing Yun gave each of these pagodas a name, and together they form a complete outline of Buddhist practice.

Words of Venerable Master Hsing Yun

The central stupa of the Main Hall and the Four Noble Truths Stupas are constructed in the Indian "stupa" style. As we moved outwards, I designed the eight pagodas in the Chinese pagoda style, and named each one:

- *The "One Teaching Pagoda," is a recognition that all teachings are in the human world. This is the Humanistic Buddhism I have been advocating.*
- *The "Two Assemblies Pagoda," to refer to the assembly of monastics who have left home, and the assembly of laypeople who remain at home, who both walk down the same path of spiritual cultivation.*
- *The "Three Goodness Pagoda," to refer to doing good deeds with one's body, speaking good words in one's speech, and keeping good thoughts in the mind.*
- *The "Four Givings Pagoda," to refer to giving people confidence, giving people joy, giving people hope, and giving people ease.*
- *The "Five Harmonies Pagoda," to refer to the harmony of joy within oneself, the harmony of cooperation within the family, the harmony of respect between self and other, the harmony of unity in society, and the harmony of peace throughout the world.*
- *The "Six Perfections Pagoda," to refer to the aspiration for enlightenment and practicing the six perfections.*
- *The "Seven Admonishment Pagoda" to refer to the five precepts against killing, stealing, sexual misconduct, lying, and consuming intoxicants, with the addition of prohibitions against gambling and violence, constituting the Seven Admonitions.*
- *The "Eightfold Path Pagoda" to refer to the Buddha's doctrine as represented in the Noble Eightfold Path: Right view, right thought, right speech, right action, right livelihood, right effort, right mindfulness, and right meditative concentration.*

Give People Joy, Give People Ease

The eight pagodas are symbols, but they stand for more than what is described by their names. They are not simply religious slogans. They represent something active and dynamic, like the air itself. The spirit of the "Four Givings" can be seen everywhere. During the conceptualization of the pagodas' design, Venerable Master Hsing Yun was in constant dialog with people and the environment. His comprehensive intelligence is evident in every corner of the pagodas, because he has always felt that when people come, one must give them joy and ease.

At first, the design for each pagoda only used the terraced, vertical structure reminiscent of traditional pagodas. But later Venerable Master Hsing Yun felt that, "There should be a ground floor. Our visitors are not merely looking at the exterior as they walk by. We must welcome them into the pagoda, where they can drink tea and look around for a while. They can also keep out of the sun and find shelter from the wind and rain. This pagoda is to be shared by the Buddhas above and the human beings below. This increase in space and extension in meaning are not for the sake of one single individual. Rather, it is done for everyone as a whole. I believe that I should work hard to make it so."

The first floor of each of the eight pagodas is set with a covered walkway that circles around the entire complex, allowing for free and easy access in weather fair or foul. On the second floor, one can walk outside, onto the roofs of the walkways below. One can also make their way to the neighboring pagodas. As one walks along the grounds, the ground slowly slopes upwards toward the bell and drum towers, all the way to the Four Noble Truths Stupas. Strolling along the way, one can take in the panoramic view: the circling corridors created by the Buddhist pagodas and the sweeping vistas are exquisite. With the trees on either side thick with leaves, it is as if one were walking down a green passageway.

Venerable Master Hsing Yun is always thinking of everyone, visiting the construction site daily to witness the progress first hand and inspire the workers.

In consideration of the people who become tired touring this vast parkway, whose feet become sore, or who are handicapped, electric vehicles are constantly circuiting the outer loop road. One can board at any point, and disembark at one's destination.

Measuring the Distance with One's Own Body

Everyone needs to use the restroom, and Venerable Master Hsing has inspected each and every restroom, particularly those reserved for the handicapped. He even did some onsite testing, measuring the distances with his own body, rather than with tape measurers, compasses, or statistics.

The locations of the restrooms were repeatedly reconsidered. It was assumed that people coming to the Buddha Memorial Center from Fo Guang Shan would make the restroom their first stop. The tour buses coming on long journeys would bring many people who would also wish to relieve themselves as soon as they disembarked. Consideration was also given to the tour bus drivers who had been driving long distances and could not leave the bus unattended for extended periods. They too would need restrooms nearby. Thus, additional restrooms were built outside the major buildings, as conditions required. But how many restrooms would suffice? Venerable Master Hsing Yun made an estimate using the volume of visitor traffic at Fo Guang Shan, such as the restroom usage during a four-hour period during a major event. He made use of his experience in managing space.

Realizing that many visitors would be traveling with their families, and that there were sure to be seniors included, Venerable Master Hsing Yun said to the engineers, "You young people don't understand how hard things are for old folks. Walking step-by-step up a flight of stairs takes a lot of effort."

Thus, ramps were built instead of stairs, making all locations more accessible.

When one comes to tour the Buddha Memorial Center, anyone would want to take a few pictures as a souvenir, but they might not necessarily find the best spot to take in the entire panorama. This is why Venerable Master Hsing Yun designed the "Grand Photo Terrace," ensuring that a camera lens could capture the grandeur of the entire Buddha Memorial Center. Anyone standing at the terrace would have the perfect background. Wheelchair ramps were also installed here, making the terrace accessible for the handicapped.

The Noble Eightfold Path Is the Path for Life

The shared theme for the eight pagodas is the Noble Eightfold Path. As Venerable Master Hsing Yun sees it, the Noble Eightfold Path is the most straightforward, most practical method of spiritual practice.

"Recognizing the truth of the principle of cause and effect in one's daily life is to have right view. Keeping one's thoughts in accord with the Dharma from moment to moment is to have right thought. Maintaining a kind expression and compassionate speech so that others are happy and gain trust in you is to have right speech. Ensuring that one's actions are moral and proper and that they do not harm others is to have right action and right livelihood. Assisting the weak and distressed, enjoying doing good deeds and charitable work, acting virtuously, and refraining from acting unvirtuously is to have right effort and right mindfulness. Being calm and collected in the face of adversity, and applying wisdom in judging and resolving

The Photo Terrace consists of thirty-seven steps, representing the thirty-seven factors of enlightenment.

matters is to have right meditative concentration. The Noble Eightfold Path covers the essential points of faith and morality. Not only is it a method of practice to attain liberation, it is a moral standard that everyone should observe as a part of their everyday life."

Aside from the "Open Palaces" that exhibit Buddhist artifacts from the third story up, the eight pagodas have other functions. Each pagoda is designed to be used by different groups. Venerable Master Hsing Yun gives one such example, "The first floor of the One Teaching Pagoda is an activity center and meeting place for young adults. The first floor of the Two Assemblies Pagoda has been designed as a recreation area for children and teenagers, containing many facilities suitable for youngsters. When parents bring their children here, they will find this area has been designed specifically for them, so that parents can go off and pay homage to the Buddha, transcribe Buddhist sutras, or participate in other activities without fear. The first floor of the Six Perfections Pagoda exhibits the accomplishments of the trust fund and examples of my 'One Stroke Calligraphy.' It is my hope that the connections formed by my calligraphy will bring in more donations for the Public Education Trust Fund, so that it can continue to operate for the welfare of society. The first floors of the Seven Admonishment and Eightfold Path pagodas, situated closest to the Mountain Gate, are visitor centers, welcoming guests with tea and providing them with various services."

Setting Off down the Noble Eightfold Path

When people arrive at the Buddha Memorial Center, they pass through the Front Hall at the main entrance, reaching the Great Path to Buddhahood. And with this, they are setting off down the Noble Eightfold Path. The seven admonitions mean to shun all killing, stealing, sexual misconduct, lying, consuming intoxicants, gambling, and violence; thus one can develop the aspiration for enlightenment and practice the six perfections: giving, morality, patience, diligence, meditative concentration, and *prajña* wisdom.

The eight pagodas outline the overall plan for Buddhist cultivation.

People from all five continents of the world begin with happiness within themselves, and then proceed to having harmony within the family, followed by respect between self and others. They should contribute to harmony in society and to world peace, finding confidence, joy, hope and ease in each other. Everyone will speak good words, do good deeds, and keep good thoughts, thereby purifying physical, verbal, and mental karma. Together, the monastic and lay communities take refuge in Humanistic Buddhism, returning to the very first teaching, the Four Noble Truths, and by doing so, stand before the Buddha.

In this manner, one step at a time, they advance towards where the Buddha resides, and draw near the Buddha's heart.

When You Appreciate Venerable Master Hsing Yun's One Stroke Calligraphy

The Buddha was an educator, and the Buddha Memorial Center is like a school. It is hoped that each and every person who comes here will be able to acquire some insight into life. The ground floor of the Six Perfections Pagoda contains an exhibit of Venerable Master Hsing Yun's "One Stroke Calligraphy." This is an example of how architecture is used to purify physical, verbal, and mental karma as taught by the Buddha: by doing good deeds, speaking good words, and keeping good thoughts.

Venerable Master Hsing Yun's One Stroke Calligraphy contain maxims and adages that direct people towards good and proper conduct, as well as encouraging people to follow the principles taught by the Buddha. For example, some pieces say *jixing gaozhao* (吉星高照), "Auspicious Star Shining High Above," *zuo ziji de guiren* (做自己的貴人), "The One Who Helps You Succeed is Yourself," *fuwu rensheng* (服務人生), "Live a Life of Service," and *huashi yiren* (化世益人), "Change the World and Benefit Humanity," to name a few. These examples show how One Stroke Calligraphy is working to purify and educate society.

Words of Venerable Master Hsing Yun

It is my hope that the connections formed by my One Stroke Calligraphy can generate an increase in donations for the Venerable Master Hsing Yun Public Education Trust Fund, so that it may continue to contribute to the welfare of society, as well as bring good fortune to those who make donations. It is my hope that devotees take a piece of my heart home with them. This is what I devoutly pray for.

Brush in Hand and Ink Prepared: All Done in One Go

At the Yunju Building at Fo Guang Shan, works of calligraphy are displayed throughout the Office of the Founding Master, so that the sayings contained within them flow forth like endless clouds.

Towards the end of the summer of 2009, Venerable Master Hsing Yun was virtually blind. He stood facing a new batch of his own calligraphy, hoping that his disciples would choose a few pieces that could be exhibited. Everyone carefully selected a few pieces. From the nearly two thousand works of calligraphy, only two hundred were picked. Venerable Master Hsing Yun expressed his deep regret, "To do calligraphy well is not easy at all! My eyesight is poor and my hand shakes as well. No matter how hard I try, I still can't write well. Putting on an exhibition this way wouldn't be fair to anyone."

He continued to wield his brush, practicing his calligraphy diligently every day. After he had accumulated four thousand works of calligraphy, he was still dissatisfied with his own work, and most of it was discarded in a pile.

One evening he called in his disciples and said, "Bring over the discarded calligraphy and tell me what's wrong with them."

Looking over one piece, there was a problem with the distance between the characters.

Looking over another piece, there was a problem with the overall spacing.

The next one had a page layout problem.

Then there were also crooked lines, flawed strokes, faded ink, ...

The problems with each piece were pointed out while Venerable Master Hsing Yun listened to each and every word, taking them to heart.

Most people would assume that examining ten or twenty pieces would give a fair idea of what the problems were. One to two hundred pieces of calligraphy would certainly pinpoint any problems. But Venerable Master

Hsing Yun did not stop there. He had his disciples continue to review his calligraphy, and as they continued pointing out mistakes, he kept on listening.

Works of calligraphy flitted through the air, revealing one flaw after another. This one was considered for a minute, this one for fifteen minutes, yet another for an hour. The examination of calligraphy works went on past midnight, and then on into the wee hours. They had flipped through no less than one thousand works of calligraphy. It was 2:30 am the next day.

Venerable Master Hsing Yun never stops his pen.

Thousands of works of calligraphy scrutinized, followed by thousands of moments of self-reflection. On a night such as this, one becomes pure and tranquil. The one master, five disciples, and one thousand calligraphy works became linked in spirit, just as if they were reciting the Buddha's name, or sitting in meditation.

At 2:30 am, this eighty-four-year-old man finally came to a stop. His disciples thought that their teacher would probably return to his room for a well-deserved rest. To their surprise, he finished another fifty works of calligraphy before 6:30 am, covering his desk, chair, and floor with them. The various problems raised the previous night were no longer to be found: his calligraphy style was now completely transformed.

It was at that moment, when the night shifted to dawn, that Venerable Master Hsing Yun, through his lines of calligraphy, awakened to the rhythm of the world. His compassionate mind connected to the continuous cycle of rejuvenation of all things. He created the unique style we now call "One Stroke Calligraphy," a work of calligraphy complete in one continuous stroke.

Venerable Master Hsing Yun explains the style in this way, "Since I can no longer see, I can only calculate the distance between each character and complete it in one gesture after I've wet my brush. If I do not finish with the first stroke, then I will not know where to put the second stroke. I can only rely upon my own mental estimations. No matter how many characters there are in a phrase, they all must be done in one stroke. This is the only way I can achieve success. That is why it is called 'One Stroke Calligraphy.'"

The Life of Ink to Be Always Cherished

After developing One Stroke Calligraphy, Venerable Master Hsing Yun continued his daily practice of writing calligraphy. Each day he would use whatever bits of free time he had left over from his teaching schedule to ply his art with brush and ink. He would find time to work maybe two or three times a day, creating more than fifty works of calligraphy at a stretch, in total over one hundred each day. What bold, vigorous energy must there be in someone who, at the advanced age of eighty-four, achieves such a stunning level of productivity!

Later on, Venerable Master Hsing Yun took up the challenge of couplet writing. Since these tend to be longer inscriptions, he needed someone to pull the paper as he wrote. This presented yet another difficulty. The speed at which he wrote the calligraphy had to be in perfect sync with the speed at which the person moved the paper. Otherwise the rhythm would be

The exhibition hall of the Fo Guang Yuan Art Galleries provides a brief biography of Venerable Master Hsing Yun.

broken. Additionally, the disciple who came and pulled the paper for him was not always the same person. Different people have different rhythm and timing. Whenever a slow rhythm was changed for a fast one or vice versa, Venerable Master Hsing Yun would have to adjust. Eventually he learned to adapt instantly, no matter who was pulling the paper. Venerable Ru Chang, general director of the Fo Guang Yuan Art Galleries, commented, "Venerable Master Hsing Yun no longer retains a sense of self. He is able to forget the self as he practices calligraphy, attaining a higher state."

One day, Venerable Ru Chang had set out the ink, writing brush, ink stone, and paper before Venerable Master Hsing Yun so that he could begin his work. In order to ensure that the writing brush was sufficiently moistened with ink, Venerable Ru Chang completely filled the ink stone. Venerable Master Hsing Yun began writing, producing more pieces than usual, and spending more time than usual. His disciples could not bear to see their aged teacher laboring away with his brush when he'd already exerted himself for so long, so one of them reminded him, "Master, why have you written so much calligraphy today? Don't you want to rest for a while?"

Looking at his disciples, he replied, "I haven't used up all the ink yet. It would be a pity if you just dumped it out. I can write much more with this. It is the ink's purpose in life to be written with."

Venerable Master Hsing Yun cherishes objects as though caring for his own body, and leaves nothing to waste. The remaining ink saw yet another fourteen calligraphy works born from his brush. Only when transformed into written characters does the ink have a meaningful existence. This is but another way that Venerable Master Hsing Yun "cherishes life."

A Continuous and Ever Present Connection to Writing

And so it was that in the short span of two months, Venerable Master Hsing Yun used up seven bottles of ink, went through seven writing brushes, and completed nearly nine thousand works of calligraphy. The pace he had set made it difficult for the paper suppliers in the surrounding areas to keep up with their deliveries.

His disciples were constantly reminding him, "You've done so much, master. Please rest. You can write some more tomorrow!"

And Venerable Master Hsing Yun would always reply, "Don't tell me to rest. I don't know how much longer I can write. So I'll write more as long as I can do so."

Venerable Hsin Pei, the abbot of Fo Guang Shan, described him in this way, "Venerable Master Hsing Yun is a committed bodhisattva who never rests." His constant and unceasing effort with One Stroke Calligraphy, without pause or interruption, is a perfect reflection of his life. For these interconnected characters, what is continuous is not merely a devoted attentiveness to the calligraphy process, but also the longstanding connection of others to Venerable Master Hsing Yun, a lifelong writer and calligraphist.

Speaking of writing, Venerable Master Hsing Yun's earliest memories can be traced back to his childhood years, as he first began his education. In the monasteries of his early life, as a monastic, his teachers were extraordinarily strict disciplinarians. They were always admonishing him not to open his eyes and look around: "What are you looking at? Is there anything that belongs to you?" Thus, at a young age he would often keep his eyes closed and not look around for ten days, even half a month. Such was his monastic education, both rigorous and austere. Amid the fires of the war with Japan, the monastery was so poor that they did not have food to eat, let alone money to buy paper and brushes for writing.

After his arrival in Taiwan, his teaching duties had him writing characters on blackboards while his magazine editing and book and article drafting had him writing characters with a pen. Due to these factors, his connection with writing was as close as pen to ink, resonating throughout all his various mental calculations and his interactions with others. This was especially true in 1953, when he took up residence at Leiyin Temple in Ilan, Taiwan. In order to decorate the plain, whitewashed walls of the main shrine for the annual seven-day retreat, Venerable Master Hsing Yun would buy the cheapest paper, upon which he would write inspirational slogans to encourage people to practice chanting, and then place them on the walls. He did so every year for twenty-six consecutive years.

Amid the Fragrance of Brush and Ink, a Moment Is a Thousand Years

But the real application of ink and brush for creating works of calligraphy came during the 1980s, while Venerable Master Hsing Yun was lecturing in Taipei.

One day, as the Emperor Liang Repentance Dharma Service was being conducted at Pumen Temple, a certain devotee walked up to Venerable Master Hsing Yun during a break and quietly offered a red envelope. Upon seeing that the red envelope contained 100,000 NT$, Venerable Master Hsing

Yun, who has never been willing to accept offerings from devotees, hastened to return it. But the devotee steadfastly refused to take it back. Venerable Master Hsing Yun recalled the old saying, "proper etiquette requires reciprocity," so he picked up some calligraphy he had just written which read *xin xie xing zheng* (信解行證), "faith, understanding, practice, and realization," and gave it to him. The devotee was overjoyed and announced his good fortune in the Buddha hall. Envious, four hundred people participating in that day's repentance service emulated him, coming in droves to plead with Venerable Master Hsing Yun: "We too will make an offering, would you please give us your calligraphy?"

As he could not bear to oppose the wishes of the devotees, Venerable Master Hsing Yun inscribed more than four hundred works of calligraphy that day. The next day, yet another Dharma service was held, in which about four hundred people were also to attend. Upon hearing what had happened the day before, they too came in droves, asking for calligraphy, each offering 100,000 NT$ in a red envelope. Venerable Master Hsing Yun, never in the habit of spending money, had suddenly acquired tens of millions in cash. How best to utilize it? He described his own reasoning at the time:

"Rather than saying I have spent my life as a monk, it is more accurate to say that I have spent my life as an educator. At the time, we were beginning preparations in Los Angeles to raise funds to build the University of the West. This money could contribute greatly to the cause. This was the first time I realized that, regardless of whether the writing was good or not, I could use this connection with calligraphy to build up the University of the West. This buoyed my confidence in calligraphy."

With the donations from Venerable Master Hsing Yun's calligraphy, the University of the West was founded, creating the "Manifesting the Meaning of Coming to the West" campaign. Twenty years later, it became the first university constructed by the Chinese community to become accredited by the Western Association of Schools and Colleges (WASC).

After wetting his brush, Venerable Master Hsing Yun works on creating masterpieces. (Photo by Cai Rong Feng)

Venerable Master Hsing Yun's famous One Stroke Calligraphy.

The wish to found educational institutes was fulfilled by calligraphy. And when the Lunar New Year came, the traditional Chinese Spring Festival of spiritual transformation, Venerable Master Hsing Yun wrote scrolls bestowing blessings of good fortune, nurtured by the human heart. More than fifteen years have passed since 1996, since the two-hundred thousand copies of *ping'an jixiang* (平安吉祥), "Peace and Auspiciousness" were printed in the first run. Every year since, millions of these New Year greetings are printed, to make positive connections with the larger society. And so the phrases *qianxi wanfu* (千喜萬福), "Infinite Blessings for the New Millenium," *shanyuan haoyun* (善緣好運), "Good Connections Bring Good Fortune," *miaoxin jixiang* (妙心吉祥), "A Wondrous Mind Brings Auspiciousness," *zide fenfang* (子德芬芳), "Prosperous Future Generations," *weide fuhai* (威德福海), "Awe-Inspiring Virtue and Ocean of Prosperity," *qiaozhi huixin* (巧智慧心), "Skillful Wisdom and Enlightened Mind," have become phrases repeated year after year. Venerable Master Hsing Yun's calligraphy has developed through the years. Great words of blessing and auspiciousness now grace the hearts of every family and household, in every village and town.

Public Service Continues Onward, a Consistent Process

In 2008, Venerable Master Hsing Yun donated all his income and royalties from writing, a sum totaling 30,000,000 NT$, and established the "Venerable Master Hsing Yun Public Education Trust Fund" to advance social services.

One day, after completing a few works of One Stroke Calligraphy, a disciple made a recommendation: "Master, you've done so much 'One Stroke Calligraphy,' you could put them up for charity sales. This could become the source of funding for a public trust fund!"

Venerable Master Hsing Yun could not contain his misgivings, "Would this calligraphy work do? Probably not!"

The disciple encouraged his teacher, "Yes, it would! You have hopes for the 'Three Acts of Goodness Campaign' public trust fund, as well as the promotion of good works in the areas of philanthropy, culture, education, and mass media. In the future, these must be carried on every year. If you were to strengthen the funding assistance through the charity sales of your One Stroke Calligraphy, this would be a wonderful thing!"

The disciple's good intention was motivated by a sense of social service, and after pondering the matter for some time, Venerable Master Hsing Yun agreed.

Looking back over the years, Venerable Master Hsing Yun has shown his work at various calligraphy exhibitions, both at home and abroad. Every time, he has nurtured people's hearts with resounding approval. One could say that with the fragrance of brush and ink, he has ensured that the Buddha's light shines everywhere, and that the Dharma waters flow forever. The ultimate shape of that one stroke in his distinctive One Stroke Calligraphy is the crystallization of a lifetime tempered with activity, a consistent practice that extends from the past into the present, and on into the future.

Compassionate Giving, One Piece of His Heart

The first floor of the Buddha Memorial Center's Six Perfections Pagoda exhibits the accomplishments of the Public Education Trust Fund and One Stroke Calligraphy. Venerable Master Hsing Yun has said, "It is my hope that devotees take a piece of my heart home with them."

Using his heart as a metaphor to convey the gift of the Dharma possesses a deep significance.

As a young monk, his teachers yelled, "What are you looking at? Is there anything that belongs to you?" Indeed, nothing can be called his, for all of it is to be given away.

Venerable Master Hsing Yun has given away his writing income and royalty fees, entrusting them to funds for the public good.

Venerable Master Hsing Yun's One Stroke Calligraphy is displayed in the Six Perfections Pagoda.

The historical and cultural artifacts that people have donated to him throughout his lifetime have been given away, every piece donated to the Underground Palaces of the Buddha Memorial Center. They have been turned over to Buddhism as a whole, to be shared by everyone.

His time and his energy have been given away as well: Even as his eyesight fails and his hands shake, he still practices his calligraphy day and night, his brush never pausing.

Venerable Master Hsing Yun always says that his Chinese characters are ugly, but within these characters, there is the Dharma: the Dharma sayings of ancient sages, Buddhist verses, the *gongans* of the Chan School, contemplations on the nature of emptiness, and Humanistic Buddhism. He hopes people will not look at the shape of his characters, but rather look at the thoughts he has put into them. He hopes to emulate the heart-baring arhat of the Buddhist sutras.

"Because in my heart lies the spirit of compassion. I can show it to you."

When You Imagine
the Underground Palaces

When you come to the Buddha Memorial Center, you can see the Main Hall, you can see the copper Big Buddha, you can see the Four Noble Truths Stupas, the eight pagodas, and so on. However, there is one area here that cannot be seen immediately. These are the underground palaces.

Called *digong* (地宮) in Chinese, these time capsules of Buddhist cultural artifacts are modeled after ancient Chinese tombs of treasures. The Buddha Memorial Center has forty-eight underground palaces located directly under the Main Hall. Inside them, thousands of cultural artifacts are stored for safekeeping. Traces of the passage of time and memories of life from around the world are preserved here in pristine condition for future generations to see.

New generations are constantly being born. Time is like a river, flowing ever onward. If you have ever considered or pictured this "linear aspect" of life, you will come to realize what inspired the design of the world of the underground palaces. Venerable Master Hsing Yun's design tells us how life is a river, forever renewing itself in an endless cycle.

Words of Venerable Master Hsing Yun

In the future, one of the forty-eight underground palaces at the Buddha Memorial Hall will be opened every one hundred years. With forty-eight of them, this means four thousand eight hundred years will pass before they will all have been unearthed. Many people feel that they can't possibly live to see the opening of an underground palace. But when you think about it, haven't you already seen how the cultural artifacts were stored in the underground palace? Even if we may not see one of them opened, we can still contribute artifacts to the underground palaces. In one hundred, five hundred, two thousand, or even four thousand years, when we return again in some future lifetime, we will see the treasure that was deposited there in the past. How meaningful that will be!

Just as a river flows east to the ocean, so too do human beings live according to the flow of time. It is like the succession of the four seasons. Once winter has passed, doesn't springtime come again? Life is an unending cycle of lifetime after lifetime. How many times one will come back in the future depends upon one's karma and vows. Life in fact extends over many lifetimes, so we must have confidence in ourselves. I firmly believe that, in the future, many people will come back to the Buddha Memorial Center to witness the grand opening of an underground palace.

A Parrot from a Hundred Million Years Ago

Can you imagine the expanse of time contained within the underground palaces? Among the cultural artifacts stored in the underground palaces at the Buddha Memorial Center is an ancient rock that resembles the head of a parrot. The rock is covered with layer upon layer of fine lines, a testament to

The parrot-shaped fossil.

the passage of time, like the development of the earth's crust.

The donor of the parrot-shaped rock was Hu Yang Xinhui. Her husband's oil company discovered this ancient rock while drilling along Siberia's Irtysh River in the former Soviet Union. Geologists studied the fossil and determined that it is up to one hundred million years old. Hu Yang Xinhui saw this fossil as the crystallization of the earth's ancient beauty, and donated it to the underground palaces. In the future, humanity will be able to see evidence of the evolution of life and the mysterious changes to the environment and climate over millions of years.

Just as a fossil is a manifestation of the earth's extensive history, Venerable Master Hsing Yun has endowed the Buddha Memorial Center with an important mission, to serve as an account of history. With the goal of preserving an account of faith, life, and culture, the underground palaces have collected various artifacts that are of great historical, informative, contemporary, and commemorative value. This includes Buddhist artifacts, cultural artifacts and inventions, items representative of Taiwanese and other world cultures, and so on.

Cultural artifacts of Buddhism are an important part of the collection. However, in order to endow the collection stored in the underground palaces with more significance, the Buddha Memorial Center has put out a public call to assemble treasures from society as a whole. Any cultural artifacts that represent the shared history of humanity are eligible to be preserved in the underground palaces.

The largest donor to the underground palaces is Venerable Master Hsing Yun himself, who has donated more than three thousand cultural artifacts.

"I have turned over to Buddhism everything that everyone has ever presented to me over the course of my lifetime, donating it all to the underground palaces."

In Venerable Master Hsing Yun's eyes, these inanimate cultural artifacts are actually imbued with a life of incomparable richness, representing the history, culture, and art of the distant past. Venerable Master Hsing Yun states that: "What is collected in the underground palaces are not treasures of gold, silver, or gems; but rather the treasure of knowledge."

And If People a Thousand Years Hence Want to Know ...

The cultural artifacts excavated from the underground palace of Famen Temple near Xi'an, China, have enabled people to learn about the culture of the Tang dynasty (618-907 CE). The discovery of Buddhist texts stored at Dunhuang has meant the reappearance of precious Buddhist artifacts preserved for more than one thousand years. These discoveries surprised the world. Venerable Master Hsing Yun is looking thousands of years into the future.

"As the present moves one step at a time toward the future, the cultural artifacts of the Buddha Memorial Center will offer something for later generations to reflect upon and study, so that they will have a more concrete understanding of the tools we used, our lifestyle, and the popular trends in our society."

The treasures placed into the underground palaces at the Buddha Memorial Center include a large number of Buddha and bodhisattva statues. Among these, there is the copper relief statue of Maitreya Bodhisattva in

A Thai Buddha statue.

Maitreya Bodhisattva in contemplation.

contemplation. This statue is set in a state of contemplation, with a crown on its head. Its right hand gently touches its cheek, and the right leg is bent inward so that the foot is resting on its left knee. It is identical to the statue of the bodhisattva at Hōryū Temple in Japan, a statue considered a national treasure. This is a significant connection, representing the Dharma's path of transmission from India to China, and then from China to Japan.

Thus, this image of Maitreya Bodhisattva in contemplation not only symbolizes the transmission of Buddhism over the past twenty-six hundred years, it also represents the all-important future. When this image of Maitreya Bodhisattva is excavated in the future, it will serve as evidence across time and space that the Buddha descended into the human realm and brought liberation to living beings.

If people one thousand years from now wish to know about the rich historical and cultural value of Buddhism, they can examine the Thai Buddha statue, with its halo of wisdom blazing above its head, and the Burmese jade Buddha, depicting a monastic robe through the use of simple, well-defined lines. Both of these works constitute the properties of humanity shared with their own contemporary aspects.

If people one thousand years from now wish to know about our current worldwide faith in Avalokitesvara Bodhisattva, they can examine the Ajaya

The *Three Treasured Buddhas of the Main Shrine.*

Ajaya (All-Victorious) Guanyin

Guanyin statue. This piece is a slender, graceful figure standing bolt upright, and displays many of the characteristics of the artisans of China's Yunnan Province. It is truly a rare piece.

If people one thousand years from now want to know about the layout and arrangement of Fo Guang Shan in its early days, forty years after its founding, they can look at the *Fo Guang Pure Land in Crystal*; Etched with high-end laser technology, one can see the Non-Duality Gate, the Main Shrine, the Great Compassion Shrine, the Great Buddha Land, and so on in the crystal. Even after all the changes to topography and architecture planned to occur at Fo Guang Shan in the centuries to come, the Fo Guang Pure Land carved inside this crystalline glass will provide a pristine view of what the temple once was. There are also the *Three Treasured Buddhas of the Main Shrine* created by artist Loretta Huishan Yang, using the lost-wax crystal casting method. In the center is the image of Sakyamuni Buddha in white, to the right is the Medicine Buddha of the East in blue, and to the left is Amitabha Buddha of the West in yellow. These are the symbols of Fo Guang Shan's faith.

Underground Palaces as Time Capsules

The objects of this age are history for the next age.

For example, during the 1970s and 1980s, Taiwanese students went abroad for advanced education. Many of them brought with them an electric rice cooker made by the Ta-Tung Corp. With it, they went out into the world, living the diligent and frugal life of a foreign student. At the time, the Ta-Tung electric rice cooker could be found in virtually every household. This single device thus came to represent the life and industrial culture of that period, becoming the lovable "Ta-Tung Mascot." It serves as a testament to the development of Taiwan's economy, as well as the indomitable spirit of the people of Taiwan as they advanced onto the world stage.

This collection of memories from the past will also include the first generation of mobile phones, rotary telephones, old radios, pagers, sewing machines, bicycles, and other such objects. The various everyday devices donated by the public will help preserve the life of this age for safe-keeping within the underground palace, telling later generations how we lived.

Then there is the instrument panel from a decommissioned American aircraft carrier. This item represents the technology aboard warships of the time. More importantly, these military instruments symbolize an ideal: The transition from war to peace, as well as demonstrating the value of incorporating Buddhism into culture.

Naturally, cultural artifacts that symbolize the glories of Taiwan and the brilliance of the Chinese are also included in the underground palace collections. These include a signed, commemorative baseball pitched by Chienming Wang, a pitcher from Taiwan who joined Major League Baseball

in America; a basketball signed by Yao Ming, China's basketball star who joined the NBA, from the first game he played as starting center; a baseball signed by Sadaharu Oh, the great Japanese-Chinese baseball player and manager in Japan; a model of the "Bird's Nest," a major venue for the 2009 Olympics held in Beijing, that symbolizes the pride of the Chinese in hosting that great occasion. All of these items have been placed inside the underground palaces.

Forty-Eight One Hundred-Year Appointments

Many of the precious cultural artifacts placed in the underground palaces are made from materials that will not decay. In the future, one palace will be opened every century. Aside from displaying cultural artifacts, donations will be solicited to help protect the cultural artifacts of the period, ensuring that the culture of humanity and the world's material assets will continue to be preserved.

As he witnessed the ceremony for the consignment of the cultural treasures to the underground palaces alongside everyday tourists, Venerable Master Hsing Yun emphasized this:

"Life does not end here. We must have faith that, in the future, when the underground palaces are opened every one hundred years, we will return here. Together, let us witness the opening of the next underground palace."

With one speech, Venerable Master made forty-eight promises, each covering the span of a century.

Venerable Master Hsing Yun employs these forty-eight underground palaces to prompt people to look toward the future. How you imagine the underground palaces now is how you will see them in the future.

The "Thousand-Armed and Thousand-Eyed Guanyin."

When You Have the Chance to Ascend to the Open Palace

When he heard that the Buddha Memorial Center had an "open palace," one child asked if it was the same celestial palace that the mythical monkey Sun Wukong wreaked havoc upon. Such a place would be quite a sight!

The open palace is actually an invention of Venerable Master Hsing Yun. Since there are sealed collections of cultural artifacts under the earth, why shouldn't there be some above ground as well? These open palaces are located in the eight pagodas. Above the ground floor, the second to the seventh floors of each pagoda are "open palaces," where treasured cultural artifacts are held for display.

As these exhibition areas become open to the public, the open palaces not only build a connection to the past, they also impart knowledge and uplift the spirit. Whether the onlookers experience a sense of wonder, or find something that resonates with them, each and every person can interact with the cultural artifacts that speak to them.

In order to capture the interest of both children and adults, the open palaces offer truly extraordinary collections. The cultural artifacts contained within are rare beyond compare. These include sacred objects of a commemorative nature, brought to Taiwan by Venerable Master Hsing Yun from the Buddha's birthplace after his first visit to India half a century ago.

Words of Venerable Master Hsing Yun

Inside the sole suitcase I brought with me on my tour of India, I had placed my clothing and daily necessities, as well as the souvenirs I bought at the various sacred sites. Aside from these, I had also wrapped and placed within the suitcase sand from the Ganges River, earth from Bod-hgaya, a brick from Deer Park, and a five-grain brick from the nirvana stupa. I brought these back to Taiwan as remembrances.

An Early Morning Just after the Rains Stopped

Nearly fifty years after this trip, all the sacred objects of the Buddha Venerable Master Hsing Yun brought back in his suitcase will be placed inside the open palace of the One Teaching Pagoda.

The construction of the open palaces has become a tangible reminder of Venerable Master Hsing Yun's first trip to India, which occurred in July of 1963, when Venerable Master Hsing Yun toured Southeast Asia as part of the Buddhist visiting delegation from the Republic of China. In the blazing midsummer heat, he pushed aside all difficulties to step into the Buddha's homeland.

It was in the morning, just after the rain had stopped, and the clouds in the sky hung white and pure. This was when Venerable Master Hsing Yun first saw Bodhgaya, the place where the Buddha attained enlightenment. He had long admired the grand India tours of Faxian (337-442 CE) during the Eastern Jin dynasty, and of Xuanzang (602-664 CE) during the Tang dynasty. Now he was emulating them: He took off his shoes and entered the Great Stupa of Bodhgaya, where he bowed deeply before the Buddha in the Buddha's own land.

Not far from there was the magnificent *bodhi* tree where, under the starlit night, the Buddha attained supreme enlightenment more than twenty-six hundred years ago. Venerable Master Hsing Yun walked in the shade of the *bodhi* tree, reflecting upon the Buddha's compassionate intention to benefit all humanity.

The *bodhi* tree is under the special protection of the Indian government. No one is permitted to break off a branch or pluck a leaf from the tree; one can only wait for a leaf to fall naturally. Venerable Master Hsing Yun's wait was rewarded when a leaf from the enlightenment tree drifted down to him. It was as if he had attained an extraordinary treasure. Another memory that Venerable Master Hsing Yun particularly treasures was the feeling of the soil on his bare feet as he circled the *bodhi* tree.

"The soil of that sacred site was so fragrant. Only someone who has experienced it themselves can truly understand the feeling behind these words."

The Buddha Is Still Teaching the Dharma Here

Once he attained supreme enlightenment and rose from his seat, the Buddha took his first step down the path to liberating living beings and traveled to Deer Park. In this serene, secluded forest grove, the Buddha taught the profound Dharma to the five bhiksus, giving the teaching which would come to be known as the "Four Noble Truths." The five bhiksus were enlightened then and there, achieving sagehood. As Venerable Master Hsing Yun gazed out from the platform commemorating where the Buddha taught, he saw the ruins of the ancient Buddhist site, filled with shattered tiles and crumbling walls. He bent down and picked up a few fragments of brick, so that this symbol of the Buddha's Dharma voice could be shared back in Taiwan.

For forty-nine years the Buddha taught the Dharma. He traveled all along both banks of the Ganges River, spreading the Dharma. When Venerable Master Hsing Yun drifted along the Ganges River in a small boat, he saw the teeming masses of living beings, the rich and the poor, the living and the dead, human beings in all their countless guises. Upon coming ashore, he cupped a handful of sand from the Ganges River. The sand was as fine as flour and sparkled with a golden light, just as described in Buddhist texts.

The Buddha spent his whole life teaching the Dharma and liberating living beings. He left the world for final *nirvana* at the age of eighty. Twenty-six hundred years later, Venerable Master Hsing Yun walked across the site where the Buddha attained final *nirvana*. There were few traces of any human presence there, and everything was quiet. Even though there was no path up the hill, he still made the climb. The hilltop was originally the location of an ancient stupa, created with bricks made from the five grains. It had collapsed long ago.

Amid the broken walls and crumbling chambers, Venerable Master Hsing Yun picked up something that caught his eye. It turned out to be one such five-grain brick. Caught up as he was with exploring the site of the final *nirvana*, there was no time for photographs. The five-grain brick remains his only memento of the site.

Breathing the Air of the Buddha's Homeland

In 1979, Venerable Master Hsing Yun personally led the "Pilgrimage to India," a tour of several sacred sites. At that time, it may have been the largest Buddhist pilgrimage ever. In those days, India's tourism business was not well-developed. The sanitary conditions were not particularly good. Moreover, gathering information was quite difficult. Whether it was lodging or transportation, the group often had to arrive at the location before they could adequately assess potential arrangements. This was especially true for the more rural areas, where political and economic conditions were unstable. At every turn the ability of the group leaders to create contingencies was challenged. It was under such difficult conditions that the group decided to charter two planes; one to carry the people and the other to carry the pilgrims' luggage, as well as a full load of food supplies, clothing, and blankets for the local population and for Tibetan refugees.

Even today, where communications network and technology have improved by leaps and bounds, such an undertaking of foreign travel would still be extremely difficult. As he reminisced about that groundbreaking tour, Venerable Hsing Yun remarked, "At the time, the Indian government presented me with a small package of rice. They told me that this was the kind of rice the Buddha ate, and that it had been excavated during the renovation of a sacred site. I held it with both hands. Though the rice had already turned brown, its value was beyond compare."

Over the many years since then, Venerable Master Hsing Yun has traveled to India no fewer than ten times. He often says to his followers, "India

is the Buddha's homeland. As Buddhists, we should go on a pilgrimage to the sacred sites at least once in our lives. When you step upon the path walked by the Buddha, you will find that the soil is particularly fragrant. Breathing the air of the Buddha's homeland, you will feel that it is especially fresh. Thinking about the past can deepen your resolve, and undertaking the Buddha's great task of wisdom can strengthen your faith. Kneeling down before the Buddha's throne, you bask in the compassionate light of the Buddha. It frees you from the afflictions of ignorance in an instant. Our humanity is constantly being elevated. Here is where the value of human life is recognized."

The Cultural Artifacts of the Eight Pagodas: The Open Palace Treasuries

For those who have yet to personally visit the sacred sites of Buddhism, the open palaces present an opportunity to view these Buddhist artifacts and to give people a glimpse of their precious spiritual energy. Aside from the ground floor of each pagoda, which is set aside for visitor services, the second to the seventh floors in each of the eight pagodas are designated as open palaces, modeled after Buddhist treasure museums. When he was arranging the displays of cultural artifacts on each floor of every pagoda, Venerable Master Hsing Yun adopted the presentation of a quality boutique:

"On each floor only one item or category of cultural artifacts is exhibited. Items are not jumbled together or scattered about. Since there is only one item or category within each space, it becomes an exclusive piece; since there is only one, there is a focus; and since there is only one, a person will examine it more carefully. Less is more."

Each of the eight pagodas symbolizes an aspect of spirituality. In classifying the cultural artifacts, Venerable Master Hsing Yun assigned a particular focus to each one:

"The One Teaching Pagoda preserves all the sacred items of the Buddha. These include the kind of rice eaten by the Buddha, the type of vessel he would

The "Three Sacred Rice Grains".

have used for drinking, and the type of alms bowl he would have used for begging. There are also monastic robes woven with gold, a brick from the platform on which he taught at the Deer Park, a five-grain brick from the *nirvana* stupa, golden sand from the Ganges River, and so on. The footprints made by the Buddha and the mementos he touched have always been hard to find, yet these sacred items have a connection with Taiwan, and so I have gathered them together in the One Teaching Pagoda. Now, visitors can come to see the history and culture of the Buddha's home country."

"The Two Assemblies Pagoda preserves the Dharma of the two assemblies of the faith, the monastics and the laity, such as multiple Buddhist sutras, palm-leaf scriptures, and several dozen editions of the Buddhist canon. These are texts that I have accumulated day by day, month by month, and year by year, over the course of my lifetime. Now, all of them are on display here for the public. The Three Goodness Pagoda contains magnificent depictions of the monastic order, including images of the great bodhisattvas, arhats, important practitioners, and hundreds of eminent monks, ranging from ancient times to the present. Be they copper statues, woodcarvings, painted drawings, or photographs, all are on display."

When You See Mañjusri Bodhisattva's Gift

Most people like to receive gifts. Gifts can be a blessing, and are a way to share something beautiful. The open palaces of the Buddha Memorial Center serve as such gifts, and are meant to be shared with everyone in the world.

There are many cultural treasures on display in the open palaces; some have been kept by Fo Guang Shan for many years. Now that conditions are right, they are being shared with the public. The community itself has also collected many artifacts, and now that conditions are right, these are being shared with the rest of the world.

Each heartfelt item has its own special set of circumstances. One particular item, a golden robe of the Buddha, can be traced to Mañjusri Bodhisattva. This item of profound significance ties together a spiritual connection spanning a thousand years: from China's Tang dynasty to the Korean kingdom of Silla in the past, and from Fo Guang Shan in Taiwan to Tongdo Monastery in South Korea today.

Words of Venerable Master Hsing Yun

The Tongdo Monastery is one of the main temples of South Korea's Jogye Order. The temple is also called the "Temple of the Buddha Gem," and was made a sister temple of Fo Guang Shan in 1982. The process of reproducing the golden robe of the Buddha was an undertaking that required the utmost care, from the recitations of mantras and the Buddha's name by the monastic community, the demarcation of a special area, and the wrapping of the gold threads and the fine stitching. It is an extraordinarily rare and precious gift.

The Bodhisattva's Verses on Mount Wutai

To explain the significance of this particular golden monastic robe, we must take ourselves back to the remote past, into the Tang dynasty. In 636 CE the Korean Vinaya Master Jajang was studying in China.

When he made a pilgrimage to Mount Wutai, Master Jajang devoutly worshipped Mañjusri Bodhisattva for seven consecutive days. One

Gold-woven monastic robe.

night, he dreamed that Mañjusri Bodhisattva recited many verses to him, but no matter how hard he tried to understand them, they remained incomprehensible. Just then, a monastic appeared before him. This was a manifestation of Mañjusri Bodhisattva, who not only explained to him the meaning of the verses, but also presented him with a golden monastic robe and alms bowl, as well as a relic of the Buddha's skull.

In 643 CE, Vinaya Master Jajang returned to the Silla Kingdom in what is now modern-day Korea. In 646 CE, he founded the Tongdo Monastery. There he enshrined the relics of the Buddha handed to him at Mount Wutai. The main Buddha hall at the Tongdo Monastery does not have a statue of the Buddha, but rather contains the Buddha's skull relic upon an altar. Because of this, the temple is also known as the "Temple of the Buddha Gem."

Tongdo Monastery is one of the main monasteries of the Jogye Order of Chan Buddhism (known as *seon* in Korean). The Jogye Order received royal patronage during the Silla and Goryeo periods (918–1392 CE) and became the dominant school of Buddhism. Over the course of thirteen hundred years and several dynasties, the temple has expanded with each new generation. At present, the temple contains a total of thirty-five buildings and

In September 2009, Venerable Jeongu personally delivered the gold-woven monastic robe to Fo Guang Shan.

pagodas, precious local artifacts from more than a dozen locations, and a legacy of more than seven hundred local cultural artifacts. Indeed, the temple can be considered a museum containing a multitude of riches.

Presenting a Golden Robe to Fo Guang Shan

In 1982, Tongdo Monastery and Fo Guang Shan formed a bond as sister temples. This senior institution, more than thirteen hundred years old, and the barely sixteen-year-old youngster Fo Guang Shan, were henceforth joined together in a deep bond, interacting with each other quite frequently.

In 2003, Venerable Master Hsing Yun paid a visit to Tongdo Monastery. The abbot at the time brought out the golden monastic robe specially for Venerable Master Hsing Yun to see. Gazing at the thousand year-old robe before him, given by Mañjusri Bodhisattva himself, Venerable Master Hsing Yun could not help but offer up great words of praise to Tongdo Monastery for its extraordinary connection to the Dharma.

Venerable Jeongu, the former abbot of Tongdo Monastery, once visited Fo Guang Shan as a guest lecturer. He admired Venerable Master Hsing Yun to an extraordinary degree. Ever since his visit in 2007, Venerable Jeongu tried to think of what gift he could give to Venerable Master Hsing Yun.

"The only way I can express my esteem and respect for Venerable Master Hsing Yun is to present another golden monastic robe to him and to the Buddha Memorial Center."

This idea was realized in September of 2009. Leading a group of monastics and devotees from Tongdo Monastery, Venerable Jeongu personally presented a golden robe to Fo Guang Shan. The monastic and lay communities at Fo Guang Shan lined the route in respectful welcome. Representing Fo Guang Shan, the robe was received by its abbot, Venerable Hsin Pei, who presented in return a Burmese palm-leaf Buddhist sutra from the Fo Guang Shan collection.

Making the Cloth from the First Thread of Gold

During his talk, Venerable Jeongu mentioned that the original golden robe enshrined in Tongdo Monastery had been passed down for many years to the present. Since the robe was protected by its gold thread embroidery, the robe still retains its flexibility even after more than twenty-six hundred years. It has been preserved in excellent condition.

In recreating the golden monastic robe at Tongdo Monastery, Venerable Myeongju sewed the robe, while Venerable Undai blessed it with mantra recitations. The cloth itself was provided by Seo Eunsuk, a specialist in the weaving industry.

Seo Eunsuk spent nearly two months looking for the gold thread to make the cloth. The search took her from South Korea all the way to Japan. However, the real difficulties were yet to come. In comparison to most thread, gold thread lacks elasticity, and tends to be shorter in length. This greatly increases the time spent joining threads when weaving the cloth. In order to ensure that the cloth remains soft, the gold threads must be wrapped in silk before being carefully applied, little by little, using a traditional hand-loom. Only thirty-five centimeters of such cloth can be woven a day.

The copy of the gold-woven monastic robe presented by Tongdo Monastery as a gift to the Buddha Memorial Center.

Owing to its extreme delicacy, the gold thread will break if it comes into contact with even the finest particle of dust. This was why Seo Eunsuk chose to set up a special tent within the factory to serve as the weaving area and prohibited people from casually entering. In this manner, she worked for days. Starting from scratch, she spent two whole months before she could finish weaving enough cloth to replicate the golden monastic robe.

Though the weaving process was quite difficult and complex, being a Buddhist, Seo Eunsuk was happy and grateful that she was able to participate in the production of the golden monastic robe.

A Seventy-Year-Old Venerable Does the Recitations and the Sewing

Once the cloth was completed, there was the sewing stage, which was done at Tongdo Monastery. In order to produce the golden monastic robe, Tongdo Monastery had a new building specially constructed. All four sides of the structure were demarcated with mantras from such texts as the *Great Compassion Mantra*. Eminent monks and great worthies conducted the consecration ceremony, respectfully beseeching generations of patriarchs to bless and protect this special area. Throughout the entire process, Venerable Undai sat in meditation and recited mantras, praying that the process of producing the robe would not encounter any problems.

Only the three people producing the monastic robe were permitted into this sacred space. To enter they had to wear specially-made clothes and socks in order to guarantee that their bodies and clothing were clean. They even had to change clothes when they went to the restroom.

Though he had more than twenty years of experience in sewing monastic robes, Venerable Myeongju had reached the advanced age of seventy, and had not performed any needlework in over thirty years. Only through meditation could he recall the robe-making methods taught to him by his teacher when he was nineteen. The gold thread presented difficulties during the sewing process, as the gold thread was as fine as silk and dazzling in the light. Given Venerable Myeongju's advanced age, this put a terrible strain on his eyes. In addition, gold thread is not as pliable as silk thread. This made the sewing process even harder. Every day, Venerable Myeongju began work after breakfast. Yet the task still took him fifteen whole days. Being 144cm in length and 120cm wide, the golden monastic robe appears identical to the original article.

The monastic robe is also called the "field of merit robe" because of the many interlocking patches which resemble rice fields. Altogether, the golden monastic robe has two hundred and fifty of these fields, woven into a grid-pattern. In order to ensure that the merit circulates like water in a field, each field on the merit grid is pierced with a hole. Each of these holes is sewn with nine stitches. During each stitch, one of the sacred names of the Buddha is chanted. To Venerable Myeongju's surprise, the shoulder pain and backache he had been suffering from disappeared, as he sewed, and his body felt supple and at ease. Aside from expressing his gratitude to the Buddha for this blessing, Venerable Myeongju observed, "This golden monastic robe could not have been completed without the accumulated power of Venerable Master Venerable Jeongu's vows, or the dedication of the weaver and the sponsors."

What Mañjusri Bodhisattva Is Telling People

In the *Three National Legacies*, one of the great national treasures of the Korean people, it is recorded that this act of recreating the monastic robe is suggestive of how the faith and spiritual focus of the Buddha's disciples is nourished and fostered. Every gold thread, every stitch sewn, every field of merit, every recitation of the Buddha's name, and every mantra are gifts that come from Mañjusri Bodhisattva, telling people that spiritual practice can be advanced in every little action.

From Mount Wutai in China to the Silla Kingdom, from Tongdo Monastery in South Korea to Taiwan's Fo Guang Shan, the connections created by this monastic robe form a bond for all those who walk along the path to Buddhahood, one that will not be extinguished in even a thousand years.

When You Meet
the Eighteen Arhats

In Buddhism, the word arhat refers to a person who has no afflictions. Among the millions of people who lived at the time of the Buddha, only a few are called *arhats* in the sutras, having attained such a title.

The most well-known of these are a group called the "eighteen *arhats*," recorded in the *Record on Dharma Abiding,* translated by Xuanzang (600-664 CE) in the Tang dynasty. These are the arhats who protect the Dharma in the Buddha's name, and each one had his representative attributes and stories.

The set of arhats used since ages past contains only men, yet the set of eighteen arhats at the Bodhi Wisdom Concourse contains statues of three women who were arhats: Mahaprajapati Bhiksuni, Utpalavarna Bhiksuni, and Bhadra Kapilani Bhiksuni. This revolutionary stroke of creativity not only highlights the Buddhist teaching of equality among all living beings, it also demonstrates the contemporary status of equal rights between the sexes.

Words of Venerable Master Hsing Yun

Buddhism must keep up with the times. These three bhiksunis, Maha-prajapati, Utpalavarna, and Bhadra Kapilani, are enlightened beings who are already arhats. This is made clear both in the sutras and in historical records.

The contributions made by the female monastic order have been essential to the growth of Buddhism in Taiwan. Even when we look at Buddhists around the world, women are clearly in the majority. When these women see that female monastics have been welcomed into the ranks of the eighteen arhats, they will know that women too possess the potential to become Buddhas. Is this not another step forward for Buddhism? The Buddhist teachings are not here to constrain people. They are here to support and liberate them. This is not a special effort to stand up for women; I'm simply upholding the truth.

Ananda, foremost in
having heard much.

Rahula, foremost in
esoteric practices.

Aniruddha, foremost in
heavenly vision.

The Offering of an Eye

In the Kingdom of Magadha, in southern India, there lies a secluded and peaceful village with green hills and clear waters. This was where Sariputra was born. From an early age, he was the wisest among his peers. At the age of eight, he was well-versed in literature and was elevated to the position of treatise master for his astounding eloquence. At age twenty, Sariputra was the disciple of a non-Buddhist teacher. It was there that he met a fellow disciple Maudgalyayana, and the two became the best of friends.

One day, Sariputra met Asvajit Bhiksu, one of the Buddha's first five disciples. Seeing his extraordinarily dignified conduct and deportment, Sariputra went up to him and asked, "Who is your teacher, and what are his teachings?"

Asvajit Bhiksu replied, "Sakyamuni Buddha is my teacher. He teaches that all phenomena are produced by causes and conditions, and all phenomena pass into extinction through causes and conditions. He also says that all conditioned phenomena are impermanent, and so phenomena arise and pass into extinction. With birth and death ended, there is the tranquility of nirvana."

As soon as he heard this, Sariputra experienced a great realization. All his past confusion regarding life and the universe were suddenly swept away.

Sariputra, foremost in wisdom.

Maudgalyayana, foremost in supernatural powers.

Mahakasyapa, foremost in austerities.

After he returned, he took Maudgalyayana with him and followed the Buddha's path. Henceforth, the two of them became the chief disciples of the Buddha.

Sixty *kalpas* before that, during one of Sariputra's previous lifetimes, a heavenly being took the form of a young man and appeared before him in tears, explaining that he needed the eye of a spiritual practitioner to cure his mother's illness. Thereupon Sariputra plucked out his left eye and offered it. The young man said that what he needed was the right eye, and so Sariputra plucked out his other eye as well.

To Sariputra's surprise, the young man said his eye was smelly and dirty, and threw it to the ground. Blind and ridiculed, Sariputra felt like giving up. Just then, many heavenly beings appeared in the sky. They explained that they were testing his commitment to the bodhisattva path. As soon as he heard this, Sariputra felt ashamed of himself. But his resolve to become a Buddha, and benefit others, was rekindled. In that moment, he resolved to never stray from the bodhisattva path.

After ceaseless cultivation for sixty *kalpas*, Sariputra was able to see the Buddha and hear his teachings, becoming foremost in wisdom among the Buddha's disciples.

A Row of Arhats Never Seen Before in All the World

Just as Sariputra was foremost in wisdom, each of the Buddha's ten great disciples has their individual specialization. There was Maudgalyayana, foremost in supernatural powers, Mahakasyapa, foremost in austerities, Rahula, foremost in esoteric practices, Mahakatyayana, foremost in debate, and Ananda, foremost in having heard much. All of them are great sages whom Buddhists know. In addition, the set of eighteen arhats at the Bodhi Wisdom Concourse at the Buddha Memorial Center include Pindola, Aniruddha, Ksudrapanthaka, Kalodayin, Purna, the Dragon Subduing Arhat, the Tiger Taming Arhat, Upali, Subhuti, Utpalavarna, Mahaprajapati, and Bhadra Kapilani.

Mahaprajapati Bhiksuni, Utpalavarna Bhiksuni, and Bhadra Kapilani Bhiksuni were specifically brought into the ranks of the eighteen arhats by Venerable Master Hsing Yun as a way of encouraging the equality of men and women in Buddhism.

Mahaprajapati Bhiksuni was the Buddha's maternal aunt. The Buddha's mother passed away seven days after giving birth to him, and he was then raised by his aunt. After the Buddha attained enlightenment, his aunt led a group of five hundred women from the Sakya clan and begged to follow the World-Honored One, joining the monastic order. This marked the beginning of the Buddhist order of *bhiksunis*, female monastics. Thus, Mahaprajapati also became the first female monastic in the history of Buddhism.

Before she left home to join the monastic order, Utpalavarna Bhiksuni suffered a turbulent life. She experienced many problems in her personal life and in her

Mahaprajapati Bhiksuni.

Pindola, foremost in merit.

Kalodayin, foremost in teachings.

Mahakatyayana, foremost in debating the Dharma.

Utpalavanna Bhiksuni, foremost among Bhiksunis in supernatural powers.

marriage. She gave up on herself, and repeatedly used her feminine charms to beguile and cheat others. Once, she met Venerable Maudgalyayana, who was unmoved by her beauty. He said to her, "No matter how grave your previous wrongdoing, my teacher the Buddha can certainly liberate you."

And so, Maudgalyayana brought her before the Buddha to repent. Her wholesome roots from previous lifetimes became manifest, and she pleaded to follow the Buddha's spiritual practice. Upon joining the monastic order, Utpalavarna practiced diligently day and night, becoming the *bhiksuni* foremost in supernatural powers.

Bhadra Kapilani Bhiksuni had been married before leaving home to join the monastic order. Her husband was none other than Venerable Mahakasyapa. Because his parents pressed him to marry, the young Mahakasyapa had no choice but to take Bhadra Kapilani into his house as his bride. As one sat at the front of the bed and the other sat

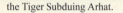

the Tiger Subduing Arhat.

the Dragon Subduing Arhat.

Subhuti, foremost in
understanding emptiness.

on the floor, the two of them discussed their desire for spiritual practice. They lived as husband and wife for twelve years, purely in name. Mahakasyapa left home to become a spiritual practitioner, and after honoring the Buddha as his teacher, he pleaded for Bhadra Kapilani to be allowed to enter the *bhiksuni* order. Upon joining the monastic order, Bhadra Kapilani was diligent in applying herself to the practice, studying long into the night. In the end she attained enlightenment and became an arhat.

A Convoluted Cultivation in the Look of the Arhats

When he designed the Buddha Memorial Center, Venerable Master Hsing Yun hoped to spread Buddhist culture through Buddhist art. He was careful in selecting the sculptor Wu Rongci out of thousands of sculptors to shoulder the great task

Bhadra Kapilani Bhiksuni.

Purna, foremost in teaching the Dharma.

Upali, foremost in monastic discipline.

Cudapanthaka, foremost in moderation.

of sculpting the eighteen arhats. Wu Rongci travelled as far as Quanzhou in Mainland China to select the best bluestone, working on this artistic project with meticulous care. With sublime creativity and masterful craftsmanship, Wu Rongci created sculptures with artistry like nothing ever seen before, bringing into this world a group of eighteen arhat statues of unsurpassable quality.

The prominent professor of history and Buddhist specialist Chen Qingxiang wrote of these sculptures:

"Among Wu Rongci's eighteen arhats, one will find the old and the young, male and female, and faces of perfect compassion along with rough-hewn faces twisted into roars. Some are standing, some sitting, and the lines denoting the folds of their clothing can be heavy or light. No two of the eighteen arhats are alike in appearance and the expressiveness of their hands and feet show the sculptor's profound subtlety. Regardless of their theme or presentation, these sculptures outstrip in every way the traditional depiction of arhats. In particular, one can understand the story of their lives from their mere appearance, seeing their complex paths of spiritual cultivation. They are truly touching, and they inspire deep thought."

When You Enter
the Buddha's Classroom

It would not be wrong to say that the whole Buddha Memorial Center serves as the Buddha's classroom.

It could even be said that one can come to learn and know the teachings of the Buddha in the mountains and rivers of the world, as well as in the workings of the universe.

The Dharma is so vast that there is nothing outside of it, and yet the Dharma is so small that nothing can be concealed within it. It is both visible and invisible, having form and no form. There exists a form of practice appropriate for each and every living being in the world. Though this may sound baffling, it is both commonplace and true.

When he designed the Buddha Memorial Center, Venerable Master Hsing Yun hoped that everyone who visited would benefit from the experience. He hoped that people would gain more than just a sense of happiness, that they could leave with a sense of inspiration that illuminates the spirit. Towards this end there are many buildings, paintings, audio-visual images, performances, and so on designed to inspire. One ancient, quiet medium that Venerable Master Hsing Yun especially excels in is bas-relief artwork, which he uses to depict stories from the Buddhist sutras.

Words of Venerable Master Hsing Yun

Oh Buddha, when I read the Agamas it is as if I hear your voice teaching the Dharma. You skillfully directed Venerable Ksudrapanthaka to sweep away the dust and dirt, you compassionately guided the cleaning worker Nidhi to purify his mind and body, you employed the metaphor of tuning an instrument to instruct Sronakotivimsa on how to practice the Middle Way, and you told the brahmin woman Ciñca what she had to do in order to prevent disaster and cleanse her wrongdoing.

Stories of the Buddha's Life

During the Buddha's lifetime, there was an untouchable named Nidhi in the city of Sravasti. He made a living carrying away dung. This was considered such a low and menial task that even children despised him. One day, Nidhi was carrying buckets brimming with dung out of the city to be dumped. When he saw the dignified visage of the Buddha in the distance. Nidhi felt so ashamed of his dirty appearance that he immediately turned around and walked the other way.

He could never have guessed that just as he was about to leave the city, he would encounter the Buddha yet again. The Buddha gently called for him to stop, and Nidhi, with his buckets of dung hanging on his pole, was so ashamed he did not know what to do. The Buddha asked him, "Would you like to join the monastic order?"

Having never been addressed so kindly before, Nidhi was both startled and overjoyed. But when he thought about his lowly status, he could not help but question how he could possibly qualify for the monastic order. But the Buddha said with a smile, "The Dharma is vast and limitless. Anyone may cultivate and gain liberation, no matter who they are."

For the first time in his life, Nidhi felt hopeful. He followed the Buddha back to the Buddha's monastery at Jetavana. After hearing the Buddha's initial teachings, he became a stream-enterer. Then the Buddha taught him the Four Noble Truths, and Nidhi Bhiksu immediately became an arhat. His afflictions had been completely eliminated, and he both attained liberation and realized supernatural powers.

Another disciple of the Buddha was Sronakotivimsa Bhiksu, also called "Two-Billion Ears." Before he joined the monastic order, he was a skilled musician. When he heard the Buddha teaching the Dharma, he was so deeply moved he joined the monastic order, shaved his head and donned the robes of a novice. So began his life as an ascetic, a life of frugality and few comforts.

Converting Angulimalya

Accepting Alms Equally

Compassion towards Nidhi

Deeply beloved by his parents, Sronakotivimsa had an extremely sheltered upbringing and found his body unable to endure the rigors of ascetic practice. Furthermore, he did not appear to be making any progress towards enlightenment. This left him quite distressed.

When the Buddha learned of Sronakotivimsa's predicament, he said to him, "You're practicing so fiercely all by yourself, but you do nothing but sitting meditation. Let me ask you, if you were to play an instrument, if the strings are too tight, what will happen?"

Sronakotivimsa answered, "If the strings are too tight, they will break."

"And what if they are too loose?"

"There will be no sound."

The Buddha then explained this analogy, "Spiritual practice is like playing a stringed instrument: one cannot be too tight nor too lax. Being either too tight or too lax will create problems. Relax your mind, for one should seek the Middle Way in everything."

Sronakotivimsa faithfully followed the Buddha's instructions, and his mind became calm and peaceful. Not long after that, he attained enlightenment and became an arhat.

Taking Home Some Illuminating Inspiration

There are twenty-two bas-reliefs set in the walls lining the walkways on either side of the Bodhi Wisdom Concourse. Each depicts a story from the Buddha's life, including the stories of Nidhi and Sronakotivimsa. They tell

Chairs line the plaza, providing visitors a place for rest if they need a break.

stories of how the Buddha went out among the people and applied his wise and compassionate mind to transform society at every level.

No matter who he encountered, be they kings, queens, great ministers, the poor, beggars, or slaves, no matter where they came from, even in the crudest, most remote corners of the land, all became students in the Buddha's classroom. In Venerable Hsing Yun's mind, the Buddha is the greatest educator there ever was. To emulate the Buddha, the Buddha Memorial Center was designed to be one big classroom.

Venerable Master Hsing Yun's design emphasizes the needs of the people. For example, every one of the bas-reliefs depicting stories from the Buddha's life has an explanatory plaque in both English and Chinese. The font is designed to be large enough so that even senior citizens can read the plaques with ease. Furthermore, Venerable Master Hsing Yun designed them to be placed below the bas-relief on a slanted sill. Aside from being at a better angle for viewing, this design prevents visitors from trying to use the sill as a seat, encouraging guests to maintain a sense of proper decorum.

Many chairs have been installed throughout the complex, so that sightseers can take quick breaks. However, you will never find any long benches. Venerable Master Hsing Yun feared people would try and lie down on the benches, which would impinge upon the sublime dignity of a Buddhist temple.

Such structures encourage people to maintain the dignity of the center through their actions and thoughts. These are some examples of the subtle and detailed arrangements that Venerable Master Hsing Yun designed within the Buddha Memorial Center.

Walking into Scenes of the Buddha's Life

Feeling as if he had been endowed with a special purpose, the famed artist Shi Jinhui carefully and skillfully created twenty-two bas-reliefs depicting stories from the life of the Buddha, built on a scale suitable for the Buddha Memorial Center.

Shi Jinhui admitted to himself that he was facing the greatest challenge in his career. For this series of bas-reliefs, he did not limit himself to Eastern or Western styles of art, but rather focused on depicting the essence of the Buddhist stories: their loving-kindness, their compassion, their joy, and their equanimity. When the bas-reliefs are viewed as a whole, one can see that he has adapted to the unique style of the Buddha Memorial Center and has thus blended many diverse cultures. Observed in detail, one can see that he attempted to travel back twenty-six hundred years, to the time of the Buddha. By bringing himself into the Buddha's life, Mr. Shih could see through the eyes of the people in the painting, see the Buddha's appearance, hear the Buddha's voice, and realize the Buddha's teachings first-hand. He would often wake in the middle of the night, struck with a flash of inspiration that had manifested in a dream. He would immediately jump out of bed to make a draft, recounting the scene as if he had experienced it himself, employing the most suitable composition, line, and image.

Shi Jinhui tells these true stories of the Buddha in artwork filled with dramatic tension. These twenty-two stories have been transformed into twenty-two bas-reliefs arrayed along the walkways on either side of the concourse. As visitors walk past them, they pause, transfixed in wonder as they gaze upon the depictions. They find themselves transported into the time and place of the Buddha, and into the depths of his heart. In his words, Shi Jinhui hopes that these depictions of stories of the Buddha's life will help people understand the Buddha's spirit of compassion, and his unwillingness to give up on any living being.

Buddhist Verses Set in Stone

Just as there are twenty-two bas-relief sculptures from the Buddha's life, there are also twenty-two calligraphic verses from the ancient sages inscribed at the Buddha Memorial Center that spread the Buddha's compassion and wisdom. Their purpose is to enable people to understand the Buddha's humanity and his compassion for all living beings. They also serve as examples of literary and artistic beauty, supplementing the atmosphere of the Buddha Memorial Center.

Venerable Ru Chang, general director of the Fo Guang Yuan Art Gallery, says that Venerable Master Hsing Yun has made promoting Humanistic Buddhism his life's mission, and has done so by doing worldly tasks in a way that goes beyond the worldly. One particular example is Venerable Master Hsing Yun's efforts to use culture and education to transform society, particularly in developing Buddhism through the arts. The presence of Buddhist verses throughout the Buddha Memorial Center is an example of using the artform of calligraphy to express profound Buddhist principles.

Since he knew his calligraphy would be used in the Buddha Memorial Center, Venerable Master Hsing Yun made a special effort to carefully select poetic verses and prose quotations from the Buddhist sutras that praise

Dharma words of the ancient sages, carved on Shanxi black granite.

the meritorious qualities of the Buddha. One such example appears in the *Flower Adornment Sutra*:

> All the water in the great oceans can be consumed,
> All momentary thoughts can be counted,
> Space can be measured, winds can be bound—
> The state of the Buddha cannot be fully described.

Here is another memorable verse from a great sage of the past:

> Many in the Buddha land have minds at ease,
> Watching the birds daily fly out and return on their own.
> Seeking something is not as good as having nothing to seek;
> How can advancing be superior to retreating?

Here is a selection from the *Xizhai Pure Land Poems* by Venerable Fanqi (1296-1370 CE) of the Ming dynasty:

> Let go of body and mind and the Buddha appears before you,
> One's ears are always filled with the sound of the Dharma proclaimed.
> The wind through the tree branches plays the song of the unborn—
> Contemplate the sun; always shining, never night.

Then there are also selections from the *Sutra on the Life Stories of the Buddha*, the *Sutra on Cause and Effect through the Three Time Periods*, *The Pure Rules of Baizhang*, the *Yogacara Flaming Mouth Dharma Service*, and many more. A total of twenty-two verses from sutras and ancient sages have been inscribed on a tablet of Shanxi black granite, specially selected for this purpose. This ensures that Venerable Master Hsing Yun's dedication to spreading the Dharma through art will become an enduring tradition.

The Production Process as an Edifying Experience

The calligraphic artistry of Venerable Master Hsing Yun is quite forceful and precise in both layout and spacing. Therefore, carving these characters into a material as hard and rigid as black granite presents a high degree of difficulty. However, one of Taiwan's master stone carvers, with twenty years of experience, managed to create an accurate rendering of Venerable Master Hsing Yun's calligraphy, capturing the beauty of its lines and spacing.

Venerable Ru Chang relates, "During production, everyone was trying to ensure that the Buddha Memorial Center conveyed the Buddha's humanity. Thus, we first did a few trial stone inscriptions for Venerable Master Hsing Yun to look at. Some were in black, some were in white, some were painted in gold, and some had no coloring at all. These examples were laid out in a row, and together, everyone shared their thoughts. Venerable Master Hsing Yun is a very open-minded individual, and so everyone at Fo Guang Shan could join in the deliberations. The views of the devotees, the views of the Buddha's Light International Association members, and the views of scholars were also brought forward, considered, and summarized. Then, everyone cast a vote, and the matter was decided. Here we can clearly see Venerable Master Hsing Yun's spirit of openness and the subtlety of his dedication. The entire process was an edifying experience."

When You Quietly Appreciate the Life Protection Murals

The protection of life is a form of compassion, for to abstain from killing is the most fundamental teaching of the Buddha.

Today, the practice of protecting life has grown to encompass more and more, including protecting the environment. Not only must individual lives be protected from harm, the environment itself must be protected comprehensively so that all the people who live within it are safe.

Living without concern for the environment has long been one of the most harmful things to the planet. It is the slow killer of mother earth. It is impossible to completely protect the environment, due to the propensities and selfishness of human beings. People treat neither the environment nor others with kindness and compassion. Ultimately, they end up not treating themselves with kindness and compassion either.

The kindness and compassion that the Buddha has taught people for more than twenty-six hundred years means unconditional loving-kindness and universal compassion. This is entirely in accord with the ideals of environmental protection. Putting such ideals into action requires that they be instilled into people from an early age.

Words of Venerable Master Hsing Yun

The eighty-six color murals depicting the protection of life were selec-
ted from Feng Zikai's Protection for Living Beings, and are arrayed
along the outer walls of the long walkway. The murals emphasize the
sanctity of life. Parents can bring their children along to appreciate
the murals and develop their sense of compassion, which will have a
positive effect on their growth.

The Extremely Large Paintings on the Wall

In this painting, there is a willow tree; in its shadow, a young boy is lying on a bench reading a book. It is a peaceful, happy scene, a vibrant image of spring. Just then, a swallow appears, trailing down with the breeze and landing on the pillow of the boy reading a book. It is not the least bit afraid.

This is one of the drawings from *Protection for Living Beings,* drawn by the famous Chinese cartoonist artist Feng Zikai (1898–1975). The poem inscribed on this painting is:

> The swallow flies to the pillow,
> No longer avoiding people out of fear.
> Only because there is no aggression in the mind
> Can it be as pleasant as a spring breeze everywhere.

The poem and the original calligraphy were written by Venerable Hongyi (1880-1942), an eminent monk of the early Republican era. The artistic mood of the entire painting is relaxed, and the wonderful relationship between the bird and the boy is extraordinarily moving.

Feng Zikai was a man with a soft, tender heart, and his *Protection for Living Beings* contains a total of eighty-six such pictures and poems. Reproductions of these paintings have been painted onto the outside wall of the northern and southern walkways of the Buddha Memorial Center. They show that life should be cherished, and exhort people not to harm living beings.

Venerable Master Hsing Yun says of Feng Zikai, "He was a pioneer in advocating environmental ecology. After taking refuge with Venerable Master Hongyi, Feng Zikai spent the rest of his life creating *Protection for Living Beings.* His compassion for all living beings is vividly illustrated in his paintings, creating a moving experience with the beauty of his work, while at the same time teachings others the merit of protecting life."

The success and influence of *Protection for Living Beings* is a precious gift left to humanity by Feng Zikai and Venerable Hongyi. Venerable Master

The extremely large paintings on the wall, depicting the protection of life.

The Buddha Memorial Center presents the *Protection for Living Beings* for even more people to appreciate.

Hsing Yun has made a special effort to collect authentic versions of the illustrations from *Protection for Living Beings* and share them with everyone at the Buddha Memorial Center. It is his hope that through such artistry, people will learn more about Buddhism, become closer to the Dharma, and treat living beings and everything in the world with compassion.

Environmental and Spiritual Preservation

The propagation of the principles of environmental protection and the protection of life are not limited to paintings on the wall. They are demonstrated through our actions. In October of 2010, the General Conference of the Buddha's Light International Association was held at Fo Guang Shan. In his keynote address entitled "Environmental and Spiritual Preservation," Venerable Master Hsing Yun made an earnest appeal to humanity to practice the compassionate vow to liberate living beings:

"Buddhism is a religion that possesses a profound consciousness of environmental protection. Through the words and deeds of Sakyamuni Buddha and the various great bodhisattvas as recorded in the sutras, we can see Buddhism's early advocacy of protecting life through environmental protection and preserving the planet. If we are to spare humanity from descending to the level of environmental refugees, it is time for us to stand up and become the vanguard of environmentalism."

To save the planet, we must first emphasize environmental protection. Venerable Master Hsing Yun underscores this in a single sentence, indicating the critical juncture of our current problems of environmental protection: "Environmental protection depends upon the awakening of humanity. To begin, we must practice spiritual preservation."

During his speech, Venerable Master Hsing Yun emphasized how Amitabha Buddha was a pioneer in the protection of the mind and body as well as environmental protection. The Pure Land he created ensures the mental and physical well-being of all who seek shelter in it, and the purification of body, speech, and mind. Over the generations, eminent monastics and great sages of Buddhism have planted trees, built and repaired roads and bridges, dredged rivers, and preserved natural resources. In expounding Buddhist sutras and teaching the Dharma, they have exhorted everyone to protect life and set living creatures free; they have advocated such ideals as vegetarianism, cherishing one's blessings, and caring for material possessions. They can be held up as a model of the finest in volunteer workers for promoting environmental protection.

For this keynote address, Venerable Master Hsing Yun took great pains to collect data and statistics, compiling them into a handbook for the attendees. In order to help everyone understand the material in detail, Venerable Master Hsing Yun asked several people, including Venerable Hui Chuan, president of Fo Guang Shan's Supervisory Council, to read the entire document out loud during the meeting. During the nearly hour-long process, Venerable Master Hsing Yun paced about the meeting hall, like a class instructor patrolling the classroom. The auditorium was suddenly transformed into one big classroom, in which two thousand people listened in rapt attention to the lecture.

Protecting the environment and protecting life are surely some of the most pressing issues for humanity today.

When You Smile in Understanding at the Chan Art and Stories

Living in this busy, stressful, and chaotic society, no one is free from physical and mental stress, or the conflict of interpersonal relationships. In this demanding, suffering-ridden life, everyone can use a laugh and a bit of relaxation: look at the white clouds in the sky, the flowers blooming on the ground, take a look at an ancient legacy given to us by the Buddha: Chan.

Chan is a wonderful thing. Once it enters your life, every movement becomes filled with vitality and every action becomes easy and unrestrained. Since Chan is open to all, a thing of peace, sometimes it only takes a look, a smile, or some small motion to bring on an experience of clear insight or some sense of realization, dispelling worry and bringing about peace.

Chan is wisdom; it is humor and compassion. It is not distant or remote. In order to ensure that the public can enjoy the profound meaning of Chan teachings, the Buddha Memorial Center has taken the Chan paintings by the husband and wife duo of Gao Ertai and Pu Xiaoyu, based on *Hsing Yun's Chan Talk*, and engaged the sculptor Ye Xianming and the painter Chen Mingqi to recreate them as a series of forty bas-reliefs. These are on display along the outer walls of the northern and southern walkways.

Words of Venerable Master Hsing Yun

Chan is like a painting that brings beauty to the world. Chan is like salt that makes things more appetizing. Chan is like a flower that brings people joy. Chan is like rouge that can make one bright and beautiful. Chan is humor, it is the natural world, it is our minds, and it is our original face. Chan is the root of Humanistic Buddhism.

Drying Mushrooms in the Sun

In a certain Buddhist monastery, there was a Chan master, more than eighty years old. One day, he was hunched over under the bright sun, drying mushrooms. When Chan Master Daoyuan, abbot of the monastery, saw the old master he said to him, "Senior elder, you are getting on in years now. There's no need for you to do such hard and strenuous work anymore. I can get other people to do this work for you."

Without hesitation, the old master replied, "Other people are not me!"

Master Daoyuan went on trying to persuade him, "That's true enough. But if you want to work, there's still no need to do so when the sun is out!"

The old master asked, "If I don't dry the mushrooms under the bright sun, then you're saying I should wait for a cloudy or rainy day to do the drying?"

The old Chan master's simple yet powerful answer fully demonstrates how Chan is a part of life. Even the act of drying mushrooms is a part of the pure Chan mind. Menial tasks are not to be done by others, nor are

Chan Art and Stories is the largest series of cement bas-reliefs in Taiwan.

they meant to be put off until tomorrow. They are for the present moment. Chan is getting to know one's true self through daily chores, and seeing first-hand how Chan points directly to the mind.

The Moon Cannot Be Stolen

Chan Master Ryokan Taigu (b. 1758) lived in a crude hut at the foot of a mountain; his life was quite simple. One night as he returned home, he ran into a thief who was ransacking his hut. When he saw the master return, the thief was so frantic that he did not know what to do.

Chan Master Ryokan Taigu spoke to the empty-handed thief in an affable manner, "Can't find anything to steal, huh? I think you may have wasted your time coming here. How about you just take the robe I'm wearing?"

The thief grabbed the robe and took off. Now bare-chested, Chan Master Ryokan Taigu watched the thief running in the moonlight. He spoke with a profound sense of regret:

"The moon is so bright and beautiful, too bad there's no way for me to give it to you."

The "beautiful moon" symbolizes the brightness of every individual's intrinsic nature. If one can come to know the treasure that lies inside, what need would there be to take anything from others? The Chan master's sense of pity was actually an expression of regret over how people have forgotten the treasures within themselves.

The Largest, Cement Bas-Relief Unequaled in All of Taiwan

Work on the "Chan Art and Stories" bas-relief series was jointly led by the sculptor Ye Xianming and the painter Chen Mingqi, who managed the project team that created the largest cement bas-relief project in all of Taiwan.

With twenty years of experience as an artist, Ye Xianming employs traditional techniques fused with concepts from modern art. Using the labor-intensive yet long-lasting clay sculpting techniques, Ye Xianming was able to convey the themes of the Chan mind and Buddha nature in a fresh and lively manner. For the project, Ye Xianming worked quickly, shaping the cement directly on the walls of the Buddha Memorial.

"One has to quickly determine and control the thickness with great precision. The sculpting process must be completed within three to four hours, because the cement will not wait."

The emotions in the facial expressions and hand gestures of the figures, in particular, proved to be a real test of the artist's skills.

Creating cement bas-reliefs puts the artist's skills to the test.

The completed cement sculptures were then adorned by the marvelous brush of the color painter Chen Mingqi. By his hands, the works came alive. It was as if the people depicted in the Chan stories could walk right out of the wall.

Chen Mingqi explains, "Since the artwork is already rendered in three dimensions, the effects of lighting are already present. The person doing the coloring must be very clear about what areas remain in shadow, and should not be emphasized. This is quite different from painting done on flat surfaces."

In comparison to the original drawings, the colors on the wall paintings are richer. This was done for the ambience of the Buddha Memorial Center and to mitigate the effects of exposure to sunlight. Thus, a richer style of coloration was adopted in order to ensure that the colors would last longer. At the same time, the rich colors heighten the three-dimensional effect of the bas-reliefs, making it possible for visitors to appreciate the artwork quite clearly, no matter what angle they view it from. Thus, one can gain insight into the spirit of Chan.

When You Gaze upon the Wall of Benefactors: A Thousand Temples, A Million People

Across the large walls are inscribed many names in closely spaced characters. Some of the names are ancient and elegant, some are not as sophisticated, and some are trendy and fashionable. Some consist of generations of ancestors of a certain family name, or the name of the benefactor's beloved pet. All of these names represent the benefactors who offered their aid and devotion to building the Buddha Memorial Center.

Someday, perhaps an elderly woman from one of these benefactor's households will bring her son, daughter-in-law, grandchildren, and great grandchildren to this wall. With the help of her descendants, this elderly woman can find her own name, inscribed neatly alongside those from the past four generations of her family.

Most of the elderly grandmothers on this island of Taiwan are simple, hard-working folk. They make their silent contributions to their families, children, friends, and neighbors. They have spent their lives being called "mom," "granny," "grandma," and so on. Some may have even forgotten their own names. But now they can see their own name, returning to their primary school days when the teacher called out that name. In truth, they are students: Students who spent a lifetime devoutly listening to the Buddha's instructions.

Who knows how many families, how many individuals, and how many temples have their names inscribed on this wall? How many stories are there to be shared? They have all been brought together in one great act of merit, to be seen by their distant posterity.

Words of Venerable Master Hsing Yun

When one Buddha appears in the world, a thousand Buddhas are arrayed in support. It is because of the help of all of you that we have the Buddha Memorial Center today.

Every name here marks an individual who has donated to the Buddha Memorial Center.

Every Single Name is Teaching the Dharma

With contributions from society, the help of senior members of the Buddhist community, and the myriad positive connections formed with more than a thousand temples, Venerable Master Hsing Yun was able to build the Buddha Memorial Center. His gratitude to each and every one of these groups exceeds whatever can be expressed in words. This long, long wall is his way of expressing his thanks.

Each name, every line, indeed, a whole swath of names are accompanied with depictions of sacred *mudras* of the bodhisattvas, along with selections from Venerable Master Hsing Yun's *Humble Table, Wise Fare*, inscribed by famous native and overseas calligraphists from Taiwan, Hong Kong, Japan, and South Korea. All of these have been deeply carved into the Shanxi black granite, forming a continuum like a gushing river: each and every drop of its spray sparkles in the light, soundlessly surging onward as it rolls along both sides of the Great Path to Buddhahood, becoming the northern and southern walkways that protect visitors from the weather. Each walkway is 254 meters in length.

Of the thousands of temples and millions of individuals, every benefactor has their name inscribed on this wall, coming a step closer to the Buddha.

As Venerable Master Hsing Yun sees it, these names are parts of the Dharma; they are all expressions of gratitude for the Buddha's kindness. Every grain of sand, every block of stone, every brick, every tile, every beam and column, indeed, the entire Buddha Memorial Center itself is the manifestation of the will of the faithful. When people have the connection to come here, when they see the impressive buildings and experience the power to move others, they can feel a sense of gratitude, and become a part of this great undertaking. This multiplies the good deeds and the kind thoughts invested into this building. Along the corridors of time and space, the goodness and beauty of Buddhism are passed on generation after generation.

The names of thousands of temples and millions of individuals have each been inscribed into this wall rich with merits, so that their names can exhort others to generate the wholesome aspiration for enlightenment.

When You Immerse Yourself
in the Serenity of Vulture Peak

> The Buddha is on Vulture Peak, but do not seek afar.
> A Vulture Peak is found within our minds.
> Everyone has a Vulture Peak pagoda.
> One should cultivate underneath this pagoda.

Where is Vulture Peak? It can be as far as distant India, thousands of miles away; and yet it is as close as our true intrinsic nature, nestled within each person.

Twenty-six hundred years ago, the Buddha expounded the sutras and taught the Dharma on Vulture Peak, while many of his disciples sat in meditation in the caves. Now the Buddha Memorial Center also has a facsimile of "Vulture Peak," containing hundreds of small caves that have been dug out to serve as isolated spaces. Within their confines, there is a desk, a sleeping couch, and a bathroom, provided to devotees so they can engage in spiritual cultivation sitting up or lying down. These humble amenities help to recreate the spiritual symbol of Vulture Peak.

Because everyone is able to practice on their own and free the mind of worries, wherever they are becomes Vulture Peak.

Words of Venerable Master Hsing Yun

I have traveled to India's Vulture Peak on six separate occasions. Each time, I was extremely excited, as if I were coming that much closer to the Buddha. It is our hope that the Buddha Memorial Center can bring one to the ancient sight on Vulture Peak, where a million human and heavenly beings came to listen to the Dharma. The hall becomes a spiritual structure, endowed with significant historical importance.

Looking Back at That Year: A Vow Never Forgotten

More than twenty-six hundred years ago, the Buddha taught the *Lotus Sutra* on Vulture Peak. A million heavenly and human beings, the bodhisattvas from the ten directions; and the eight classes of heavenly beings: *devas, nagas, yaksas, gandharvas, asuras, garudas, kimnaras,* and *mahoragas* all gathered there to listen to the Dharma.

Nearly fifty years ago, Venerable Master Hsing Yun made his first trip to India, and to Vulture Peak.

It was a burning summer day in 1963, amid the oppressive heat. When the car arrived at the foot of Vulture Peak, the first person to head off up the mountain was none other than Venerable Master Hsing Yun himself. He recalls his excitement as he made those first steps toward the summit of the mountain:

"I was finally visiting Vulture Peak. I thought about that grand assembly of millions of heavenly and human beings who were present when the Buddha taught the Lotus Sutra here. But now the mountain was desolate and barren. How can one not feel a sense of regret?"

Filled with many different emotions at his first sight of Vulture Peak, Venerable Master Hsing Yun paced back and forth. Just as he was leaving, he turned back for another look, and silently made a vow to Vulture Peak:

"In gratitude for the Buddha's kindness and to commemorate this visit to Vulture Peak, I vow that henceforth I will redouble my efforts, working with greater diligence and perseverance as I spread the Dharma for the benefit of living beings."

Since that day, a half-century has passed, and Vulture Peak can now be found at the front right side of the Buddha Memorial Center. Its lush vegetation and its verdant forest scenery enhance the many small caves, welcoming visitors as they search for the Vulture Peak within themselves.

Bodhgaya in India

The Magnificent Assembly on Vulture Peak Never Ended

Having accompanied Venerable Master Hsing Yun on his subsequent pilgrimages to India's Vulture Peak, Venerable Tzu Hui recalls, "Upon reaching Vulture Peak, one's heart expands, bringing one closer to the universe. It is as if one is becoming one with the world. The Buddha once said that the assembly on Vulture Peak will never end, that it will continue on forever."

It continues to this very day. One night, during an assembly of two thousands members of Fo Guang Shan, Venerable Tzu Hui told the crowd, "Tonight we gaze with our heads raised, and see the beauty of the sky. It is particularly beautiful at dusk, when many laypeople are doubtlessly taking pictures of the sky with their cameras: the iridescent clouds were inconceivably extraordinary. I believe that all the Fo Guang people here today were present at the assembly that year on Vulture Peak. Here, we meet again."

During that sunset mentioned by Venerable Tzu Hui, a cool, fresh drizzle was falling from the sky. At the same time, sunlight suffused the scene. Rays of light danced about, while the iridescent clouds glittered in a plethora of dazzling colors. Venerable Master Hsing Yun decided this was the ideal condition for a few words:

"All of you speak of seeing the miracle in the sky. I would like to avail myself of this topic to tell you all something. The place in which the Buddha Memorial Center is situated has always been either baked by the sun or drenched by rain. But the sunlight today is mild and gentle, and the rain fairly light. This is the kind of weather in which the Buddha's light shines, the Dharma water is sprinkled about, and cool breezes are gently blowing. Everyone came to Fo Guang Shan through various forms of transportation, such as riding on planes, in trains, or automobiles. Now if the Buddhas, bodhisattvas, arhats, spirits, and deities want to come and participate, then what form of transportation do they take? They come drifting in on the wind, riding on the rain, or atop thunder and lightning. The Executive Director for the Buddha Memorial Center, Mr. Fu, is a graduate of the Department of Civil Engineering at Taiwan National University. He said that he clearly saw the iridescent clouds and the rainbows in the sky that occurred during our gathering. Today we had wind and rain, so I think the Dharma protector spirits have come to join us. This is a gathering of heavenly and human beings, and is no less than another magnificent assembly on Vulture Peak. Why not make a wish now? Let us all wish for the opportunity to assemble back here in the future."

When You Hear
the Water Sounds of the Ganges River

Taiwan is a beautiful island, with many mountains and rivers. One particular waterway winds its way along the north side of the Buddha Memorial Center, its clean headwaters teeming with life. For a long time now, it has been remembered proudly in the collective memories of the local residents, and has come to be known as the "Ganges River."

Though it is not the Ganges River of India, the mother of all the children of the earth, this beautiful river flows beside the Big Buddha, coursing around the Four Noble Truths Stupas and the eight pagodas, tying together the various facilities of the Buddha Memorial Center.

The sounds of the river are like the words of the Buddha, and the music of flowing water teaches the Dharma. The river's waters move like life itself: the river has its ripples, waves, and surges, just as life has its ups and downs, its gains and losses, and its rises and falls. Gazing into the water's clear depths, one can gain much insight into life. One's thoughts drift back to twenty-six hundred years ago, when the Buddha traveled along the Ganges River, liberating living beings.

Words of Venerable Master Hsing Yun

For many dynasties, the flowing waters of the Ganges River have run through India, carrying the sounds of the Dharma as spoken by the Buddha down to this day. It will even bring these sounds with it into the future, spreading outward in all directions.

A Conversation Beside the Ganges River

For forty-nine years the Buddha taught the Dharma. He was always on the move, bringing spiritual enlightenment wherever he went. His footprints could be found on both sides of the Ganges. One day, the god of the Ganges appeared before the Buddha, and angrily reported that he was being treated rudely by Pilindavatsa.

Pilindavatsa was a disciple of the Buddha. In five hundred of his previous lifes, he had been born into noble Brahmin households. Because of this he had built up a habitually arrogant and scornful character. Whenever he came to the Ganges River, he would always command the river god in a contemptuous manner:

"Hey! Servant girl! You'd better hurry up and stop the river so I can cross."

Every time the god of the Ganges River was addressed in this tone, he became upset. After he could bear it no longer, he went to the Buddha to complain.

The Buddha listened to the god of the Ganges and then sought out Pilindavatsa and told him, "When you ask someone for help, you speak in a haughty manner. It is very rude to address someone as 'servant,' you should apologize to the god of the Ganges immediately."

Pilindavatsa admitted his fault, "I did not mean to belittle or humiliate him. I meant no harm."

He then returned to the god of the Ganges and apologized, "Hey! Servant girl! I'm sorry! Don't be angry—I apologize for how I treated you.

The god of the Ganges was even more incensed. "See? He's still calling me his servant girl!"

The Buddha explained: "Pilindavatsa is doing so unintentionally. He does not mean to belittle you. His arrogant tone comes from the negative habitual tendencies he has accumulated over many lifetimes."

Even though he was an arhat, Pilindavatsa still had subtle negative habits. These negative habitual tendencies require a profound level of cultivation before they can be purified. The Buddha shared his teachings and liberated many people on either shore of the Ganges, from the kings and great ministers, the powerful members of society, down to the slaves and untouchables at the lowest levels. Everybody was able to receive nurturing from the Dharma waters of the Buddha's wisdom and compassion.

The "Ganges River" at the Buddha Memorial Center serves as a symbol of Buddhism's support, and naturally merges the surrounding environment with the recreated Vulture Peak to the south, and the recreated Ganges River to the north. Venerable Master Hsing Yun has bestowed upon this Ganges River a leisurely charm.

"The flowing waters of the Ganges River supply the needs of those who come here in pilgrimage, one can even sail a boat upon it and play with its waters."

The sounds of the river are like words of the Buddha. In the murmuring of its flowing waters there circulates the never-ending music of the Dharma.

When You Wander through the Jetavana Grove

People who arrive at the Buddha Memorial Center at the height of spring will have the opportunity to witness the breathtaking array of flowers planted across the Buddha Memorial Center. The whole site becomes one vast garden.

Many people use the red, orange, purple, yellow, and green flowering plants in the foreground of their pictures, while in the background are the surrounding mountains, forests, the eight pagodas, and the Big Buddha. Imagine a young person who takes a picture with their cellphone and immediately sends it off to their friend.

"Where is this?" the friend may ask.

"Jetavana Grove."

"Shouldn't the roads be paved with gold?"

"If it were I couldn't be here."

"What are you doing now?"

"I'm paying homage to the Buddha, enjoying the cool air, and viewing the flowers!"

"You can see flowers anywhere. What's so special about these?"

"If you heard how the master talks about them, you would know they're quite special."

Words of Venerable Master Hsing Yun

From a single flower, one can see the spirit of the six perfections:

The flower opens to display its beautiful appearance, giving those who see it a sense of happiness. It brings joy to others. This is how the flower practices giving.

The flower always opens under certain conditions, during a certain season. This is something it will never violate or overstep. This is how the flower practices morality.

Before a flower blossoms, first it is a seed. Buried in the earth, it must endure darkness, dampness, and isolation, before it emerges from the ground. After blooming, the flower must withstand wind, rain, frost, and snow, and even the injuries caused by insects. This is how the flower practices patience.

No matter how long or how short the flowering season, a flower will always endeavor to spread its fragrance and display its beauty. Even when it withers, it is transformed into nutrients in the soil in preparation for next year's growth. It will even leave behind its seeds, ensuring the continuation of life. This is how the flower practices diligence.

The flower silently opens, revealing its serenity, harmony, and perseverance. This is how the flower practices meditative concentration.

Flowers come in a myriad forms, varying in color, size, and fragrance. It is a source of unceasing wonder. This is how the world of flowers contains unlimited prajña-wisdom.

The five Bhiksus in the Jetavana Grove.

Partly Hidden and Partly Visible within the Forest

Having accompanied Venerable Master Hsing Yun on many visits to India, Venerable Tzu Hui described the Jetavana Grove of the Buddha's time:

"It was a large forested park, filled with flowers and trees. The monastery had many buildings, including lecture halls, classrooms, monastic dormitories, meditation rooms, and medical clinics. Its planning was very thorough, leaving it lacking in nothing. From historical accounts and calculations made using remnants of the ruined walls, we can see that the Jetavana Grove was the largest center of Dharma transmission in the time when the Buddha lived and taught in north India."

Of the forty-nine years the Buddha taught the Dharma, twenty-five of them were spent at the Jetavana Grove. Some of the most well-known Buddhist sutras, such as the *Amitabha Sutra* and the *Diamond Sutra* are accounts of the Buddha's teachings given there. For example, the *Diamond*

The lush Jetavana Grove propagates the Dharma through its plants and flowers.

Sutra begins: "Thus have I heard. At one time, the Buddha was in the city of Sravasti at the Jetavana Monastery."

The Buddha resides in India's Jetavana Grove just as the Buddha resides in Taiwan's Buddha Memorial Center. Here, Venerable Master Hsing Yun has built an emerald green Jetavana Grove, so that the flowers and trees of the earth preach the Dharma to living beings.

Under the guiding principles set down by Venerable Master Hsing Yun, Venerable Tzu Hui personally designed the landscaping for the Jetavana Grove, located on the left side of the Main Hall. Glowing with a scholarly demeanor both within and without, possessing an urbane elegance, this senior monastic of Fo Guang Shan describes how she herself spent the days planting trees in Jetavana Grove, a task she found very enjoyable:

"Venerable Master Hsing Yun envisioned that the landscape would contain a large forest that partially obscures the buildings. During the construction of Fo Guang University he told me that he hoped that it would be a

Once news spread that the Buddha Memorial Center needed plants, trees came flooding in from every direction.

forested university with lots of trees and grass. That way the teachers and students could effortlessly walk out of the classrooms at any time and hold class under the trees. It was a beautiful setting for academic studies. Here, too, the Buddha Memorial Center reflects this love for vibrant green scenery."

As she spoke of these scenes of nature, Venerable Tzu Hui became even more animated and expressive.

Together, these great trees form a green canopy. Under this leafy shade, one can enjoy a leisurely stroll, ponder deep thoughts, or quietly sit and read. One can listen to the hum of insects and the song of birds, to the very rhythm of nature amid such tranquility. Venerable Master Hsing Yun's design sensibility is reflected in how these buildings exist in harmony with nature.

The Children's Grandpa Tree

Generally speaking, landscaping usually entails enormous costs: The planning, the cost of trees, plants, and the planting itself are all quite expensive. From the very outset, Venerable Tzu Hui was worried: "It's such a huge area. Where would we get the trees? Trees are expensive. Quite a lot of money must be spent on purchasing them. However, something special happened. As soon as people heard that the Buddha Memorial Center was planting trees, the trees came flooding in from all directions. There were trees that had to be moved as old buildings were remodeled or new roads opened up. A flurry of trees that needed to be resettled were moved here. But the real miracle was what happened to these trees: whether they came from public institutions, private institutions, or donated by individuals, their survival rate after replanting soared to ninety-nine percent. Truly, this is a land that nourishes life!"

The fifty *bodhi* and banyan trees had originally been at the Houhong Public Elementary School in the Gangshan District of Kaohsiung County for twenty to thirty years before they were moved to the garden. They came with the blessings of the teachers and students, with wishes that they would settle down and take root at the Buddha Memorial Center.

For many years now, under the direction of Houhong Elementary's principal Huang Xiaozong, every class has chosen a particular tree to care for. They would take on the responsibility of caring for the tree, and this instilled in them the importance of cherishing the planet. In time, the children came to care for them deeply. On the day before the trees were to be moved, the children held a "prayers of gratitude" activity, in which they made little cards containing their heartfelt wishes:

"Grandpa tree: I wish you a safe journey!"

"Grandma tree: Hope you will live a long, long life!"

"Oh great, great trees: Thank you for making oxygen for us! Thank you for blocking the hot sun and supplying us with cool shade. We will always think of you, so don't forget us either! We will go to Fo Guang Shan and visit you all!"

Li Hancun, the general manager for Houhong Elementary School, recalls, "The children were actually very attached to these trees. Some were so overcome with emotion that they hugged the trees and cried. That was something I had not expected. We considered many places when selecting a site to transplant the trees to, and it just so happened that the Buddha Memorial Center was asking for donations of trees. We believe that Fo Guang Shan will take good care of these trees."

After some time, Li Hancun came to the Buddha Memorial Center and saw the *bodhi* and banyan trees so missed by the teachers and students. They were already forming new buds, green and full of life. He was extremely happy, and immediately picked up his camera to capture this inspiring example of vitality flourishing under the sun, so that he could show the children how the plants have grown. He said, "The children will certainly be happy to see the trees growing so well."

Just like the children's grandpa and grandma trees, all the trees donated to the Buddha Memorial Center came imbued with the fond memories of their original owners, regardless of whether the trees came from large families, municipal or county governments, or from nurseries, forestry stations, corporate sponsors, or private individuals. Once planted in the Buddha's garden, they confer their blessings upon the earth with their brimming life force, as well as sheltering visitors from the sun.

All the Flowers and Trees Teach the Dharma

Venerable Master Hsing Yun is always thinking of the bigger picture. This is as true for trees as it is for people. He deeply understands a tree's circumstances. For example, in order to save two old-growth trees inside the building area, the Buddha Memorial Center blueprints were redesigned to provide room for these trees, so that it now exhibits a sloping curvature.

All the trees planted in the garden area were personally selected by Venerable Master Hsing Yun. Every tree has a meaning of its own.

The *bodhi* trees planted along the Buddha Memorial Center's Great Path to Buddhahood tell the story of one certain enlightened being. Twenty-six hundred years ago, the Buddha was sitting under a *bodhi* tree. As he entered deep meditative concentration, his spirit became pure and untainted. On the night of the eighth day of the twelfth lunar month, he gazed upon the stars and attained enlightenment, becoming the Buddha of supreme, perfect enlightenment. The *bodhi* tree, the symbol of enlightenment and wisdom, is a beautiful tree. Its leaves resemble hearts, symbolizing the affirmation of finding the meaning of life after having listened to the Dharma. Before Buddhists began creating statues, the sacred and auspicious *bodhi* tree was a symbol with which disciples remembered the Buddha.

The small-leafed tropical almond trees arrayed in front of the eight pagodas grow as straight as pencils. Their branches are distinctly layered and extend horizontally outward from the trunk in all directions. Their multi-leveled, parasol shape gives them a certain graceful charm. When all the leaves have fallen during the autumn and winter, their stark delicateness provides yet another captivating scene.

The rosewood trees along the Ganges River and the Japanese White pine trees in front of the Main Hall remain green throughout the year. The camphor trees in the Jetavana Grove exude a naturally pure fragrance that brings peace to visitors.

Every corner is planted with numerous trees. Venerable Master Hsing Yun cares for each one of them as if they were family heirlooms, clearly instructing the gardeners to water the trees in a timely manner. Once, after he'd returned from a trip abroad, he noticed the condition of the trees, and went to speak with the caretakers.

"Yesterday I received a phone call from a tree. It complained that it hadn't drunk any water in a long time."

This comment by the venerable master is both humorous and deeply compelling.

Every single tree and every blade of grass are the Buddha's Dharma body. Every flower and every leaf are the wondrous truths of the Buddha. Aside from planting trees, Venerable Tzu Hui also planned a long trellis of flowers that meander along the Ganges River.

Well-regarded in academic and cultural circles for her capability, Venerable Tzu Hui is highly skilled in Dharma services and administrative affairs and is entrusted with multiple offices. On this occasion, she demonstrated her creativity by working with flowers, letting her imagination unfurl by planting bougainvillea.

"At the place where the Jetavana Grove borders the Ganges River, we planted a long row of bougainvillea; its length is the same as the distance between the Main Hall and the Front Hall. Bougainvillea is a plant perfectly suited to the climate of Southern Taiwan. Once it blooms, it will flower for up to half a year. A species of creeping vines, the bougainvillea blooms so that the colors of the flowers intermingle with the green vines in a riotous profusion: there are purple flowers, white flowers, red flowers, moss green flowers similar to taro in color. Some flowers even bloom in two colors. They vie with each other's beauty, so alluring a competition that it cannot

Here, there is beautiful scenery, invested with deep emotion.
Religious tranquility infuses the setting.

be fully appreciated. We have been collecting various kinds of bougainvillea and are breeding them with different colors, as well as single or multi-petal variants. We have even managed to collect some rare varieties. As I see it, we are growing them for a purpose. We hope that one day the bougainvillea will become a defining feature of the Buddha Memorial Center. When the Taiwanese people think of bougainvillea, they will think of the Buddha Memorial Center. Bougainvillea bloom vigorously, such that once the buds open, the flowers form a vibrant profusion of colors. Just imagining this fills me with joy.

Serenity in Everything Seen and Heard

Be it the flowers, the trees, or the buildings, Venerable Tzu Hui had drafted blueprints for the unique scenery that unfolds around the Buddha Memorial Center:

"Venerable Master Hsing Yun often speaks about the Pure Land. In it, there are various kinds of fantastic birds that produce marvelous songs day and night, as well as seven layers of trees, bejeweled with flowers and leaves formed of seven kinds of precious gems. To emulate this, we will plant some Kassod trees to attract butterflies, while birds twitter and chirp up in their branches. It will be just like early morning at Fo Guang Shan, where the song of birds rouses us from sleep. Some marshes have already been created in the garden area, where frogs have now made their home. The sounds of their call are loud and clear. We are planning to place some stones in the pond, so that when the river is flowing, people can hear the murmuring of the water. The sounds of the river are like the words of the Buddha, and the mountains are like the Buddha's pure Dharma body. It is hoped that the Buddha Memorial Center will have scenic vistas worthy of artistic inspiration, as well as a sense of religious serenity."

Venerable Master Hsing Yun once put it clearly, "Everyone with faith has some kind of practice. Bowing before the Buddha, sutra or mantra recitation, and words of praise are only one aspect of spiritual practice. In order to truly practice comprehensively, one must cultivate the six sense organs."

The eyes are exposed to only that which is wholesome and pure; the ears listen only to sounds that are wholesome, fair, and true; with our every breath, we stand between heaven and earth: regulating the breath, regulating the body, and regulating the mind. With the sense of smell, we welcome in the minute particles that dance through the air. Different trees breathe differently. Grass that has just been cut also gives off the fresh smell of grass, while the fragrance of flowers needs no explanation.

"In the future, we will also plant Yulan Magnolia trees and Osmanthus. Yulan Magnolias are splendid looking trees with beautiful leaves. Osmanthus gives off a subtle fragrance in autumn."

Venerable Tzu Hui admits that she herself is quite an admirer of Zhu Ziqing's (1898-1948) poem "Spring":

> Little grasses stealthily bore up out of the dirt—
> So soft, so green.
> Go look
> In the garden, in the fields,
> Covering all in one great patch after the other.
> Sit there, lie down there, roll over a couple times ....

When You Sit Down in the Water Drop Teahouses

The Water Drop teahouse has a long, rich history. It is a story born from Venerable Master Hsing Yun's gratitude.

Having grown up in Buddhist temples, Venerable Master Hsing Yun lived a hard, poor life. When he was around seventeen or eighteen, his previously healthy body was suddenly struck with serious illness. He vomited, defecated, and was pushed to the brink of death. For almost two months, he could not eat even a single grain of rice, though he scarcely had enough food to begin with.

Knowledge of his condition was passed on until his own master learned of it. Hsing Yun's master sent someone a great distance to deliver a half bowl of salted vegetables to him. To people today, a half bowl of pickled vegetables is next to nothing, but at the time it was a rare and valuable delicacy. Overcome with gratitude, Master Hsing Yun tearfully ate this bowl of pickled vegetables, internally making this vow:

"Master, in the future, I will work to spread the Dharma for the benefit of living beings, and I shall expand and develop Buddhism. This is how I will repay you for your kindness!"

Words of Venerable Master Hsing Yun

The Water Drop teahouses derive their name from the gratitude expressed in the old saying "a drop of water's worth of kindness repaid with a gushing spring." We must all repay that drop of kindness from our parents, our teachers, and our country with a gushing spring. Only a grateful life can be a rich life.

Walking into the Fragrance of the Camphor Grove

There are a total of three Water Drop teahouses within the Jetavana Grove of the Buddha Memorial Center. One of these is the Camphor Grove Tea House.

The camphor tree is a type of tall evergreen tree that gives off a faint fragrance. It is also called the "scented camphor." In the correct conditions, its branches and trunk can grow to extraordinary thickness, and live for hundreds of years. As the camphor tree grows in size, it does not push toward the sky. It extends outward in all directions, its branches and twigs reaching away from the trunk and covering the ground beneath it in shade. Its fruits and seeds are plentiful, nourishing the birds that roost in its branches.

Building a Water Drop teahouse within this beautiful camphor grove creates another type of scenery. Following the secluded path, one walks straight into the shade within the camphor grove, where one will find a crescent moon.

The crescent-shaped Camphor Grove Tea House was the creation of Venerable Tzu Hui. Known as a great talent within the Buddhist community, this senior Fo Guang Shan monastic is deeply influential in the areas of education and culture. In the last decade, she has also left her beautiful mark on many architectural designs, including the Fo Guang University, Junyi Elementary School in Taidong, and others. In addition, one can see the spark of her creativity in the Water Drop teahouses of the Buddha Memorial Center.

The crescent-shaped Camphor Grove Tea House.

"Three Water Drop teahouses were built in Jetavana Grove. The more involved I was in building them, the more interested I became. I even happily picked out the color of the windows and laid out the climbing vines along the rooftop," explains Venerable Tzu Hui. "The flowers along the rooftop hang down over the red Chinese-style window lattices, like a village girl wearing a wreath of flowers in her hair. It is a beauty both refined and natural."

Having visited the construction site several times over the course of many years, Venerable Tzu Hui often finds herself scrutinizing the buildings. She often thinks that:

"Just as with someone's eyes on their face, whether the exterior of a house is beautiful or not depends upon how the windows are set. If the windows are set in a pleasant manner, then the house itself will look good; otherwise, it will not. The windows are like the spirit of the house, and with the installation of elegant wooden frames, the view outside is transformed into a painting. In effect this is 'borrowing' the scenic beauty of Nature. The Flower Adornment Sutra says: 'The mind is like an artist who can paint all things.' I believe this to be true. Whenever I am making plans, as soon as an idea forms, the whole picture is there. This is why sometimes I am so happy that I cannot sleep."

Water and Bridges for Quiet Contemplation and Lively Conversation

As designed by Venerable Tzu Hui, the Camphor Grove Tea House stands next to a pool of deep, emerald water. This serves not only as an aesthetic presentation, it also serves to regulate runoff from heavy rains. In this clean, orderly environment, one can relax and enjoy a cup of tea, or perhaps a light meal. From the windows near the water, one can see the emerald ripples that ply across its surface. Here, one can quietly contemplate as one pleases, or engage in lively conversations with a close friend. Venerable Tzu Hui envisioned it as such:

"Whether someone is a tourist who has come to take in the sights or a pilgrim who has come to venerate the Buddha, it is our hope to offer modern people a garden in which to rest, one that is both religious in spirit and yet possesses a natural, scenic beauty. On holidays, the whole family can come visit the Buddha Memorial Center and spend the whole day sightseeing."

As there is water, so too is there a bridge. An arching bridge connects the long northern walkway with the Camphor Grove Tea House. Venerable Tzu Hui decorated the bridge with some clothes: She made racks on the railings on either side of the bridge in which she planted hanging plants with

One can take a break and enjoy a meal and tea at the Tea House.

flowers, a display no less vivid than exploding fireworks. When seen from a distance, this hanging curtain is like a waterfall of green, like willows hanging along the banks of the pond waving their long, delicate branches.

"Over an even larger pool, I designed a Water Drop teahouse that hangs over the water, like a waterside pavilion or terrace that floats on the surface of the pool. The third Water Drop teahouse is a circular structure built for the express purpose of offering takeout meals, making it easier for guests to grab meals on the go."

As locations where visitors can rest their feet, enjoy some tea, and take their time and eat a meal, the Water Drop teahouses serve as a supporting structure to the other facilities in the Jetavana Grove and vice versa. Venerable Tzu Hui and Venerable Master Hsing Yun each have their own unique taste. Venerable Tzu Hui describes, "Venerable Master Hsing Yun made it a point to emphasize that several small-scale stages should be erected about the Jetavana Grove. This way, if a family comes here for an outing and the mood strikes then, the children can go up to perform on the stage for the enjoyment of the sitting adults; or mom and dad can go up and sing songs while the others applaud and share in the fun."

Now that the stages of fun for the entire family have been prepared for them by Venerable Master Hsing Yun, the singing and the sounds of laughter merge together with the grove, drawn into its luxuriant growth of flowering plants and profusion of rocks and trees.

When You Step into the Front Hall

Most Buddhist monasteries and temples have a mountain gate. The traditional mountain gate is a gated entrance, symbolizing the passage from the mundane world of ordinary existence into the awakened world of the Buddha. The Buddha Memorial Center also has a mountain gate, but it is different from that of most temples'. Breaking with the traditional styles of architecture and layout of the past, the main entrance of the Buddha Memorial Center is called the "Front Hall." In Chinese, it is called the *lijing dating,* "Reverence Hall," because after one enters one begins to pay reverence to all Buddhas.

This is a 50,000 square-foot building, with three floors above ground and one floor below ground. It is like a castle, erected in front of the Buddha Memorial Center. Thus, as visitors from around the world disembark from their cars and prepare to leave the chaotic, noisy mundane world to make their entry into this pure, sacred, and majestic Buddhist site, the Front Hall is a place where they can transition and reorient their minds. Here, services will be provided to satisfy or treat every personal or material need.

Words of Venerable Master Hsing Yun

The society of tomorrow must be a society for service. As visitors enter the Buddha Memorial Center through the Front Hall, they will be welcomed with all sorts of services. At the same time, they will be presented with the sight of the pagodas and the Big Buddha, a view certain to move their spirit.

Meeting Demands with Generous Service

Upon arriving at most Buddhist temples or monasteries, many people will worry about breaking some taboo, and are reluctant to tour the grounds. Perhaps it is due to the sense of sanctity, or perhaps it is because they are unfamiliar with the surroundings. The Front Hall of the Buddha Memorial Center serves as a welcoming center, easing the visitors in with a more familiar atmosphere. As soon as visitors enter, they are greeted with the familiar sight of various forms of information, maps, banking and post offices, senior-care and child-care services, wheelchair rentals, and eateries. Also at this location, one can apply for guided tours. This ensures that people can make their visit with confidence and clarity.

Venerable Master Hsing Yun has thought of everything. Long distance travelers, people crossing great distances by plane or automobile, will doubtlessly be hungry or thirsty. The Front Hall offers "good health porridge" free of charge, to bring one good health and fortune. While one is standing around the Front Hall, one can also take a look at the giftshop, or visit the bookstore on the second floor, its vast collection guaranteed to satisfy any reader. In this room, the fragrance of the books entwines with the aroma of tea. The truths of Buddhism are annotated in everyday language while philosophy is explained in simple terms, allowing all to use these texts to nourish their spirit.

Another special feature of the Buddha Memorial Center is the "Buddhist marriage ceremony." The Five Harmonies Pagoda not far from the Front Hall offers a wedding photography service. Buddhism emphasizes establishing a Buddhist family life, as embodied by the Layman Vimalakirti and the Elder Sudatta, prominent laypersons during the time of the Buddha. When a newly married couple comes to the magnificent architectural achievement that is the Buddha Memorial Center and vows before the Buddha to become a *bodhi* family, they are promising to support each other and to treasure the connection between them, until old age and death. This is the meaning of the idea of "enhanced marriage" promoted by Venerable Master Hsing Yun.

The Welcome by the Lion and Elephant Clans

Before stepping into the Front Hall, you will see two groups of statues, one on either side of the main entrance welcoming visitors as they arrive. On the right side is an adult elephant, leading a herd of small younger elephants, while on the left side is a large lion surrounded by three cubs.

Both the lion and the elephant have symbolic meanings in Buddhism. The elephant represents noble dignity, for the Buddha rode a white elephant into his mother's womb. Thus, the figure of an elephant is used to commemorate the Buddha's birthday, the day that he descended into the human world.

The lion is the king of beasts. Peerless in its world, it is the ruler of its realm. In many Buddhist sutras, the lion is a metaphor for the Buddha's fearlessness and majesty. The sound of the Buddha preaching the Dharma is known as the "lion's roar," for his words could wake living beings from their dreams. Then, they can finally be themselves, understanding their own lives with pure awakening.

The white elephant commemorates the Buddha's arrival to the human world.

The lion represents the Buddha's majesty.

The Front Hall

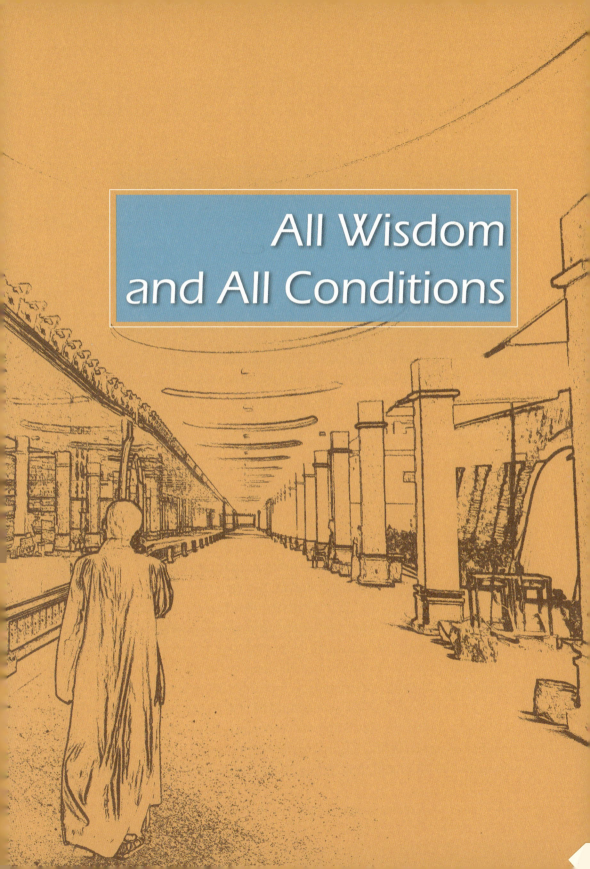

All Wisdom
and All Conditions

To Embody Humanistic Buddhism through Architecture

It's not just architecture, it encompasses everything:
No matter how creative he became, how innovative he became,
The venerable master has never strayed from the Dharma,
nor changed himself to fit popular taste.
This is the one fundamental law he adheres to.

—— Venerable Tzu Hui

Architecture for Everybody

In the words of Le Corbusier, the great modernist architect, "a house is a machine for living in." Having followed the Venerable Master Hsing Yun for more than half a century, Venerable Tzu Hui has come to understand this: "The reason why Venerable Master Hsing Yun's designs make people feel so comfortable is that the houses he builds are not different from how he acts or what he says. No matter what he does, he begins by considering everybody. Everything is considered in terms of what everybody needs."

Venerable Tzu Hui gives an example of how Venerable Master Hsing Yun goes about designing a building. He considers every aspect of its construction. For example: Who will the building's occupants be? What are the measurements for the width and height of the space? What will the distribution of plants and trees be? How will the building be integrated into nature? How will it support the congenial relationship between oneself and others? And how must it be designed to exist in harmony with people and nature?

Venerable Tzu Hui accompanies Venerable Master Hsing Yun at the construction site (second from the left).

"Venerable Master Hsing Yun pays extraordinary attention to these things. This is why his buildings are so comfortable for people. On one occasion, a school principal from Japan mentioned how the structures that he builds reflect him as a person: very grand, very spacious, and with an expansive capacity for tolerance. In my mind, Venerable Master Hsing Yun does not only care for people, he cares for all living beings, including animals. If a stray dog appears, he will take it in and give it a home. Even if crippled and ugly, as soon as it falls ill, he will bring it to the veterinarian. Even the people at the veterinary hospital say that dogs that reach Fo Guang Shan are truly fortunate. In the past, there was a bodhi tree in front of the Treasure Bridge that had been blown down during a typhoon. Venerable Master Hsing Yun had it propped up and stabilized using a brace. Every day, he would personally go to look after it. Later on, it grew even taller. From his sense of compassion and concern for living beings, one can clearly see his philosophy regarding architecture and all things."

Merging into a Oneness with Nature

No matter which temple invites him to preside over a Dharma service, give a Dharma talk, or present a lecture, Venerable Master Hsing Yun always first goes to the main shrine to pay homage to the Buddha. Before the event begins, he then visits the kitchen to convey his regards to the volunteers for their efforts. If a visitor were to make an offering of some high-quality fruit, Venerable Master Hsing Yun is sure to share it with those working in the kitchen.

Venerable Tzu Hui recalls, "Venerable Master Hsing Yun is very mindful of these easily overlooked individuals. In his early days running a kindergarten, when it was time to change the wall drawings each semester, there would be volunteers who would come to help with the drawing. He would care for the volunteers as soon as they arrived, bringing refreshments, brewing tea, and serving milk. Later on, when Venerable Tzu Chuang and I ran a magazine and published books, an older writer, Mr. Chu Chiao, edited for us on a volunteer basis. Whenever he came in for his monthly visit, we would mobilize the entire staff to respectfully welcome him in. All his life, Venerable Master Hsing Yun has treated people in this fashion."

The way in which Venerable Master Hsing Yun treats all living beings as if they were his own family is manifest in the architecture. In Venerable Tzu Hui's mind, his brilliance lies in how the buildings and nature are blended together into one.

When speaking of pagodas, one imagines a structure that rises straight up, one level at a time, soaring to the clouds. If it is poorly designed, it will resemble a smokestack outlined against the sky. Venerable Tzu Hui has visited the Buddhist pagoda at Tianning Temple on Mainland China more than a dozen stories tall, yet not unsightly in any way:

"I think it's because it has ornate eaves at every story, with bas-reliefs of bodhisattvas and cloud-dragons exquisite beyond compare. Starting from the bottom, the eaves gradually become smaller, shrinking one level at a time with a set, rhythmic beauty. I have always been fond of the artistry of Buddhist pagodas, for they are suggestive of a certain poetic touch. Sometimes a cloud will drift over the pagoda, and sometimes a crescent moon will be hanging near its spire. The Buddhist pagodas are compatible with every aspect of nature. One can take a sunset, and the presence of a Buddhist pagoda standing against the sky will deepen that sight into something extraordinarily expansive. I think even the most advanced modern buildings should be able to meld itself with the daytime cloudscape and the changing scenery around it. This is the architectural principle behind the Buddha Memorial Center."

The sight of the standing pagoda casts the mind afar.

(From the left) The first patriarch Bodhidharma, Huiyuan of Mount Lu, Daoxuan of Mount Nan, and Subhakarasimha.

They'll Understand Once They Walk through It

There is no separation between architecture and scenery, no separation between architecture and human beings, no separation between oneself and others, no separation between one's own mind and the Buddha's mind, and no separation between the human world and Buddhism.

Venerable Master Hsing Yun has said that Fo Guang Shan promotes "Humanistic Buddhism," but this term is not easy to define. If defined in a conventional way, Humanistic Buddhism may seem mundane and ordinary; but if it is defined with profound, complex concepts it becomes difficult to understand. Since its ideas are so profound, stories are often employed to illustrate its meaning. One must speak of profound ideas in a simple, artful way. Venerable Tzu Hui experienced this idea deeply:

"Since the founding of Fo Guang Shan, Venerable Master Hsing Yun has made it his purpose in life to make the profound and impenetrable Dharma understandable to people. In his lectures, writings, or even the various

(From the left) Jiaxiang Jizang, Huayan Xianshou, Xuanzang Sanzang, and Tiantai Zhiyi.

construction projects he worked on such as the Buddha Memorial Center, Venerable Master Hsing Yun wants to make the Dharma something that everyone can understand."

This understanding does not require an extremely high intellect to achieve. Rather, it is something that even children or people with an average education can understand. In order to achieve this, Venerable Master Hsing Yun has employed sculptures as a way of depicting the deeds of the Buddha as he sought to liberate this world. He had Feng Zikai's *Protection for Living Beings* painted one by one onto a wall to serve as a modern, enlarged edition. If someone wishes to gain an understanding of Indian Buddhism and the practice of the Buddha's disciples, they can look at the statues of the eighteen arhats at the Bodhi Wisdom Concourse. If one wants to know something about the essence of Chinese Buddhism, then one can grasp the principles from the statues depicting the founders of the eight Mahayana schools.

Windows utilize nature to decorate the area.

In fact, this kind of architectural design can be traced back to the founding of Fo Guang Shan in its early stages. Venerable Tzu Hui recalls, "As early as the construction of the Pure Land Cave at Fo Guang Shan, Venerable Master Hsing Yun has considered how visitors may not have time to listen to a talk on Buddhist sutras, and even if they do they may not understand it. Therefore, it would be better to employ statues and wall paintings to convey the concepts, as they can be understood on sight."

From conception to execution, from Fo Guang Shan in the past to the Buddha Memorial Center today, Venerable Tzu Hui has observed one consistent intention, "Venerable Master Hsing Yun has come up with many unique designs, both active and passive. He can make use of lighting, apparatuses, projection, and technical forms of expression to bring one into the scene and atmosphere and allow people to experience it for themselves.

There is no need for language or words as in a long, drawn-out lecture. After someone takes a tour of this complex, their outlook and understanding will be greatly impacted."

A Spiritual Style Rich in Creativity

Known as a creative force in the Buddhist community, Venerable Master Hsing Yun expresses profound thoughts through his architectural designs. In Venerable Tzu Hui's eyes, he is a happy creator. His travels are always packed with activities, but in the gaps between meetings, lectures, site inspections, and receiving guests, he is often struck by flashes of inspiration.

Venerable Tzu Hui recalls, "Venerable Master Hsing Yun is always happily creating something. He enjoys thinking about everything all the time. Whatever the source of his creativity, it has never required any racking of the brains or strenuous effort. It's not just architecture, it encompasses everything: no matter how creative he became, how innovative he became, the venerable master has never strayed from the Dharma, nor changed himself to fit popular taste. This is the one fundamental law he adheres to."

Venerable Master Hsing Yun's creative energy often inspires those around him. Venerable Tzu Hui feels that she herself has benefited a great deal: "Take for example the construction of the Water Drop teahouses. It only took a few words from him to spark new ideas in my mind. Superficially, it seems that many of the ideas are something I thought up. But in reality, they came from the pointers offered by Venerable Master Hsing Yun, sparks of creativity that ignited my mind. Having been in his company for so long, I've grown used to these phenomena. A word or phrase from Venerable Master Hsing Yun's can develop infinite possibilities."

Learning in the Buildings, Cultivation amid Activities

"Activities are also a form of spiritual cultivation." While appreciating the architecture, examining the culture, and experiencing the art stored at the Buddha Memorial Center, people are also absorbing and learning.

——Venerable Tzu Jung

In March of 2010, amid the sounds of powerful, vigorous Dharma drums, the Chan, Pure Land, and Tantric Ceremony made its first appearance at the Buddha Memorial Center. More than twenty thousand members of the public gathered at the Bodhi Wisdom Concourse. Under the open night sky, they prayed with one voice for the purification of the human mind.

As secretary general of the Buddha's Light International Association, Venerable Tzu Jung was placed in charge of the entire event, she led the event from in front of the Buddha Memorial Center, amid the energy of Buddhist chanting and a sea of lights shining beneath a canopy of stars. It lit in her heart a sense of happiness difficult to express in words.

The light from a myriad candles had been lit. The work on the Buddha Memorial Center was now nearly completed, and the Buddha's tooth

relic had been safely kept in Taiwan for twelve years. Looking back across those twelve years, Venerable Tzu Jung can still remember every aspect of that trip to Thailand, made to escort the Buddha's tooth relic to Taiwan.

Devout Offerings and Auspicious Relics

Venerable Tzu Jung (right) and Venerable Master Hsing Yun with construction workers at the Buddha Memorial Center construction site.

After being toured through Taiwan for eight months, the Buddha's Tooth Relic returned to Fo Guang Shan on December 13th, 1998, to be enshrined in the Buddha's Tooth Relic Hall on the fourth floor of the Tathagata Hall. This created the opportunity for the public to purify themselves through worshipping the Buddha's tooth relic, revealing that the truth and purity of the Buddha was in their hearts.

Venerable Tzu Jung describes the Buddha's Tooth Relic's influence upon the public, "The Buddha's Tooth Relic is a sacred object more than two thousand years old. Most people who hear about the relic immediately understand that it is a sacred, regardless of whether they are Buddhist or not. They realize that it represents the Buddha's spirit, and so will naturally feel a sense of respect. For Buddhists in particular, seeing the relic is like seeing the Buddha. Even atheists, agnostics, and other people who see the relic only as a cultural artifact are able to appreciate what a true and extraordinarily rare occurrence it is for the Buddha's tooth relic to have been passed down for more than two thousand years, surviving to this very day. Thus, they will wish to understand it and see it. This underscores its exalted historical and cultural value."

The *Prajña Sutra* states: "Since the Buddha's body and the Buddha's relics have been imbued by the merit of the perfection of prajña-wisdom, all the heavenly and human beings in the world worship them with reverence and praise them with devotion."

Ever since the Buddha's Tooth Relic was enshrined at Fo Guan Shan, it has actually begun to generate new relics due to the public's devout homage and worship. To date it has already generated many hundreds of relics.

Regarding this phenomena, the Venerable Tzu Jung quietly smiles and replies: "Inexplicable events in religion have occurred since ancient times. However, we must always face them as if they were the ordinary. Although we know that is an extraordinary occurrence, we have never gone out of our way to advertise this."

Speaking of sacred relics, Venerable Tzu Jung recalled something that happened many years ago: Every year, Fo Guang Shan's Shoushan Temple holds a Medicine Buddha Dharma Service. One year, during the service, sacred relics in the form of lotus flowers emerged from the candles in response to the devotion of the attendees. Numbering in the tens of thousands, this profusion of multicolored crystals glittered in the light.

Venerable Tzu Jung remembers, "At that time a few dozen people were in charge of ensuring that several hundred candles were kept perpetually lit. Whenever it became quiet, they would hear a faint noise coming from nowhere. It was only later on that they discovered that the lamp table was covered in small, multi-colored crystals. As soon as Venerable Master Hsing Yun saw them, he said that they were candle-flower relics. Looking

Eight pagodas are aligned along two sides of the Bodhi Wisdom Concourse, symbolizing the Noble Eightfold Path. (Photo by Cai Rong Feng)

carefully at the candle flames, you could see perfectly round crystals forming at the tip of the flame. When it reached a certain size, it would roll off. When we reached out our hands to touch it, it was quite solid."

The Venerable Tzu Jung recalls the grand scene at the time, "News of such auspicious signs emerging from the candles spread very quickly. Everyone wanted to see it for themselves. By custom, shoes are to be taken off before entering a Buddha hall. But in order to facilitate the large numbers of people who had come to see this miracle and to keep the entrance orderly, this rule was temporarily suspended. As a result, amidst the din of hundreds of onlookers, the candles stopped producing relics."

Venerable Tzu Jung also remembers that a reporter learned of this miracle and came rushing over to cover it. The reported interrogated them about what oil was used and what kind of lamp wick was lit, thinking that there must have been something special about them.

"In fact, it was just ordinary oil and ordinary wicks. There was nothing special about them at all. The reporter even took the some lamp oil back with him and lit it, but no relics came out of the burning candlewick. Such miraculous events like this have happened in the past, which is why we don't consider the Buddha's tooth relic's continued generation of relics to be remarkable. It is simply a product of the people's devotion."

Planning with Creativity, Spiritual Practice amid Activity

As soon as Venerable Master Hsing Yun was entrusted with the Buddha's tooth relic, he decided to find land in Taiwan to build a pagoda to enshrine it, so that anyone could have the opportunity to see and worship it. Thirteen years later, the Buddha Memorial Center was revealed to the world. Aside from serving as an exhibition hall, the Buddha Memorial Center also comes equipped with the facilities to assist in spiritual cultivation and the attainment of wisdom, as well as serving as a site for culture and education.

A skilled organizer, Venerable Tzu Jung considers every angle when planning for the various activities the Buddha Memorial Center is designed to hold. "From an educational standpoint, it increases the public's awareness of the Buddhist religion. Visitors who come here can appreciate the architecture, explore the culture, and experience the art while at the same time absorbing and learning from the experience. It also introduces visitors to the many traditions of Buddhist practice and shows them how to connect with the Buddha's heart through sitting meditation, reciting the Buddha's name, making vows, establishing profound concentration, as well as many other practices. As the Buddha Memorial Center provides such a large venue for activities, everyone fully experiences the various expressions of faith by witnessing the diverse methods of worship and devotion."

Always happy to interact with the public, Venerable Tzu Jung is adept at handling any level of planning, providing for the people's needs, and planning many interesting and diverse events. This active, innovative individual often invokes the adage "only running water can be drunk." Just as water nourishes life, these activities are meant to nourish and deepen people's spiritual practice. Inspiring others with the Dharma is nourishment for the human heart.

The first Chan, Pure Land, and Tantric Ceremony was held at night, outside the entrance to the Buddha Memorial Center, beginning a new tradition. Before the Buddha's Tooth Relic was enshrined, when the complex was still being built, participants sat in meditation to focus their bodies and minds, reciting the name of Amitabha Buddha to create a connection with all Buddhas and bodhisattvas, and used single-minded Tantric practice to remove distractions. Aside from accumulating merits for themselves, these practices also made for greater harmony in society. Venerable Tzu Jung placed herself in the midst of these activities, controlling the flow and managing the atmosphere. Harboring both religious sentiment and a concern for society, this senior member of Fo Guang Shan created an act of group practice on an entirely new level.

Venerable Tzu Jung has said, "Activities are also a form of spiritual cultivation." Bringing happiness to others is an act of merit. As night fell, thousands of people lit their lamps, simultaneously illuminating their hearts. The Buddha nature in all of us is a never-extinguishing life. Just like the incident with the candle-flower relics, as the flower of the mind reach full bloom, it will create beautiful crystallizations of faith.

The Chan, Pure Land, and Tantric Ceremony in March 2010

Bringing Together All Conditions for Collective Creativity

From the architects to the building companies to all the con-
tractors large and small, each and every one of them worked
on this project with the greatest sense of dedication, hoping to
build something that would bring happiness to everyone.

—— Venerable Man Zhou

In his article "The Origin of the Buddha Memorial Center," Venerable Hsing Yun wrote:

During the design and planning phase, I said that whoever took charge of the construction project for the Buddha Memorial Center must not be attached to their own opinions. Only someone who understands "non-self" can act in such a capacity. Later on, it turned out that Venerable Man Zhou, the executive director of Fo Guang Shan's Pure Land Culture and Education Foundation took up this responsibility.

As the head planner of this immense project, Venerable Man Zhou returned to an extraordinarily simple idea in order to practice a "non-self" approach. She recalls, "My thinking was quite simple: My master wanted me to do this job, so I considered what everyone needed with all my heart and mind. I simply did my very best to ensure its success."

Venerable Man Zhou, coordinator of the construction of the Buddha Memorial Center

More than One Hundred Design Plans

Venerable Master Hsing Yun cites this reason for the specific pre-requisite of "non-self" in the planner: "Attachment to the 'self' leads to the concepts like 'you,' 'him,' and the 'world.' It creates the distinctions between self and other, right and wrong, and winners and losers. These thoughts are incompatible with the Dharma. Only with the view of 'non-self' can one listen with attentive ears and take in the opinions of everyone. This allows for collective creativity that brings together all conditions. In the past, when I built Fo Guang Shan, I acknowledged my own ability to accept everybody's ideas, but now that we are building the Buddha Memorial Center, I find that I've grown old, and that a younger person must take up this task. And the most important quality to fulfill this task is to have a view of 'non-self.'"

In fact, from the very first proposal for the Buddha Memorial Center to the appearance of its first design draft, one can clearly see the spirit of "non-self."

Since 2003, the development of design for the Buddha Memorial Center's external appearance has undergone more than one hundred revisions.

Venerable Man Zhou remembers this process, "After each design plan was completed, we would make a report to Venerable Master Hsing Yun, the senior monastics, as well the members of Fo Guang Shan's Religious Affairs Committee. Since everyone hoped that the Buddha Memorial Center would become a spiritual guideline and stronghold for humanity around the world, as long as unanimous consensus was not achieved by the concerned voices, the design plans were revised again and again, and development continued."

By the time the committee had gone through ninety drafts of the design plan, the construction of the foundation had already been completed. Then, one day, Venerable Man Zhou said to Venerable Master Hsing Yun, "Next week we will start working on forming the overall look of the center. Once we begin, the whole layout will be set. If you have any feedback or anything you want to change, there is still time to do so."

Venerable Master Hsing Yun thought for a while.

"Is it really okay?"

Venerable Man Zhou replied, "Yes, master."

Even so, Venerable Master Hsing Yun was worried about all the effort put in by the architects and the building contractors. Venerable Man Zhou understood this, so she tried to reassure him, "The manufacturers are all willing to cooperate in order to ensure that the Buddha Memorial Center manifests itself in its most ideal form for everyone."

It was from that conversation, on that day, that a crucial moment came.

Venerable Master Hsing Yun had a sudden flash of inspiration in the Office of the Founding Master at Fo Guang Shan. Using a few bottles of mineral water, a tissue box, and some newspapers, he set out a rudimentary layout for the Buddha Memorial Center. The design plans that so many had painstakingly worked on for so many years were finally settled.

Thus they advanced, step-by-step closer to the ideal layout for the center, fleshing out the final details after a long eight years. Including the

Venerable Master Hsing Yun creates a model for the Buddha Memorial Center

original ninety drafts, the committee finally settled on the one hundred and fourteenth design plan. In every one of these plans, one could clearly see the core concept of "non-self." Venerable Master Hsing Yun made a special effort to thank the architects for their hard work, "By merging into the larger whole, the self that abides by 'non-self' becomes even greater and loftier, becoming all the more able to accomplish and complete everything."

Just Like the Taste of the Honey Peach

Finding herself trying to balance the ideals of the masses and the practical work of engineering, Venerable Man Zhou saw extraordinary coordination and harmony displayed by the construction teams scuttling across the construction site on a daily basis. Whenever any changes occurred the front-line work would immediately come to a halt, while the supporting groups, as the materials manufacturers, would immediately open up communications and search for a solution. Over these past few years, one of the most incredible things Venerable Man Zhou observed, "The manufacturers never complained. Everything was about acceptance and cooperation. In my mind, this was due to Venerable Master Hsing Yun's influence: From the architects

Every contributor wholeheartedly throws themselves into the project.

to the building companies to all the contractors large and small, each and every one of them worked on this project with the greatest sense of dedication, hoping to build something that would bring happiness to everyone."

Venerable Man Zhou knew that such efforts were extraordinarily rare and commendable. From the vast building companies down to the smallest contractors, including the manufactures of the various construction materials, all of them constituted a tightly integrated production chain, in which each link had its own specialized task. However, contractors varied in scale from large to small. For the smaller businesses with less capital to spare, the consideration of costs was certainly a very realistic problem. However, since this was the Buddha Memorial Center, the builders shed their expectations from the very start. The significance of participating in this project transcended the need for personal profit.

Venerable Hsing Yun was deeply moved, "One could say that the construction of the Buddha Memorial Center started from the self, and then transcended the self. It started with form, and then transcended form. It is the greatest example of the transformative power of Buddhism!"

Each time he toured the construction site, he would see those hardworking people. To him, it was as if he saw the students of the earth being bathed in the Buddha's teachings.

Whenever the workers saw Venerable Master Hsing Yun off in the distance, and they would stop work, stand up, and join their palms together.

Some would say, "Hello venerable master!" Some would chant, "Amitabha!" Others, somewhat more reserved in nature, would quietly smile, their eyes filled with joy. Venerable Master Hsing Yun would always give some words of encouragement, "The building of the Buddha Memorial Center is a beacon for all. Your participation in this project will be a rare and unique experience in the lives of each one of you. Thank you all for your effort."

Sometimes, when he returns to Fo Guang Shan from abroad, Venerable Master Hsing Yun would get out of the car and take some fruits he had received as a gift, such as delicious honey peaches, and bring them over to the construction site to share with everyone.

Just like the taste of the peach, these short intervals of interaction give one a taste of the sweetness and fragrance of humanity. Venerable Man Zhou put it like this: "Venerable Master Hsing Yun's thoughtfulness is really refined. It's impossible for us to pay attention to such details all the time, but he can do so quite meticulously."

Delicious Vegetables in the Bowl, the *Heart Sutra* beneath the Brush

One of Venerable Man Zhou's most profound memories was of how, early one morning, Venerable Master Hsing Yun came to the construction site. With their external appearance completed, the eight pagodas were about to undergo planning for the open palaces. Venerable Master Hsing Yun prepared to ascend the pagoda for an inspection.

At the time, the elevator had not yet been installed. Despite his poor eyesight and large frame, Venerable Hsing Yun pushed himself to climb the stairs. His disciples looked on with extreme trepidation. Each of them tried to deter him: "Master, going to the second floor will be enough, everything from the third floor on up is the same as the second floor."

Working together, everyone devotes their hearts to building the Buddha Memorial Center.

But Venerable Master Hsing Yun insisted on climbing up to the topmost seventh floor.

He carefully observed the view presented by each floor, experiencing the different lighting within each space, considering elements such as how the artifacts would be arranged, and where the visitor's line of sight would be. As he walked here and there, he pondered these questions one by one.

Venerable Man Zhou was deeply touched, "Young people wouldn't think twice about climbing a seven-story building, but an elderly person would have to ascend one stair at a time, one floor at a time. Once they've reached the top, one still would have to make the journey down. Seeing this earnest spirit of Venerable Master Hsing Yun, we realized how we must be careful, how we cannot be the slightest bit unsure of ourselves. His ascent of the building both inspired and supported everyone at the construction site."

In response, the engineering team also actively emulated the compassionate spirit of the Buddha.

"While at work, they practiced a vegetarian diet and abstained from alcohol. It was a self-imposed prohibition that demonstrated their good intentions; a wonderful gesture."

Venerable Man Zhou recalls the self-demanding demeanor of the engineering team, "Participation in the 'Million Copies of the Heart Sutra Joining the Dharma Body' was also a movement they proposed of their own initiative. Not only the engineers and contractors, even the workers began inviting others to participate in the effort with them. Every day, more people would come to register and pay the fee. More than two hundred people joined from the construction teams alone."

One Family at the Construction Site

From the very outset, extreme care was taken in selecting the building contractor who would undertake the most important role in the project. Venerable Man Zhou related in some length about the stages of that process.

Ten contractors were selected for a shortlist from among the finest in Taiwan, publicly acknowledged for their level of excellence. Next each of the ten were contacted to guage their willingness to undertake the project, and then the achievements, construction contracts, and financial structure of each company was assessed. After this process, four companies remained. Then their brief presentations were reviewed, and the on-going construction projects of each company were inspected for quality and to assess their on-site management skills. In addition, the owners of each company's completed construction projects were contacted and interviewed concerning the level of communication and cooperation between the owners and the contractors. Once the owners learned that the interviews were with regards to the Buddha Memorial Center, they all enthusiastically offered their cogent appraisals.

Only at this stage was a draft design submitted, inviting each company to give a simulation of the project, supply concrete construction plans, construction schedules, and so on. It was on this basis that we assessed the construction strengths of each company.

The three companies that passed this stage then began the quotation procedures. The bidding review was done in conjunction with the Religious Affairs Committee of Fo Guang Shan. When the bids were opened, it

Every aspect of the construction process is clearly planned. No detail is passed over.

turned out that the Ta-Chen Construction and Engineering Corporation won.

Over the years since the Ta-Chen Construction and Engineering Corporation took up its duties at the construction site in 2005, the relationship between contractor and owner has been transformed into a profoundly close friendship. Venerable Man Zhou explains, "By treating each other with sincerity, both sides can feel how this team is of one body. We do not differentiate our relationship as you the employee who wants money and we the employer who pays you. Rather, we are one family. Each has its duties to perform, but there is the shared belief that the Buddha Memorial Center is for all of us."

Venerable Man Zhou cites the example of Fu Zaixian, the Executive Director for the Buddha Memorial Center project. Every day, he would arrive at the construction site at 6:00 am, even though his work shift actually began at 8:00 am. Though he comes off duty at 5:30 pm, you could always see him there at 7:00 pm. It seemed that he was at the construction site even during the holidays. Fu Zaixian's home is in Fengyuan, yet he would become so busy with the project that it kept him away from home for prolonged periods of time.

Venerable Man Zhou would often remind him, "Mr. Fu, it's been a long time since you've seen your family. Go back for a few days."

But he would always say that it was fine, that he would make his own arrangements.

"I found such instances very touching," said Venerable Man Zhou, "Mr. Fu was really quite willing to make the Buddha Memorial Center his home. In the early morning, he would go up to the Main Shrine for the morning service, and would then go to the construction site when the service was finished. Seeing their executive director making such earnest efforts, his subordinates naturally did their utmost wholeheartedly."

Time, Space, and Human Relationships

As the one responsible for the overall planning of this project, Venerable Man Zhou excelled at managing the project schedule and budget. Her method of management integrated all aspects, and all the coordination between the work teams and the scheduling of work processes were set out clearly and smoothly in her detailed plans.

Generally speaking, all it takes is more than one group before there forms a division of views. A conflict of opinion is something that cannot be avoided. Yet the Buddha Memorial Center project was able to cordially achieve overall consensus on all matters. As Venerable Man Zhou observes, "This was the result of everybody communicating with sincerity. I feel that whatever the case, conflict must be allowed to occur in human relationships, for it is only through conflict that we can observe, confront, and resolve problems. Lack of conflict is merely the facade that everything is going well. My job is to ensure that the channels of communication operate smoothly and mediate between the various viewpoints, so that everybody can be happy."

In her wise mediating of interpersonal interactions, Venerable Man Zhou experienced a deep realization regarding the architecture, "Venerable Master Hsing Yun's design is very free-flowing, and the planning for the flow pattern is very clear. Shouldn't we deal with people in the same way?

As long as some space is left between oneself and others, then one can walk about freely and not bump into a wall."

The very route leading to the Buddha Memorial Center can bring about this realization. There are many ways to reach the Big Buddha. One can travel the Circle Drive, or proceed from the Front Hall along the covered walkways, past the eight pagodas, and head directly towards the Main Hall. The whole route consists of one uninterrupted space, without any twists or turns. The whole area is well-balanced and solid, and very well-defined. As large and vast as the garden areas are, as long as one is sure of the direction, one will not get lost, no matter where one walks.

This clear and open layout is actually the product of careful planning with skillful wisdom and the enlightened mind. Venerable Man Zhou cites an example: The Grand Photo Terrace features thirty-seven steps, representing the thirty-seven factors of enlightenment, The "thirty-seven factors of enlightenment" are a set of foundational Buddhist teachings, and includes the four bases of mindfulness, the four kinds of right effort, the four bases of supernatural power, the five faculties, the five powers, the seven factors of enlightenment, and the Noble Eightfold Path. These constitute the bodhisattva practice for seeking wisdom, achieving liberation, and attaining Buddhahood.

Venerable Man Zhou points out the significance of this design, "Venerable Master Hsing Yun's Grand Photo Terrace is a clever manipulation of space: the Main Hall ahead is constructed in the Indian style, while the eight pagodas behind are done in the Chinese style, symbolizing how the Dharma was spread from India to China, while this location itself is a manifestation of Humanistic Buddhism. People standing on the photo terrace can take a picture in the direction of the Main Hall and have a background in the style of India, If they turn around to take a picture in the direction of the entrance,

The special design of the Buddha Memorial Center gives it a fluid appearance with clear-cut, well-defined features.

then their picture will be framed by the Chinese style pagodas, against imperial style buildings. This demonstrates Venerable Master Hsing Yun's creativity, while at the same time showing the path of Buddhism over time. In this way, the development of Buddhism is communicated as a spatial progression."

A Faculty Advisor for the Architecture Department

To Venerable Man Zhou, creativity is the fountainhead of architectural design. Without it, building a house is just a matter of piling wood.

"Following Venerable Master Hsing Yun's path through architecture has taught me to think outside the box and stimulate my latent creativity. That is why so many consider him the mentor of Fo Guang Shan's architecture department."

In the early years of Fo Guang Shan's founding, the design and decoration of every building was born from Venerable Master Hsing Yun's imagination. Despite having never received a diploma in his life, nor studied architecture, Venerable Master Hsing Yun regularly finds himself creating new plans as he stands by the road or sits at the construction site. One time,

In the Jetavana Grove, one can see delightful carvings of small novice monks everywhere.

on his way back from a site, he declared a new realization, "It turns out my greatest interest in life is construction engineering."

Over the past decades, Fo Guang Shan has created branch temples all over the world. The building of the Buddha Memorial Center has also taken such a long, long time. Since it was constructed on a hillside, the procedures required by law were protracted and complicated, and included a business plan, a development plan, and a water and soil conservation plan. Only after these plans were examined and approved could the contractors apply for the necessary building and use permits. Only after land apportionment has been completed could the building permit be processed, allowing construction to commence.

Having personally experienced this whole process, Venerable Man Zhou observes, "I've been at the construction site for the Buddha Memorial Center for eight or nine years now. Since accepting this position in 2002, I've spent the whole time by Venerable Master Hsing Yun's side. From him I've lear-ned about administration and planning. My experiences in these areas have been very profound."

Whenever there was a change in the plan, whether it was the slightest change to surface area, elevation, or position during the building process, then the applications for licenses needed to be resubmitted in accordance with the law and run through the entire process of legal regulations again. This procedure often takes more than half a year. To outsiders, such a pro-tracted and complicated process would really seem far too onerous, but Venerable Man Zhou can encapsulate her attitude in a single sentence:

"As long as you are happy to do it, it is not a hardship."

A Feast of Multifaceted Art for Giving People Joy

As Venerable Master Hsing Yun sees it,
Buddhist practice is not about suffering,
the human world should be a happy and joyful place.
Modern life is very stressful,
so when people come to Buddhist temples,
what they are seeking is spiritual tranquility and ease.

—— Venerable Ru Chang

The Buddha Memorial Center teaches the Dharma to all. As to exactly how these buildings propagate the Buddha's teachings, Venerable Ru Chang, the person in charge of the overall aesthetic of the complex, summarizes it in five facets:

"First is directly spreading the faith. Second is culture, which at the Buddha Memorial Center is a combination of Buddhist culture, global Chinese culture, and Taiwanese culture. Third is education, as demonstrated by the Buddha Memorial Center's Life Protection Murals or the Chan Art and Stories, which teach guests about life and character building through their beauty. Fourth and fifth are recreation and tourism. These five

Venerable Master Hsing Yun is the director of planning for the Buddha Memorial Center.
To the right is Venerable Ru Chang.

approaches ensure that people of all ages and from all social strata can see, hear, and enjoy something beautiful."

Generally speaking, paying homage to the Buddha, participating in Dharma services, and engaging in group practice are the main reasons why Buddhists go to Buddhist temples and monasteries. At the Buddha Memorial Center these activities can be performed at the buildings along the central axis of the center: the Big Buddha, the Main Hall with its three shrines, the central stupa, the Four Noble Truths Stupas, and the eight pagodas. However, Venerable Ru Chang says there is more:

"The surrounding facilities such as Jetavana Grove and the Water Drop teahouses will draw in even more people. Here they can stroll about, drink

Small stages set in the grove for parents and children.

tea, enjoy family fun, exercise, and go on outings. Visitors can enjoy the tourist and recreational activities in a relaxed manner, while practitioners can quietly explore their inner selves. This environment, suitable for both active and quiet activities, is not just a place from Buddhism, but rather something that transcends Buddhism."

Three Major Areas of Excitement That Draw Close to Life without Any Separation

Venerable Master Hsing Yun is the mastermind behind the design of the Buddha Memorial Center. Constantly at his side, Venerable Ru Chang describes Venerable Master Hsing Yun's thoughts on Buddhist practice, "As Venerable Master Hsing Yun sees it, Buddhist practice is not about suffering, the human world should be a happy and joyful place. Modern life is very stressful, so when people come to Buddhist temples, what they are

seeking is spiritual tranquility and ease. That's why we put rocking chairs in Jetavana Grove, allowing people to relax and let go of everything as they gently rock to and fro. We also planted many trees, as well as setting up several stages through this elegant forest, so that friends could relax around these stages while relishing tea, or a whole family could perform on these stages and enjoy a good time."

The Song dynasty artist Guo Xi (*ca.* 1020-1090 CE) wrote in his treatise on landscape painting, *Lofty Sentiments of Forests and Springs*, "There are mountains for walking, for viewing, for wandering, and for living."

As one leisurely wanders through the Buddha Memorial Center, one can freely enjoy the impressive Buddha statues, the endless wall murals, the elegant calligraphy displays, and the magnificent buildings. One can freely walk among the eight pagodas. In the forests of camphor and banyan trees, one can enjoy the scenic wonders of the garden park and the gentle fragrance produced by its plants and trees. It is a truly delightful experience. If a half-day visit fails to satisfy, then one can stay another day or two, to fully enrich one's experience.

Aside from Jetavana Grove, the Front Hall and the Water Drop tea-houses, additional facilities have been built to welcome our visitors. All living beings need food. You can't do much on an empty stomach, for one needs energy and stamina to appreciate the beauty of the environment and pursue a spiritual practice.

"The Front Hall offers everything one could need: eating, drinking, browsing, meeting locations, waiting sites, as well as shops and bookstores. One is surrounded by beautiful scenery both near and far," Venerable Ru Chang offers her further analysis, "Since everything here is part of life, people will not feel out of place. There is no sense of distance between the visitors. Schools come here on their field trips to learn about life. In the Water Drop teahouses, the public comes to hold meetings for their book clubs, their bird watching societies, and their photography associations. All kinds of recreational activities have already formed close associations with each other under the beautiful and relaxing ambience of the Buddha Memorial Center."

Experiencing the Beautiful Scene Right in Front from Five Angles

As a specialist trained in aesthetics, Venerable Ru Chang possesses a detailed understanding of the Buddha Memorial Center's aesthetic construction. She points out that the garden area is on a continuously rising slope. On its own, this would make the design look uneven. But the symmetrical design of the four stupas, the parallel walkways, and the opposing two entrances produce a sense of order. As one walks amidst the beautiful long walkways, every doorway they pass will demonstrate how the Buddha Memorial Center uses the beauty of the surrounding natural landscape. Every entrance serves as a picture frame, capturing the lush green mountains, the dazzling sunlight, the vivid flowers, and occasionally, vibrancy of other fellow tourists.

The Buddha Memorial Center is designed so that one can witness the beauty of light and shadow at any time of the day. The rising sun reflects off the Buddha's golden features, while the glow of twilight frames the Buddha from behind. The iridescence of the rosy clouds moves the profusion of people who witness it. Whether morning lights and evening shadows, or when the moon shines bright and clear, beams of light play upon the yellow roof tiles and the cream-color stone surfaces. From a distance, it looks as if the ground was paved with gold.

The architecture, sculpture, painting, and calligraphy create a beautiful atmosphere that naturally brings peace to the mind. When one's mind achieves calm, one is better able to appreciate the beauty of the content contained within. Venerable Ru Chang cites some examples: The Front Hall

offers good health porridge to all visitors upon arrival. This is a beautiful gift, exchanging the pleasantry of tea for porridge. The many names on the Wall of Benefactors represent the beauty of donations contributed in kindness. The various exhibitions and artistic creations are a veritable feast of the many different flavors and styles of Buddhist art.

The Beauty of the Eighteen Arhat Sculptures

Before the eighteen arhats were placed at the Buddha Memorial Center, before the stone sculptures were transformed from images of faith into artistic creations, there was the search for the artist. This proved to be a difficult and delicate process.

Venerable Ru Chang searched within Taiwan and abroad for a craftsman capable of the task. She recalls, "The Buddha Memorial Center is a project of historic scale and is international in its character. To create a piece of Buddhist artwork that would be representative of the times is no easy task. Even more so since we are expecting the sculptor to free themselves from the traditional formulas and endow the eighteen arhats with a new vitality. This makes the project considerably more difficult. It was very fortunate indeed that we found Wu Jung-tzu.

Wu Jung-tzu did not agree to the task immediately. But after he had visited the Buddha Memorial Center, he was quite amazed at the extraordinary karmic opportunity presented to him. It was as if his forty years of sculpting experience was all accumulated in preparation for the eighteen arhats. He spoke frankly about his own feelings, "These are works for the ages. If this opportunity had come ten years ago, I probably would not be able to accomplish it. But now that I've reached the age of sixty, I've honed my skills to their finest. I'm confident I can do a perfect job!"

Even the placement of the Eighteen Arhats was an enormous task.

At the age of twenty-three, Wu Jung-tzu apprenticed himself to the famous teacher Pan De from Fuzhou to learn his art, marking the beginning of his career as a wood sculptor. Having only received a primary school education, Wu Jung-tzu returned to school at the age of forty-five at the prompting of the scholar Han Baode. There, he devoted himself to his studies until he'd achieved a graduate school degree. When he became the sculptor for the eighteen arhats of the Buddha Memorial Center, Wu Jung-tzu demanded extremely high standards from himself.

Having observed him throughout the course of the project, Venerable Ru Chang recalls, "Mister Wu came to understand in depth the spirituality and character of each of the eighteen arhats, so as to better present their external qualities from within. Take for example Ksudrapanthaka, who attained enlightenment while sweeping the ground. His sculpted form includes his famous broom and the gestures of his hand. Even the folds of his clothing reflect the motion of his sweeping. Looking at the structure of the human form, sweeping is a sideways action, and so Mister Wu has carefully considered how to depict

the bending of the arhat's arms and legs. Sweeping the ground also covers one with dust and dirt, and so the surface layers of Ksudrapanthaka's statue is gritty, a contrast with the smooth exterior of the other arhats. Each of the eighteen arhats possesses a fine level of detail. They each have different head shapes, different postures, and different expressions. Even if the sculptures were not identified by name, one could still see the act that brought them enlightenment in their unique qualities and actions."

In order to work on the eighteen arhats, Wu Jung-tzu journeyed all the way to Quanzhou in Mainland China to select the best *qingdou* granite, which he used to carve each of the four-meter tall sculptures. Wu Jung-tzu resided on the site for more than a year and a half, giving up his teaching career in Taiwan, declining other projects, and canceling any of his exhibitions. In this way, he focused his attention on creating something entirely new, working hard in partnership with the local stonecutters versed in the traditional portrayals of the arhats. Even though this cross-straits project raises the costs, Venerable Ru Chang relates, "Venerable Master Hsing Yun insisted on doing it this way. He hoped such structures could propagate the Dharma through their profound aesthetic appeal."

The Beauty of Concrete Sculpture So Supremely Difficult

"Stories of the Buddha," "Chan Art and Stories," and the "Life Protection Murals" are the three major sets of bas-relief artwork at the Buddha Memorial Center. The one who turned these three great series of two-dimensional paintings into three-dimensional works was none other than the artist Ye Xianming, a cement sculptor with more than twenty years of experience.

As Venerable Ru Chang points out, one of the unique aspects of cement sculpture is that the materials are easily procurable, but its fast-drying nature means that it is difficult to work with. One cannot set a composition beforehand. Once the cement is obtained, one must immediately shape it on the wall with speed and precision so that the three-dimensional effects of the semi-relief are made manifest.

"This technique was transmitted to Taiwan from Mainland China some years ago, but has since been lost in China. Only Taiwan preserved this technique. Mister Ye is one of the finest practitioners of this medium. He is meticulous about the overall presentation of his works. When he undertook this project, Mister Ye even made a trip to personally invite his mentor to come and join him in the planning of the line, angle, and visual appearance of the bas-relief. Mister Ye even participated in the weekly Buddhist sutra study sessions and practiced his own mental cultivation, so as to increase the artistic significance of his work."

Actually, Ye Xianming began practicing Chan a decade ago. During this project for the Buddha Memorial Center, he became better able to focus and more aware of his own drives and motives. Ye Xianming explains, "I do my very best in honor of the Buddha. To me, this was a process of introspection. The spiritual benefits I gained were completely unexpected. It is my hope that those who see my works will come to understand the wondrous effects of Chan!"

The lion and elephant families at the entrance to the Front Hall are also the cement artworks of Ye Xianming. The lion and elephant, each six meters tall and six meters wide, represent his finest artistic creations in twenty years. Heralded as the largest guardian statues in any Buddhist temple or monastery in all of Taiwan, these groupings of lion and elephant sculptures started out as steel frames before being tightly covered in steel mesh so that the cement would adhere to the frame. Once the overall shape was formed and after the detailing was finished, the sculptures were then colored using the "terrazzo" method.

Venerable Ru Chang talks about the aesthetic appeal of this technique, "Before applying the pebbles in the terrazzo style, one must first make a layout that clearly defines the areas to be colored on the bodies of the lions and elephants. Then, yellow, white, and black crystalline stones are mixed with the cement an d applied to the body of the frame. After the cement has hardened, the surface is washed with a wet sponge. After all the cement slurry has been wiped away, the natural beauty of the colored stones will appear."

Chan Arts and Stories

Like the Beauty of Colored Landscape Paintings

After the cement sculpting for the "Life Protection Murals" and the "Chan Art and Stories" bas-relief series were completed, the task of covering them in vibrant colors required the skills of the painter Chen Mingqi.

Venerable Ru Chang talks about the difficulties involved in coordinating the cement sculpture with the coloration: "If the cement sculptor does not have a good grounding in painting techniques, then they will be unable to present the three-dimensional effect; and if the painter does not understand the principles of cement sculpture, then they will be unable to boldly draw distinctive lines. Together, the painting of Chen Mingqi and the cement sculpture of Ye Xianming reflect each other's brilliance, forming a successful partnership."

Bas-relief exhibits perspective, chiaroscuro, coloring, and line. Painting upon them requires a different technique than that used for flat surfaces. This presents a fundamental difficulty. However, this is not the biggest problem. Venerable Ru Chang cites as an example the eighty-six Life Protection Murals: "The problem lies in the fact that the viewer is moving and that the walkway is on an incline. If done in the typical fashion, the square frame of each mural would appear askew as visitors approached. Later on, we used circular frames to avoid this issue. However, a continuous series of circular frames would lead to sensory fatigue, so we inserted a calligraphy work between every four or five murals, enabling one's vision to relax through the added variety."

There were, of course, many more problems than these. With so many pictures lined up side by side, how could we avoid the colors clumping together into a chaotic mess and avoid making them too monochromatic and thus appear unappealing? Chen Mingqi came up with this solution. The colors moved from red, to orange, to yellow, to green, to blue, to indigo, and to violet, increasing or decreasing by degrees. This enabled the application of colors to achieve harmony even in change.

Having painted in Buddhist temples since childhood, Chen Mingqi would go home every day to practice calligraphy, which developed into a habit in his adult life. His background in line drawing is very solid, and he continues to develop both his watercolors and oil painting, in which he blends together traditional and modern techniques. Venerable Ru Chang observes, "Mister Chen is very careful about his painting. Every day he climbs up the steel frame and begins to paint. He could be up there the whole morning. He could spend several days just painting the wood grain of a bed. When he's done, it is as beautiful and detailed as a Qing dynasty work. Mister Chen is a very quiet person, and he sets very high standards for himself. He deeply cares for his works. When I'm at the construction site, I always watch him from a distance, worried that I would place pressure on him. His drawings are truly of great quality, and bring happiness to everyone.

Engineers taking measurements.

Behind the Touching Beauty

However, even after color, line, chiaroscuro, and perspective, beauty is not yet achieved. To bring this beauty to viewers, electromechanical equipment, fire protection, air conditioning, worker safety regulations, cost budgeting, and so on are necessary. This turned out to be a big test for Venerable Ru Chang, who had a background in arts, not engineering.

Construction sites are places of professionalism. Initially, Venerable Ru Chang lacked a clear understanding of the specialized terminology. However, she had come to learn their terminology and become highly adept at holding business meetings. She can communicate and coordinate, as well as bargain, supervise, evaluate, and take charge of scheduling, dealing with any and every situation that comes her way.

The Six Perfections Pagoda

"The biggest pressure is time," Venerable Ru Chang admits of the fifteen construction projects she managed, most of the contractors and designers had no knowledge of Buddhism, "It took me two, sometimes three times longer than usual to explain the spirit of the Buddha and the unique characteristics of Buddhism to them. The contractors were the hands that carried out the work, while Venerable Master Hsing Yun was the brain that conceived and created it. His ideas came in written form, and we were the ones who had to transform them into paintings and three-dimensional works. We were tasked with transforming them into an interactive exhibition space."

Take the permanent exhibit of the Life of the Buddha for example. Venerable Ru Chang describes how after listening to Venerable Master Hsing Yun's ideas, more than thirty discussions on how to present it were held. This translated into repeated changes. The presentation method and the

technical considerations would all affect the design of the aesthetic appeal, determining whether or not what was imagined could be manifested into a concrete result.

"We depended upon the heavenly Dharma protectors, as well as the support from countless devotees, including the guidance and assistance from many advisors. Our success was facilitated by the positive connections from all quarters, working in concert with each other."

The Buddha Memorial Center has made a break from Buddhism's traditional forms of architecture, but the spirit of the Dharma pervades its every corner. Venerable Ru Chang came to this realization:

"Venerable Master Hsing Yun's first consideration is where we can find happiness, and what are the needs of people and of everyday life. In his mind, Buddhism is not just what is said in the Buddhist sutras. The tranquility of the spirit, the language of non-confrontation, harmony in the home, and congeniality among colleagues all constitute the teachings of the Buddha. In advocating the Buddha's thought, be it the Four Noble Truths, the Noble Eightfold Path, or the twelve links of dependent origination, he does so to apply the Dharma for the benefit of living beings. We are simply using the forms of aesthetics to present the language of Buddhism."

Positive Connections
Create a Wonderful Life

"In this world, good things are infectious, for one good cause can create another. We have seen here how many good things can come one after another."

—— Venerable Man Yi

On one occasion a ninety-year-old man was visiting the Buddha Memorial Center. As he entered he began walking, looking, and listening carefully to the explanations of the tour guide. Then, suddenly, he lifted his wrinkled face and began to cry.

Venerable Man Yi, Executive Director of the Fo Guang Shan Benefactors Board, rushed over, very concerned, and asked, "What's wrong, sir?"

"I'm so fortunate to still be alive," the old man said in a somewhat excited tone, "Otherwise I would not be able to see this building."

Having spent a lifetime devoutly reciting the Buddha's name, he felt that having the positive connections to be here and witness the construction of the Buddha Memorial Center had given him the opportunity to give his own small contribution. He continued to exclaim, "I'm very fortunate, very fortunate indeed!"

From the second floor of the Front Hall, one can see the entire Buddha Memorial Center.

Similarly blessed was an eighty-year-old woman. She had traveled far and wide to collect donations for the center's construction, and as a result ten people made a positive connection with the Buddha Memorial Center. Some people made their donation in one lump sum, while others donated in installments, which were personally collected at their door by this old woman each month. Seeing how full of joy and energy she was, people would ask her, "How old are you?"

She would reply crisply, "I'm eighty."

Many would feel embarrassed and said, "And here you are, having to come back each month to collect my installment. Let me pay it all now so we won't be troubling you so much."

To which the elderly woman would say, "It doesn't matter. I walk simply to remind everyone of this wonderful opportunity. In this way, people who make their donations can fulfill their merit, and for that I am happy."

There are many different opinions as to what makes a wonderful life. There have been instances when people who were just about to buy a house have a sudden change of heart, and instead donate their wealth to the Buddha Memorial Center, thinking, "If I buy a house, then I would have it, but I'm actually in no rush. I should first ensure that the Buddha Memorial Center has all that it needs. I want to leave behind some token of significance to mark my life. Also, I'll be joining everyone in Buddhism, and leaving this wonderful institute for future generations."

Children are our future, and they so often grow to imitate the words and deeds of the adults around them. There have been children who, seeing that their parents donated money, declared, "I want to donate too!"

The parents would remind the child, "You know you'll have to use your own money if you want to make a donation!"

The child remains certain and replies, "Each month I have six dollars in allowance, so I can donate two." Isn't their innocent enthusiasm adorable?

Good Things Are Infectious, for One Cause Can Induce Yet Another

In this world, good things are infectious, for one good cause can create another. We have seen here how many good things can come one after another." As Executive Director of the Fo Guang Shan Benefactors Board, Venerable Man Yi has seen the workings of merit on a grand scale, but also has experienced in detail how even the smallest good thoughts shine forth:

"Just now, I brought in the donations from the donation box. Although there was only a few dollars, I still feel that it is a good contribution. This money is an expression of kindness from the people who come here. While the Buddha Memorial Center was under construction, there was a donation box set up at the eight pagodas service office. I made a point of going there every day to collect the donations. Regardless of how much money was put into the box, it all represents the positive connections that people are making. We must ensure that these connections take root here at the Buddha Memorial Center."

This practice highlights how Venerable Master Hsing Yun thinks about donations. Venerable Man Yi recalls, "Venerable Master Hsing Yun has said, 'What comes from all directions, supports undertakings in all directions. The generosity of thousands of people creates connections for thousands of people.' Large donations are worthy of gratitude, but small contributions can show the same depth of devotion. Regardless of the donation's size, it acts as a cause which becomes connected to the Buddha Memorial Center as a condition. With the connection of cause and condition comes joy, the joy of coming here to learn about Buddhism, and of making this place a part of their lives."

No matter what amount one donates, one forms a connection to the Buddha Memorial Center.

The Buddha Memorial Center embodies the spirit of the Buddha.

Venerable Man Yi strongly believes that any individual can make a positive connection with the Buddha Memorial Center. Some people have limited resources, and may only be able to make a donation in installments. Venerable Man Yi gives such an approach the same praise, "The job of handling these donations is complicated, in that the monthly installments have to be kept track of, the contributions recorded on the computer. This requires hiring additional staff. However, I feel that paying in installments is a beautiful thing, for if people wish to see the Buddha Memorial Center completed, we should see to it that their wish is fulfilled. Each time I see a donation form coupled with one or two dollars, I feel that people's hearts are truly beautiful. This one dollar could be someone else's one thousand dollars. The good connections that people form are not differentiated by size or potency, and there is no need to make comparisons between people's good karma. During the Buddha's time, there were those who specialized in collecting donations from the poor. A single donation could enable the poor to escape their poverty by laying down positive causes for auspicious results in the future."

Fo Guang Shan believes in investing its wealth in its devotees, emphasizing that giving must be done without hardship and without regret. This is a principle that Venerable Master Hsing Yun taught everybody.

The Collective Creativity of Good and Kind Thoughts

Giving need not be about money. To donate money is one form of contribution, but to donate one's effort and work is also a very praiseworthy form of participation.

Wave upon wave of volunteers regularly appear from all over the country. As dawn breaks, they come in tour buses to Fo Guang Shan, ready to perform communal labor such as pulling weeds, digging up rocks, and tidying up the gardens. Sometimes, they help with the sweeping, window cleaning, wiping the tables and chairs, and boiling water to make tea for the tourists who are coming to visit. They may even begin to sing, greeting the guests with their bright smiles.

On this smooth expanse of land, swaying flowers sweeten the air with their fragrance. The brightness and clarity of the field brings peace to the spirit. In the smiles of others, one can find warmth. This form of contribution brings in even more contributions, gathering thousands upon thousands of good and kind thoughts from every direction, creating an endless chain of connections. Serving as a guide for the visitors who come to Fo Guang Shan, Venerable Man Yi has personally experienced this motivating force of continuous connections:

"I discovered that there are an extraordinary number of people who have been inspired by Venerable Master Hsing Yun, inspired by the architecture, and inspired by all the positive connections as a whole. Some people walk in and are stunned by the immensity of the site. They feel that by contributing to this Buddha Memorial Center that they could then share in its glory."

In the effort to form positive connections, even the mahogany and camphor trees are doing all they can. These two precious old trees are more than eighty years old, and were transplanted from the Anle Vihara in Taitung. Weighing nearly eighteen tons each, these trees now stand in the Buddha Memorial Center. Every one of their leaves is a Buddha, enlightening the minds of ordinary people.

In the effort to form positive connections, the workers at the construction site became involved as well. These include the builders, the construction contractors, the material suppliers, and so on, who responded to the call of the "Million Copies of the *Heart Sutra* Joining the Dharma Body" campaign of their own initiative. On one fine morning, everyone was sitting in rows along the corridor, copying out the *Heart Sutra* one stroke at a time. How long had it been since they last used a traditional Chinese writing brush? Had they ever had such a close experience with a Buddhist sutra before? Having planted seeds in the field of merit through this activity, they are witnesses to the causes and conditions surrounding this once-in-one-thousand years project. Here, they were wielding the traditional writing brush with great effort, a sight hardly ever seen at construction sites, which made the scene all the more impressive and moving.

In the effort to form positive connections, the Water Drop teahouse's signature good health porridge can also gather in many sentiments and inspiring feelings. Upon their arrival at the Camphor Grove Tea House in the Jetavana Grove, visitors are heartily welcomed with a bowl of good health porridge as soon as they sit down. This represents Venerable Master Hsing Yun's personal wish, to bless those that come to the Buddha Memorial Center with good health and fortune. Furthermore, all the items on the menu

have no fixed price. People may donate whatever they wish, and all the income from the teahouses is donated to the Buddha Memorial Center.

All these donations and contributions have brought great energy to the Buddha Memorial Center. Venerable Man Yi says, "It is just like the process of 'collective creation' that Venerable Master Hsing Yun talks about. Only when the combined efforts of all causes and conditions are brought to bear do things turn out for the best."

The Mission Entrusted by the Buddha

Having long served at the Buddha Memorial Center, Venerable Man Yi sees the Main Hall, the eight pagodas, and the Big Buddha every day. Under the clouds and sky, she gazes off into the distance, her thoughts traveling back to twenty-six hundred years ago, when the Buddha reached final *nirvana.* She thinks about the Buddha's tooth relic, which survived the Buddha's cremation. She recalls how it survived in India for more than one thousand years, how it has been worshipped in India for several centuries, and how it has miraculously been brought to Taiwan. Venerable Man Yi explains how extraordinary this series of events is, "The tooth of the Buddha himself is actually here! Truly this came about through unbelievable causes and conditions. It is also a responsibility, demonstrating that Buddhists today are still worthy of the mission entrusted to us by Buddha. The Buddha Memorial Center represents the Buddha's spirit, and the burden of its construction is very heavy. The financing and planning of the Buddha Memorial Center required the full efforts of Venerable Master Hsing Yun, thousands of temples, and millions of devotees. As Venerable Master Hsing Yun says, 'as long as we truly are working for the sake of Buddhism and on behalf of living beings, then the contributing causes and conditions from all quarters will naturally bring success.'"

A Wise Measure Even an Architect Admires

"Venerable Master Hsing Yun possesses a deep understanding of architectural space. Each and every area is based upon the requirements of the Dharma and the needs of the people."

—— Li Guanghui

Three times a day, every day, Venerable Master Hsing Yun came to the construction site of the Buddha Memorial Center.

The first inspection tour sometimes begins as early as 6:00 am, though sometimes as late as 9:00 am. When Venerable Master Hsing Yun arrives, sometimes he will visit the construction office made out of shipping containers, or perhaps under the corrugated steel awnings, or even on the construction platform itself. As he sits, he looks out over the gigantic construction area, his mind swirling with ideas.

Such a sight has become quite commonplace for Li Guanghui, who has been supervising this construction project for many years. He recollects, "Venerable Master Hsing Yun comes here early in the morning, sometime even earlier than me. He walks around, looks about, and thinks over what he sees. Then he walks out. He'll come again at noon, and then once more in the afternoon. His visits are not a disturbance, in fact, upon learning that he has arrived, we hurry to meet him and listen to any instructions he has

for us. Any time Venerable Master Hsing Yun is at Fo Guang Shan, he will come to see us. Sometimes, after returning from a trip abroad, he would enter the site, even as late as at eight or nine at night, to examine the construction before returning to his residence."

When Venerable Master Hsing Yun arrives, the architects, structural engineers, water conservation engineers, electrical engineers, environmental engineers, and so on, will bring him an item-by-item report addressing specific information in detail, current problems being faced, and construction progress, which includes every flat surface, every vertical surface, and every measurement. Then they will present their conclusions professionally and accurately.

During its construction, Venerable Master Hsing Yun visited the Buddha Memorial Center daily.

The Architect's Architect

When people see the majestic, symmetrical design of the eight pagodas, they would probably not guess that in the original design, the towers only had a vertical main structure. The base structures were later added by Venerable Master Hsing Yun. Since the pagodas only had this main structure, they appeared too aesthetically simple. Li Guanghui closely observed Venerable Master Hsing Yun's conceptualization process, "He had already designed the bases for the eight pagodas, but what dimensions would fit the bases best? If they were too small, they would be unable to serve their functions. If they were too big, then the proportions would appear wrong. But Venerable Master Hsing Yun had a clear idea in his mind, and simply uttered the figure of 6,120 square feet. The instant we heard this number, we all thought that it was too big. But as soon as we drew it into the plans, the proportional

Venerable Master Hsing Yun designed the eight pagodas. The depths of his wisdom is truly unfathomable.

dimensions of the whole structure completely transformed the entire look. His wisdom on the macro level is truly extraordinary."

Having the fortune to participate on temple construction projects for Fo Guang Shan since the 1990s, Li Guanghui has deeply admired Venerable Master Hsing Yun's eye for architecture.

"Experiencing the entire architectural space from every angle, one can appreciate the ingenuity of Venerable Master Hsing Yun. Oftentimes, he tells us a number, and as soon as we integrate it into the plan, we see that it is a perfect match, both as an expression of the Dharma and as a structural measurement. It is as if he has his own built-in measuring stick, one that is extraordinarily precise. In my mind, he is an architect's architect, for he is more accurate than us professionals."

Even though he possessed an "internal measuring stick," Venerable Master Hsing Yun is committed to the idea of collective creativity. He believes that the Buddha Memorial Center belongs to the public, not to any individual, or any single organization. Thus, aside from his discussions with the engineering staff, he also holds meetings at the construction site with members of the monastic community.

With the sky as their roof, they sit on the ground. As soon as Venerable Master Hsing Yun has taken his seat, all his disciples also sit down. His purpose here is to fully appreciate the building. Together they experience the Buddha land in the human world, as they watch the rolling white clouds and listen to the sound of the wind in the forest. So long as the idea or approach is conducive to bringing serenity to people's minds, anyone can offer their opinion, bringing forth the collective wisdom of the group.

A Breakthrough in Building Technology

Though people can see the solid build and intricate appearance of the central Main Hall, few could imagine the complexity of its construction.

Discussing its architecture, Li Guanghui reveals the technology that outsiders cannot see: "Generally when constructing large assembly spaces, including large and small arenas, the roof area is sealed off and cannot be used. But the Main Hall has transcended that limitation. The Great Enlightenment Auditorium inside the Main Hall is an assembly hall that can accommodate two thousand people, a magnificent and impressive sight. A staircase leads up from this location, reaching level by level to the very top of the hall. Here, there are four main supports and eight major beams, which must meet very precisely in one place, where they are fixed with steel structural elements. The superstructure is built upon this. Can you imagine how they are fixed? There can be no deviation from the central axis, nor can there be any deviation in the superstructure. When the steel structural elements arrive here for assembly, the workers must maintain a margin of error within two millimeters in order to ensure that the screws can be locked in place, which forms the structural strength supporting the entire building. Technologically speaking, this is a tremendous breakthrough."

The exterior of the Main Hall is made up of stairs. Ascending one step at a time demonstrates one's sense of humility, as well as conveying one's admiration for the Buddha. Li Guanghui describes the process, "This involved the joining and hoisting into place of large reinforced walls, yellow sandstone, concrete, and steel structural elements. Accurate positioning and fixing them into place required the application of computer technology. It was only by using simulations with 3D models and by ascertaining the longitude and latitude coordinates that this highly complicated structure

The Great Enlightenment Auditorium under construction.

could be completed in midair. The Main Hall building both meets the requirements of space utilization and expresses a sense of lofty stability. Simultaneously, this building brings together the Dharma ideas of compassion, wisdom, vow, and practice represented by the Four Noble Truths Stupas, and spreads Dharma words via the wall of benefactors. As a whole, it becomes an intellectual journey, a religious journey, an artistic journey, an educational journey, and a journey of spiritual practice to all who come to see it. These were the plans and designs Venerable Master Hsing Yun formed through his daily inspections."

Here, everyone can see what Humanistic Buddhism means.

Architecture for Humanistic Buddhism

The overall construction plan was initially drawn up and designed by architects at the request of Venerable Master Hsing Yun. In the eight-year period between 2003 to 2010, more than one hundred renditions of the center's exterior were made, due to the various causes and conditions. Then, Venerable Master Hsing Yun was struck by inspiration, setting out the rudimentary layout for the Buddha Memorial Center using a few bottles of mineral water, a tissue box, and some newspapers. It was at that moment that the long-discussed design plan was finally settled.

Aside from its principal building, the "Main Hall", the center's layout consists of the eight pagodas in front, the Big Buddha in back, Vulture Peak to the south, and Jetavana Grove to the north. Such a layout was broad, sweeping, and lofty. Li Guanghui was there when Venerable Master Hsing

Yun first mentioned this plan, and remained there long enough to see it become a reality. He underwent the entire process first-hand.

"Venerable Master Hsing Yun possesses a deep understanding of architectural space. Each and every area is based upon the requirements of the Dharma and the needs of the people."

Li Guanghui learned much about Humanistic Buddhism from Venerable Master Hsing Yun's architectural designs.

"Most people are reverent and respectful as they enter temples, for they feel as if the sacred is something distant and unapproachable. They come with hearts bound by formality, and they leave as soon as they've paid their respects. But at the buildings of Fo Guang Shan, including the Buddha Memorial Center, there is room for more than personal worship. There is also space for educational, artistic, and social pursuits. As Venerable Master Hsing Yun says, 'Greet them when they come and bid them farewell when they go.' There is a Chan meditation hall for those who want to practice meditation. There are quarters available for those who want to request temporary monastic lodging. There are classrooms for those who wish to learn art, and there are galleries for those who want to immerse themselves in the fine arts. Those wishing to cleanse their spirits can enter the main shrine to worship the Buddha. If one is feeling a bit down, there are volunteers who will offer up a cup of Fo Guang tea to help one relax and be at ease. If one has an empty stomach, one might go to a Water Drop teahouse for a vegetarian meal. Humanistic Buddhism means planning for people's various needs in the design and planning of Buddhist temples. Because the funds to build such facilities came from all corners of the world, they are open for everyone to come and encounter the profound Dharma."

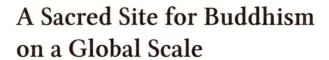

A Sacred Site for Buddhism
on a Global Scale

> *Built to various high standards and requirements, the Buddha Memorial Center possesses a strength that far exceeds the general norm. Even if it faces some severe environmental challenges in the future, I believe that this temple to Buddhism will stand for a thousand years."*

> —— Chen Yinghui

Along the inside of the northern and southern walkways, the gleaming black granite is densely inscribed with the honored names of thousads of temples and millions of people. There blocks are divided into sections, and between these sections are the sacred hand gestures (*mudra*) of the bodhisattvas, rendered in fine, elegant lines. Or there may appear the Dharma words from Venerable Master Hsing Yun's *Humble Table, Wise Fare* written in a powerful hand by famous artists of Chinese calligraphy; here are some examples:

> A bowl of compassion porridge is better than drinking precious ginseng soup,
> A cup of calming tea is better than drinking a fabulous elixir,

The Buddha Memorial Center under construction.

A mouthful of humble fare is better than dining on meat and wine,
One thought free of unwholesomeness is better than arranging a sumptuous feast.

Don't enjoy all your merit, leave some virtue to spare.
Don't say everything, leave some spare room for compromise.
Don't do everything, leave yourself some leeway.
Don't exhaust yourself, leave some energy to spare.

Using time to serve others gives one an abundance of time;
Using words to encourage others gives one an abundance of words;
Using joy to honor others gives one an abundance within;
Using strength to help others give one an abundance of power.

Chen Yinghui, the Engineering Director of the Ta-Chen Construction and Engineering Corporation for the Fo Guang Shan project, often pauses to ponder these Dharma words. As he describes it, "They are a kind of energy source."

Hardware Building, Software Design

An architect responsible for the construction of numerous public works projects, housing complexes, and electronic factories, Chen Yinghui considers the Buddha Memorial Center to be different from the traditional

Buddhist temple. Chen Yinghui describes the layout, "The Main Hall is designed in the Indian style. Its layout and the dimensions make it one of a kind, as its vaulted stories spans large distances. The eight pagodas on the other hand are designed in the Chinese style. Their coloring and shape are extremely simple, making them appear solid and reserved."

The Buddha Memorial Center was constructed with the highest quality materials. It is truly a sacred Buddhist site f the millennia.

As a sacred site on a global scale, the Buddha Memorial Center sits on a solid stratum of earth. Chen Yinghui points out, "These are ideal geological conditions, and the body of the Main Hall utilizes the highest quality construction materials. The column and beam joints are securely bound together with hoops, for every effort has been put into making the framework strong and stable. Additionally the building framework has been reinforced with a symmetrical square made of quality concrete. Built to various high standards and requirements, the Buddha Memorial Center possesses a strength that far exceeds the general norm. Even if it faces some severe environmental challenges in the future, I believe that this temple to Buddhism will stand for a thousand years."

As a professional architect, Chen Yinghui would often receive "examination questions" that would tax his imagination during his discussions with Venerable Master Hsing Yun. For example, when the public comes here they are sure to bring their children along, so what should be provided for the children? Are they any forms of entertainment that are fairly interesting, but are still educational? Do you have any thoughts or opinions as to the management of such a large area?

"Venerable Master Hsing Yun would raise such questions, and we would have to consider them and come up with some proposal," Chen Yinghui recalls, later thinking upon these questions as a form of training. "As we were working on the construction itself, we were also following in Venerable Master Hsing Yun's footsteps in visualizing the future programs these buildings would contain. He would always set the larger goals of the Buddha Memorial Center, but our group had to use our imagination for the details."

Rather than only considering what would make the most impressive building, Venerable Master Hsing Yun considered the people who would be using the facilities in the future, and tried to design the buildings for their convenience. Chen Yinghui understood that only if it were constructed with such a mindset would the building be able to respond to the needs and hopes of the people, thereby truly becoming a place of spiritual refuge.

The Locus of Motivating Force and the Source of Energy

Every day Chen Yinghui would be at the worksite, perhaps inside the stupas, perhaps up in the Sutra Repository, or perhaps in front of the Big Buddha. Concepts such as the Four Noble Truths and the Noble Eightfold Path manifested themselves as architectural hardware and became interwoven with his work. Though he does not possess a Buddhist background, Chen Yinghui now has his own understanding of the teachings on the truths of suffering, its cause, its cessation, and the path. He states frankly, "The hardships of work are a form of suffering, but are also a kind of education. The project here is very hectic. Many plans are in a constant state of flux. Though the spiritual axis remains unchanged, in order to find something better or more ideal, it may be that yesterday's decision has to be changed today. There's no preparing for it, and then there are the endless phone calls and the constant updating of the plans. That is extremely difficult. When I came here, my understanding of the fundamental principles of Buddhism did indeed begin with the Four Noble Truths and the Noble Eightfold Path."

From the Four Noble Truths and the Noble Eightfold Path to the *Humble Table, Wise Fare* on the Wall of Benefactors, Chen Yinghui gained an accurate sense of his own suffering, as well as how to effectively transform such suffering.

Therefore Chen Yinghui regularly encourages his colleagues to go and read the Dharma words inscribed upon the wall. He feels that those inscriptions are brimming with the spirit of Venerable Master Hsing Yun.

"I said to my colleagues that amongst the dozen or so of us, each is an accomplished engineer, and possesses the strength of will to overcome obstacles. But to change one's state of mind, one should try and understand more of Venerable Master Hsing Yun's sayings. We need only read them, not memorize them. When we experience their wisdom, these words will naturally flow into the mind and become the locus of motivation and a source of energy."

Personally witnessing Venerable Master Hsing Yun, a man of more than eighty years, move about the worksite every day, Chen Yinghui's sense of esteem and admiration welled up within him. He used the master as an example when encouraging himself and his colleagues, "If the old man can drive himself so hard, then how can we thirty or forty year-olds not try harder? I wonder whether or not I'll have the stamina of this eighty-five year-old when I'm just sixty-five years old! If I had such willpower, what would there be that I could not overcome? Although engineering is difficult work, as long as one walks down the correct path, then there is nothing one need worry about. Everything can be completed. This is what I have come to understand most deeply."

True Understanding, Impressions Transformed

Since he began working on the Buddha Memorial Center in 2005, Chen Yinghui has spent part of his six years working on a project in Bodhgaya, India to assist in building the Gaya Children's Home and Fo Guang Shan Buddhist College of India:

"There were about forty kids at that children's home, and the temple itself was neither grand nor imposing. It was just an abandoned workshop the devotees had loaned the monastics. In the past, I heard everyone say that Fo Guang Shan was quite wealthy, but only upon seeing these conditions for myself did I acquire a better understanding of Fo Guang Shan. Besides spreading the Dharma, Venerable Master Hsing Yun also made strenuous efforts to run schools in many countries, including places with little materials or manpower, such as India. Aside from all this, Fo Guang Shan engages in disaster relief wherever disasters have occurred. In the past, I thought monks and nuns only engaged in spiritual practice, recited the Buddha's name, expounded on the Buddhist sutras, and spread the Dharma. Now my impression of them has been totally transformed."

Architecture and Buddhism are two different fields, and there is a vast difference between them in terms of language and methods. In his venture into the land of the Buddha, it is as if Chen Yinghui has been emulating the great master Xuanzang's odyssey to the west and return to the east. He recalls, "This route that I took resembles the symbolic vocabulary embodied by the Buddha Memorial Center's architecture. The source of Buddhism lies in India, and the Buddha's tooth relic came from India to Taiwan, where it is enshrined in the Main Hall."

A Selfless and Egoless Layout So Adaptable

Venerable Master Hsing Yun issued his command, and we began digging. Originally, we were constrained by the terrain. From above, the whole base of the area appeared slanted. After he circling around the site many times, his mind was made up... Without him, this entire grand project of immense scale would not have been completed. It is my belief that no one but Venerable Master Hsing Yun possessed the boldness to give this idea form."

—— Fu Zaixian

Along the slopes of Vulture Peak, the wild grasses sparkle with crystalline beads of water as the first rays of the morning sun touch them—a picture of vigor at dawn.

Vulture peak features a retaining slope that secures the mountain. Employing green methods, the entire hillside has been safely and firmly secured with use of strong nets. With the arrival of rain and dew, the wild plants sprout, developing into a rich, dense growth in their own home soil. In comparison to crude walls made of concrete blocks, the grassy slopes not only offer stability, but also possess a gentle beauty.

A Groundbreaking Act of Creation on a Grand Scale

Fu Zaixian, Executive Director at the Buddha Memorial Center, gives Venerable Master a report on the progress of the construction.

Occupying an area of one hundred hectares, the Buddha Memorial Center extends east from the No. 21 Provincial Highway and west to the Big Buddha. Northward it circles along the Ganges River and southward it rests against the Vulture Peak.

However, this unbroken square was not made easily. Fu Zaixian, the Executive Director of the Ta-Chen Construction and Engineering Corporation for the Buddha Memorial Center, has been stationed here since 2005, during the early stages of ground preparation. No one understands better than him the difficulties of this project.

"Before we started on ground preparation, this place was originally an uneven parking lot, covered in bumps and potholes," recalling the scene in those early days, Fu Zaixian starts at the beginning. "The parking lot had an asphalt road surface, and Venerable Master Hsing Yun would often drive his electric car across the site, once, twice, even three times. He wished to plan out a foundation that was overwhelming in its size and majesty, so that the Buddha Memorial Center could be placed within it, and remain suitable for the public's needs."

One early morning, barely after 6:00, Venerable Master Hsing Yun was riding his electric car, as he usually did, over the work site's many highs and lows. A plan no one else would have conceived was forming in his mind.

Fu Zaixian describes that key moment, "Venerable Master Hsing Yun issued his command, and we began digging. Originally, we were constrained by the terrain. From above, the whole base of the area appeared slanted. After he circled around the site many times, his mind was made up. Venerable Master Hsing Yun is far wiser than we are. He had no need for blueprints. Simply by walking, by treading across the ground a few times, he could plot out the whole environment in its entirety. Only in retrospect do we now see this decision as a stroke of genius: if there had been no outward expansion, then the eight pagodas would not have been born and the circle drive could not have been completed; nor would this groundbreaking project of immense scale have been completed. It is my belief that no one but Venerable Master Hsing Yun possessed the boldness to give this idea form."

Expanding beyond the original plans for a single Main Hall, the wider base allowed for the construction of the eight pagodas.

"Next, Venerable master decided to add the Big Buddha behind the Main Hall," Fu Zaixian continues, "Once the decision to construct the Big Buddha was settled, force of presence projected by the Buddha Memorial Center became even more impressive. After it was completed, the Buddha could be seen from as far as the Formosa Freeway and Ligang."

By allowing people from afar see the Buddha, and through it see the noble and pure self they harbor within.

Inspiration Coming from Selflessness

Despite his background in civil engineering, Fu Zaixian never imagined that he would one day come to Fo Guang Shan and participate in the construction of the Buddha Memorial Center. He feels that such an honor was presented to him due to the positive karmic rewards he had cultivated over several previous lifetimes.

After the design plans have been approved, a model is constructed for a clearer image of the site.

Upon becoming involved in the project, Fu Zaixian did indeed gain some profound realizations from his work, "The only thing that doesn't change is change. As Venerable Master Hsing Yun has stated, the Buddha Memorial Center is for everybody. He emphasizes collective creativity and the wisdom of the group. After the discussions, the plan is set, at which point a model will be made, so that people can get a sense of what the fully developed building would be like. If everyone feels that changes must be made, then they are made. But these are changes that are made before the plan is executed, not the sloppy improvisations made halfway into a project. It is for the express purpose of avoiding redoing something after it is done that many changes are made to the Buddha Memorial Center beforehand."

Fu Zaixian does not deny that these changes make things more difficult, but for him, they are a source of inspiration as well: In comparison to us, the monastic community here has an even tougher job. Regardless of their level of education, they must all undergo training of mind and body through pulling weeds, sweeping the grounds, and performing various other communal labors. They do whatever needs to be done, dedicating themselves completely to Buddhism. I interact with the monastics here on a daily basis, and I often wonder, if I was one of them, would I be able to handle it? Could I dedicate every moment every day to Buddhism for ten years, twenty

七誡塔
Seven Admonishment
Pagoda

五和塔
Five Harmonies
Pagoda

三好塔
Three Goodn
Pagoda

禮敬大廳
Front Hall

八道塔
Eightfold Path
Pagoda

六度塔
Six Perfections
Pagoda

四給塔
Four Giv
Pagoc

years, thirty years, or even longer? Take Venerable Master Hsing Yun for instance. If he's not thinking about the Buddha Memorial Center, then he's thinking about Dajue Temple, the seat of his lineage, or consider how to help all human beings. Such a selfless spirit is what I should be emulating."

Holding the Compassionate Vow to Liberate Living Beings

The garden area of the Buddha Memorial Center is both wide and deep. From its east end at the Front Hall to its west end at the Big Buddha, the garden spans a kilometer, rising at a four percent incline. This means that at every hundred meters, the ground rises by four meters. After one has walked a kilometer, the height difference reaches forty meters, though it is hardly noticeable. This is because the incline rises smoothly, so subtly that one does not feel it.

But the sloping incline is not that the only thing rendered invisible. There are also invisible boundaries in place between individuals and groups. Fu Zaixian offers his praise, "Venerable Man Zhou of the Pure Land Culture and Education Foundation did an excellent job organizing the engineering

一教塔
One Teaching
Pagoda

萬人照相台
Grand Photo
Terrace

菩提廣場
Bodhi Wisdom
Concourse

本館
Main Hall

鼓樓
Drum Tower

鐘樓
Bell Tower

二眾塔
Two Assemblies
Pagoda

祇園
Jetavana
Grove

樟樹林滴水坊
Camphor Grove
Tea House

teams. Since there is more than one company involved in the construction work here, there are mechanical and electrical, masonry, planning, and fitting teams that must be coordinated with each other. Otherwise, each group will do their own thing, and nothing will fit together. These situations often occur at construction sites, but nothing like that happened at the Buddha Memorial Center. In my mind, being able to bring together all the work teams was an extraordinary feat.

Having seen one building rise after another throughout his six years here, Fu Zaixian finds it hard to suppress the happiness and sense of accomplishment he feels.

"Doesn't Venerable Master Hsing Yun have a bit of calligraphy that goes like this: 'Holding the compassionate vow to liberate living beings. One is like an unmoored boat upon the Dharma ocean. You ask what merit my life accumulated: the Buddha's Light shines across the five continents.' It is indeed such a spirit of compassion that I see before me."

Fu Zaixian keeps a small card in his notebook, the one he received when he went to the Buddha's Tooth Relic Hall to worship the Buddha. He carefully takes it out and looks at it, then very carefully returns it to his shirt pocket.

Gaining Health and Happiness in a Family of the Buddha

If any of my friends or relatives are looking for a place for recreation,
I heartily recommend that they pay a visit to the Buddha Memorial Center.
It is an excellent site for exercise, for strolling, and generally for walking about.

—— Yang Zhaojun

Standing beneath one of the Four Noble Truths Stupas, Yang Zhaojun lifts up a Buddha statue from its shipping container and drills out a hole in its back. She then identifies its location according to a numbered diagram and carefully installs it on the outer wall of the stupa structure, locking it firmly into place.

Each time she picks up a Buddha statue, Yang Zhaojun carefully examines the Buddha's facial expression, as well as its eyes, ears, and even its hand gestures. Each statue is different. She explains, "Without knowing any better, most people would guess that these are made from molds. In fact, they have all been carved by hand. Since I have had the chance to examine each one of them, I can see that the sculptors have put a lot of effort into them."

Carvings of the Buddha adorn the walls of the Four Noble Truths Stupas.

The company Yang Zhaojun and her husband operate, Shunhong Construction, was been subcontracted to do the installation work for Xianglian Stone Company. It is merely one of a multitude of teams working on the Buddha Memorial Center. The masonry work on many of the walls of the memorial complex was accomplished only through their dedicated efforts. Husband and wife arrived and left together every day, along with the four or five workers from their company.

At home, Yang Zhaojun worships the Chinese folk deities Mazu and Nuozha, and has no knowledge of Buddhism. The past two years she worked on the Buddha Memorial Center marked her closest contact with Buddhism, particularly the three months she spent installing the Buddha images on the outer walls of Four Noble Truths Stupas. She recalls, "Whenever I lift one of these statues, I feel different. Once, when I lifted a colored statue of the Buddha, I felt as if I had a special connection to the statue. I was overjoyed.

Yang Zhaojun starts to smile as she speaks, her voice expressing frank sincerity, "As I placed it on the wall, I really felt unwilling to let that Buddha statue go."

A Worksite Echoing with Song

Having worked in this business for many years and worked across many different worksites, Yang Zhaojun knows that friction between teams working on the same project is unavoidable. For example, the construction work varies in difficulty. Everyone competes for the easy jobs. But now when the easy jobs do not come to Yang Zhaojun, she finds it easier to accept:

"Perhaps we get the harder assignments because we do a much better job. When I think of it this way, I no longer harbor resentment. In fact, after viewing things calmly, everything is fine, so long as we get by. Even if we earn a bit less, it does not matter. We consider it our own contribution to the completion of the Buddha Memorial Center."

At this huge worksite, where all kinds of construction teams are stationed, one of the things Yang Zhaojun remembers most vividly is the singing voice of Venerable Man Yi, Executive Director of the Fo Guang Shan Benefactors Board. She remembers, "Venerable Man Yi is very nice and friendly. She will come to where we are working and sing for everybody. She really has a beautiful voice!"

Spreading the Dharma through song, Venerable Man Yi regularly shares the songs composed by Venerable Master Hsing Yun with everybody, such as the Taiwanese song "What is Happiness?" Each time the graceful, perfectly rounded notes begin echoing across the worksite, the whole place becomes wreathed by a clear melody. The lyrics, translated in English, are as follows:

> If you ask me what is happiness; it is actually not something difficult:
> Happiness is contentment in all things, and simplicity in all things.
> If you ask me what is happiness; it is actually not something difficult:
> Happiness is becoming a decent person, and doing things well.

What is happiness? What is happiness after all?
Happiness is freedom and ease, peace and well-being, keeping an open mind.

What is happi ness? What is happiness after all?
Happiness is good health, being free of body aches and sickness pains.

Sometimes happiness is in the palm of one's hand,
Sometimes it is in the great sea.
Sometime it's in one's heart,
And sometimes it's in one's dreams.

What is happiness after all? Saying it all would be worthless.
Happiness is when one's views begin to change.

This song tells us the secret to happiness: doing things well, being healthy, and keeping an open mind. Dharma is a way of life. This echoing melody is a blessing and an encouragement to the hard-working laborers, expressing gratitude while forming a broad array of connections for a positive future. As the voices of many hearts are joined together across the worksite, the singers and the listeners all come together to experience this happiness.

Nature's Gift

As the song brings happiness to the worksite, the sunlight also resplendently accompanies the crew. Good weather is a necessary condition for construction work, but as often happens in the Kaoshiung and Pingdong area, the mornings are bright and sunny, while the afternoons bring sudden downpours of rain. But, strange enough, as Yang Zhaojun worked under the roof

Dark clouds blot out the sun, but above the construction site of the Buddha Memorial Center, the sky remains clear.

of the Main Hall, she kept her eyes to the sky. By 2:00 or 3:00 in the afternoon, dark clouds would be rolling in from all directions, and lightning would illuminate the sky. Clearly a torrent of rain was about to come down, but as Yang Zhaojun recalls, "...the work area around the Buddha Memorial Center was the only place under a patch of clear sky! Sunlight still shone over our heads. I said to the other workers, this must be the Buddha's light that shines everywhere."

But by 5:00, having stopped for the day and walked out the main entrance, the rain immediately began to pour on to her windshield as she turns onto the main roadway. It was coming down in buckets! That patch of clear sky was truly "Nature's gift," and although she could not make sense of it, yet she remembers it vividly.

There was still another thing that Yang Zhaojun could not understand:

"My husband quit smoking without me noticing!" she said with joy that no wife could suppress.

Her husband smoked for almost twenty years. For the sake of his health, Yang Zhaojun had been constantly asking him to quit. But her husband would always say that in the construction business, cigarettes facilitate face-to-face negotiations. One always has to observe certain formalities in social interaction, which was why he was never able to quit.

She remembers, "I do not know when it happened, but one day I discovered that his pack of cigarettes had been sitting there for a week untouched. It was only after I asked did I learn that he'd already quit smoking."

What led to his decision to quit? How was he able to simply stop smoking? Yang Zhaojun asked her husband these questions, but he only said plainly, "I had no desire to smoke so I didn't."

Yang Zhaojun speculates that perhaps the atmosphere at the worksite influenced him. The person in charge of supervising Xianglian Stone Com-

pany would often remind them that the Buddha Memorial Center is a pure and sacred place. Any cigarettes butts left on the ground would adversely affect its image. No matter what the cause was, when she discusses how her husband quit smoking, Yang Zhaojun cries out with glee, "What a bonus!"

Sharing a Family of the Buddha

This was a gain in health, a gain in happiness, and a gain in well-being and harmony for the whole family. This is the "family of the Buddha" that Yang Zhaojun wishes to share with her friends and family:

"If any of my friends or relatives are looking for a place for recreation, I heartily recommend that they pay a visit to the Buddha Memorial Center. It is an excellent site for exercise, for strolling, and generally for walking about. I think the monastics are truly devoted, having put the various construction materials like rebar and cement to their best possible use." Yang Zhaojun says, candidly, "Because we come and go from this place every day, we see things quite clearly."

Historical Buildings Will Witness the Future

Venerable Master Hsing Yun has taken the spirit of compassion spoken of in Buddhist sutras and condensed it down into simpler and more accessible sayings, including the "Four Givings." Then, they have been embodied into the architecture.

—— You Shengwen

The entire complex is a classroom that allows us to enrich our spirits, so that we can constantly improve ourselves morally and spiritually.

—— Zhan Shufen

February 16th, 2010, on the third day of the lunar new year, the Buddha Memorial Center echoed with Buddhist chanting.

During the ceremony to consign the cultural treasures to the Underground Palaces, President Ma Ying-jeou was present at the Bodhi Wisdom Concourse. Amid the blessings of a hundred thousand devotees, he and Venerable Master Hsing Yun, Cecilia Y. Koo, and Yang Chiu-hsing, the governor of Kaohsiung County at the time, each in turn placed the cultural treasures into the time capsule. Monastics slowly carried the capsule into the Underground Palace, where it was then sealed inside.

The cultural artifact that President Ma had personally placed inside was the very baseball that he and First Lady Chow Mei-ching had signed together. The moment he saw this baseball, President Ma gave a look of surprise, for this was an unexpected reunion.

The donor of the baseball was none other than the famous English language instructor You Shengwen and his wife Zhan Shufen.

Leaving the Baseball to Future Generations

Zhan Shufen explains the story behind the baseball, "My husband and I were invited to attend the evening gala for President Ma's inauguration on May 20th, 2008. During that unique opportunity, we had the great fortune to receive a baseball signed by President Ma and First Lady Chow Mei-ching. Later on, we thought about how Venerable Master Hsing Yun had always been supportive of athletic activities as a way of liberating living beings. We decided to present this baseball to him as a gift. He compassionately remarked, 'It would be far too selfish of me to keep this for myself alone. I'll preserve it in the Underground Palace so that it can be shared with everyone.' Two years later, on that very day it was to be consigned to the Underground Palace, it was arranged so that the President Ma would be placing that very baseball he had signed. I am sure that when he saw the baseball, President Ma would present it with a knowing smile."

Placing these artifacts into the Underground Palace only took a few

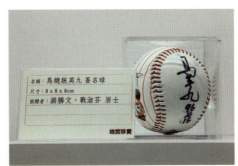

A baseball signed by President Ma Ying-jeou.

short minutes, yet the benefit it will bestow upon later generations will last for thousands of years.

Aside from this baseball, Mr. and Mrs. You Shengwen donated many other contemporary cultural artifacts to the palace, including a signed, commemorative baseball pitched at the new Yankee Stadium in New York by Wang Chien-Ming, a pitcher from Taiwan who joined Major League Baseball in America; and a basketball signed by Yao Ming, China's basketball star who joined the NBA, during his first game as starting center.

The couple loves Venerable Master Hsing Yun like a father. Whenever they travel abroad, this couple would offer whatever curiosities they discover to him. For example, they once gave him a mask of an honorable old man.

"When we looked at it from a distance, the mask looked like Venerable Master Hsing Yun."

You Shengwen also recalls a crystal-etched plum blossom she gave to him, "The piece was entitled 'An Innate Nobility that Defies the Snow,' which I thought was an apt description of Venerable Master Hsing Yun's drive to spread the Dharma, as well as his demeanor and moral integrity. I decided to buy it for him as soon as I saw it. One time, my wife even presented a square watermelon as a birthday present for Venerable Master Hsing Yun, because upon it were inscribed the words: 'Limitless Longevity.' The price of the item really doesn't matter. My wife and I just want to express our devotion."

Spiritual Practice at Fo Guang Shan Twice a Week

Their devotion is expressed not only through gifts, but also through their work, serving as teachers at Fo Guang Shan Tsung-Lin University as volunteers.

You Shengwen teaches English while Zhan Shufen teaches Chinese. Twice a week, the couple makes the climb to Fo Guang Shan to give lessons.

Each time the car passes by the Buddha Memorial Center, You Shengwen will slow down and stop for a moment:

"Every time I see it, the construction progresses a little further."

You Shengwen shares his observations over the past few years, "The eight pagodas popped up one after the other, growing taller one story at a time. I often thought about how, in the future, devotees in the tens of thousands would gather at the huge Bodhi Wisdom Concourse for events. They could enter any of the pagodas to rest or take in the sights. It is a wonderfully convenient design. Aside from demonstrating Venerable Master Hsing Yun's wise use of space, each pagoda symbolizes a different principle, such as 'One Teaching,' 'Two Assemblies,' 'Three Goodness,' 'Four Givings,' and so on. Seeing such a well-thought-out design that fully utilizes every inch of room available was quite inspirational for me."

The "Four Givings" that You Shengwen mentions are to give people confidence, give people joy, give people hope, and give people ease. You Shengwen has experienced the importance of these principles in his own life as a teacher. With students coming from all over the world, You Shengwen regularly encounters students he has taught in the past. His former students will often rush over and ask, "Do you remember me? What you said back then really gave me the drive to pursue my studies."

You Shengwen relates, "Perhaps something I had said at the podium has given confidence and hope to my students. In my mind, we should live by these principles in our interactions with others. We can at any time give people confidence, give people joy, give people hope, and give people ease. Venerable Master Hsing Yun has taken the spirit of compassion spoken of in Buddhist sutras and condensed it down into simpler and more accessible sayings, including the 'Four Givings.' Then, they have been embodied into the architecture. I think that a great individual is not a military strategist

The colors of the Fo Guang Big Buddha shift with the changes in the sky.

who takes an army into battle, nor a political leader who rules the country, rather, it is a person who can penetrate the people's spirit to constantly stimulate dynamic effects."

Seeing the weekly progress of the construction became a spiritual practice for You Shengwen, just like pouring over Buddhist sutras or cultivating the mind. You Shengwen has realized how this was its own pursuit of happiness.

You Shengwen explains, "This happiness is a sense of inner serenity. It is maintaining a pure mind that is not swayed by external circumstances. In this state, one is neither particularly overjoyed nor upset when something happens. One tries to maintain this inner sense of serenity as much as possible, and the ability to do this is an extremely important step in one's practice."

The writings of Venerable Master Hsing Yun have had a profound impact upon You Shengwen's daily spiritual practice.

You Shengwen offers an example, "Consider Venerable Master Hsing Yun's commentary on the verse from the Diamond Sutra, 'One should contemplate them in this way.' That is to say, things should be treated just as they are, not to be swayed by emotions."

You Shengwen uses the analogy of a feather, "The feather floats and flutters about, falling down onto the surface of the water. As it touches the water, ripples appear. The point is that, when something has happened, it should be treated just as it is. There is no need to add any meaningless emotions. In the past I may have gotten angry at times, blamed this person or that person for how they could have done something differently. But now, I try to see things from another angle: this is the way things are. What is important now is that I have to find a way to deal with the problem. Other emotions are unnecessary."

One Teacher, One Path: Upholding Humanistic Buddhism

Zhan Shufen too has her own thoughts concerning the Buddha Memorial Center. She has seen how Venerable Master Hsing Yun has concentrated his efforts towards cultural and educational causes:

"The interiors of the eight pagodas were designed as classrooms, some large and some small, corresponding with the differing needs of people. The courses are not limited only to Buddhist activities, but also for various specialized groups. In fact, the entire complex is a classroom that allows us to enrich our spirits, so that we can constantly improve ourselves morally and spiritually."

In her practice, Zhan Shufen has generated right mindfulness and made right vows, a decision that stemmed from a profound realization she had at Fo Guang Shan. In April of 2006, Zhan Shufen's mother lapsed into a coma as a result of her terminal liver cancer. Her children were unwilling to let their mother suffer needlessly, so they decided to bring her back to the Longevity Shrine at Fo Guang Shan, planning to send their mother off with dignity amid the solemn sounds of Buddhist chanting.

Amid the sounds of the sutras being chanted at the Longevity Shrine, Zhan Shufen's mother, who had been sleeping peacefully, suddenly called out: "There's no need for you to make all this noise. I'm not dead yet."

For the past six days and six nights she had nothing to eat or drink, and she had not taken any medicine. Miraculously, the swelling in her abdomen caused by the liver cancer gradually subsided and eventually returned to normal. Dr. Cheng Jin-shiung (vice director of the Tainan Veterans Hospital) who had been her physician for many years came to visit her. He said, "The Dharma is truly inconceivable! Here is a patient whose blood pressure could not be measured in the hospital, yet surprisingly, she survived without food or medicine."

Gazing upon the eight pagodas from the Main Hall.

On the afternoon of the sixth day, Venerable Tzu Jung came to the Longevity Shrine out of concern. She said to Zhan Shufen's family, "Why don't you all take advantage of tomorrow being the first day of a new lunar month and visit each shrine to pay homage to the Buddhas and bodhisattvas? You can make an earnest vow and pray that your mother will no longer suffer from the pain of her disease."

Early the next morning, Zhan Shufen went to every single hall and shrine, making her vows to the Buddhas and bodhisattvas and at each one prayed, "If the bodhisattvas will ensure that my mother can follow the Buddhas and bodhisattvas into the Pure Land peacefully before 9:00 this morning, the first day of the fourth lunar month, then I, Zhan Shufen will henceforth and for the rest of my life dedicate all my efforts to temples of the true faith."

That very morning, after 8:00, Zhan Shufen's mother opened her eyes and looked around at all the family members, breathing her last breath with a smile. The time was exactly 8:52 am.

Zhan Shufen remembers, "The Buddhas and bodhisattvas fulfilled my wish. My mother left this world serenely, free from fear or pain before 9:00. On the night of the seventh day of mourning, I saw my mother in a dream, dressed in the clothing of a Buddhist devotee, greeting guests. She smiled broadly and said: 'Shufen, you must keep to one teacher and one path. Follow Venerable Master Hsing Yun and uphold Humanistic Buddhism.'"

Present at This Historical Moment, Joining in the Precious Connections

In pursuit of Humanistic Buddhism, twice a week, You Shengwen and Zhan Shufen come to Fo Guang Shan. This has been going on week after week, year after year. It has been four years since they began.

During these four years, You Zhengwen and Zhan Shufen had the opportunity to witness the birth of the Buddha Memorial Center, and had the privilege of being present at this precious moment in history. You Shengwen states, "Today is tomorrow's history. The Buddha Memorial Center is the guiding line for Buddhism, for it embodies the future. This precious moment in time now lay before us. Everybody is invited to join us. Letting this opportunity pass by is to pass up planting seeds for positive karma. Think about it: It is rare enough simply to be born a human being. Rarer still is this opportunity to put our faith in Buddhism and follow in the Buddha's footsteps. Being able to plant seeds of positive karma at such a temple is a sign of wondrous causes and conditions."

A Solemn Dharma Center
for Dallying with the Flowers

We would like to thank Venerable Master Hsing Yun for creating this Dharma center. This place has allowed us to learn the Buddha's compassionate spirit, plant seeds in its field of merit, and increase our own wisdom.

—— Mrs. Zhang Jian Meijuan
and Mrs. Lin Zhang Suzhen

These are the words of a team who "plays among the flowers." Its members are housewives, but they are completely committed to the work. They are spirited and enthusiastic individuals. Every week, they set out on schedule, a dozen or so members on the team, to Fo Guang Shan, for they are the gardening volunteers of the Buddha Memorial Center.

Mrs. Zhang Jian Meijuan is the person who rallies these ladies. Each time they come to Fo Guang Shan, she is the one who drives them, picking up and later dropping off the members on her way to and from Fo Guang Shan. Mrs. Lin Zhang Suzhen is the only member of the team who works full-time, so it is only on off days that she can join others in playing among the flowers.

Bathed in Sunlight: The Spiritual Practice of Pulling Weeds

The Main Hall and the Four Noble Truths Stupas during construction.

The team consists of the female devotees of the second Niaosong Sub-chapter of the BLIA. Once, three years ago, while they were doing volunteer work, they discovered that the gardeners at Fo Guang Shan were in sore need of help. They took it upon themselves to lend a hand, forming their own team. They vowed to help with planting flowers, spreading fertilizer, trimming the branches and leaves, and taking care of the bonsai at Samantabhadra farm. Later on, when the landscape at the Buddha Memorial Center needed to be maintained, they would appear every Friday at Jetavana Grove.

The trees and plants of Jetavana Grove are widely spaced, occupying a vast area. In order to maintain such a vast garden, much work must be devoted to weeding. Pulling weeds looks simple enough, but it is not easy at all. Resembling a carpet of green wool, the zoysia grass lawns have many minute weeds growing amid the grass. Mrs. Zhang Jian Meijuan explains, "You have to carefully spread the zoysia grass open and pull out the weeds, which must be pulled out cleanly one by one. That's the only way to maintain the beautiful, well-ordered lawn."

This work requires patience and attention to detail, as well as physical stamina and endurance to heat. Sunny days in the southern part of Taiwan can be extremely hot. Mrs. Lin Zhang Suzhen describes battling the weeds under a burning sun, "We're all dressed up in our 'battle gear.' Each person has a large sun hat, washcloth, over-sleeves, and gloves. They cover the entire head, face, and body."

It seems that almost all of their time is spent bathed in the sun. They are soon soaked with sweat, and yet their minds are calm and naturally cool. They treat their work as a form of spiritual practice. Mrs. Zhang Jian Meijuan says to, "Treat the weeds like the distracting thoughts in the mind. Pulling out one weed means pulling out an affliction; eliminating one weed is eliminating one portion of ignorance. This is how I think as I work. Weeding is no different from reciting the Buddha's name. Every one of us is happy to cultivate our spiritual practice on this greenery."

The two of them jokingly declare that they are all workaholics. As soon as they start working they all try to do the best possible job. Because of this, over the past three years or so, the work on the gardens has gone far ahead of schedule.

"We 'go to work' at 8:30 in the morning," says Mrs. Zhang Jian Meijuan. With a smile, she says her volunteer work is also a "job."

"We must leave before four o'clock or so in the afternoon. All of us are housewives, so we have to hurry home to pick up the children and cook dinner. In the evenings, some of our members will also help out at the Dharma service, sort recycled materials, or serve as volunteers at the hospital."

Equal Emphasis on Practice and Understanding, Dual Cultivation of Merit and Wisdom

Whether one is pulling weeds, planting flowers, spreading fertilizer, or sweeping up fallen leaves, readying a beautiful setting for the public is a boon to everyone. Aside from their dedication to their work, this female brigade also delves deeply into the Buddhist sutras, practicing the bodhisattva path.

Mrs. Zhang Jian Meijuan says, "Fo Guang Shan holds classes to teach people about the Buddhist sutras, Chan meditation, reciting the Buddha's

This beautiful scenery is an offering to the people.

name, and joining Dharma services. One such example is the 'Million Copies of the Heart Sutra Joining the Dharma Body' campaign. Everyone has something in which they can participate. In the past, a lecture series on the Lotus Sutra held in the Devotees Building lasted three months, and our same old group came together to listen to them. Since we felt that it was important to equally emphasize understanding and practice, we all made an effort to understand the sutra as well as maintain our practice as we practice the bodhisattva path. We must cultivate both merit as well as wisdom, for that is the only way one can achieve a fulfilling and happy life."

Mrs. Zhang Jian Meijuan feels a particular connection with Venerable Master Hsing Yun's explanations of the Buddhist sutras. She thinks that a person's thoughts and ideas need to be revitalized, and delving deeply into the Buddhist sutras is the most direct and thorough method to do so. This facilitates introspection, assisting one in changing one's bad habits. Mrs. Lin Zhang Suzhen, on the other hand, has been inspired greatly by Fo Guang Shan's Buddhist chanting. Chanting and singing the Dharma with purity can aid the practitioner in achieving serenity of mind and body. One becomes immersed in the wisdom and splendor of all the Buddhas and bodhisattvas. Mrs. Lin Zhang Suzhen feels that with their gentle and profound voices, the chanting of the venerables at Fo Guang Shan can reach deeply into the hearts of the listeners.

One delves deeply into Buddhist sutras, word by word, line by line. One listens attentively to chanting note by note, phrase by phrase. Regardless of what method is used to improve oneself, the spiritual practice among the flowers and plants done by this group of Dharma sisters, guiding and supporting each other as they come and go as a team, has enabled them to attain an even greater strength. This is why none of them feel that the volunteer gardening is an obligation. Rather, they come here to play and enjoy

themselves, to the point where their minds and bodies are relaxed and free of worry, filling them with Dharma joy.

Ennobled Because of the Flowers and Plants

Each time Mrs. Zhang Jian Meijuan's husband sees her face radiant with joy, he knows that she spent the day at Fo Guang Shan.

"The changes that occurred in me have garnered me even more support from my family for the path I have taken."

Since her exposure to gardening, Mrs. Zhang Jian Meijuan has slowly come to appreciate the emotional bond she has with the flowers and plants: If they are spoken to nicely, then they will grow even more beautiful. And as one deals in this way with plants, one must use even more kind and gentle words when dealing with one's husband and children. One must make the effort to communicate in an understanding way.

Mrs. Lin Zhang Suzhen also feels the same way. Often she will say things to the flowers like, "You should bloom more beautifully. That way, even more people will enjoy you."

The gracious and courteous interaction that comes from complimenting the beauty of flowers and admiring the spirits of the fellow members of the team creates a pleasant ambience within the group. Each member of the team has experienced some miraculous transformation.

"I really admire my Dharma sister Meijuan. In the past, she generally stayed out of the sun. Even for a busy housewife like me, this gardening is a lot of hard work. But Meijuan can do it with such enthusiasm and joy. There's nothing easy about that. She has her own zoysia grass lawn in the yard. In the past, she hired someone else to tend to it. Now, she does it all by herself with a large clipper, tidying it up one patch at a time by hand."

Nourished by the beauty of the flowers and plants, nurtured by the spirit of the Dharma, everybody is full of energy and youthful vigor, even at the burning height of summer. Mrs. Zhang Jian Meijun said, "I've discovered that everybody has become ennobled and appears much younger. All their faces are aglow."

On one occasion, Venerable Man Yi, the Executive Director of the Fo Guang Shan Benefactor's Board, gave them a tour of the Buddha Memorial Center. Then she took a picture with them at the Grand Photo Terrace.

"In the picture, you could see Dharma wheels filling the sky. It was something truly incredible!" Mrs. Zhang Jian Meijun offers this explanation, "I believe that all the Buddhas, bodhisattvas, and Dharma protectors are helping us. How else could a group of women who fear sunburn and tanning have the courage to undertake such a task, and to do it for more than three years continuously? Every day there are many at the Buddha Memorial Center maintaining the scenic areas. We're just one small group among them. We would like to thank Venerable Master Hsing Yun for creating the Buddha Memorial Center. This place has taught us the Buddha's compassionate spirit, planted seeds in its field of merit, and increased our own wisdom."

The Buddha Memorial Center is truly a miracle that occurs once every one thousand years. It fuses together the positive connections from all around the world, opening the path to the field of merit and the door of wisdom to people. The human world has a Buddha land and the Buddha land is in the human world.

On August 23rd, 2011, the Love and Peace Prayer Ceremony was held at the Buddha Memorial Center (Photo by Cai Rong Feng) .

1998

02   Kunga Dorje Rinpoche acknowledges his advanced age. When Venerable Master Hsing Yun visits Bodhgaya in India, Kunga Dorje Rinpoche informs him of his intention to give him the Buddha's Tooth Relic, along with a certificate signed by twelve other Rinpoches of attesting to the authenticity of the relic. He believes in the master's vision to bring Buddhism to all living beings, and let the relic once again be seen by the world.

04/07-09   Two hundred Buddhist monastics and high-ranking officials of society gather to welcome the Buddha's tooth relic. Lead by Wu Poh-hsiung, the group flew to Thailand on China Airlines flight CI-695. After Kunga Dorje Rinpoche presents the relic to Venerable Master Hsing Yun, the group returns to Taiwan.

04/11   Regardless of their political, religious, or racial affiliations, people from all over Taiwan come to the Chiang Kai-Shek Memorial Center to welcome the Buddha's tooth relic. Venerable Master Hsing Yun hosts the ceremony. Guests include Vice President of the Republic of China Lien Chan, Premier of the Executive Yuan Vincent Siew, Straits Exchange Foundation Chairman Koo Chen-fu. During the ceremony, Vice-President Lien Chan appealed to everyone to support Fo Guang Shan, to follow Buddha's Light International Association's Three Acts of Goodness Campaign: Do good deeds, speak good words, and keep good thoughts.

2001

Fo Guang Shan acquires forty square kilometers land from the Qingtianshan, which soon becomes the site of the Buddha Memorial Center.

11/21   Accompanied by Venerable Tzu Jia and others, Venerable Master Hsing Yun personally inspects the site, beginning planning with the help of Sinotech Engineering Consultants, LTD.

2002

03/15   The "Qingtianshan Transfer of Land Ceremony" was performed at Fo Guang Shan. Qingtianshan's former general manager Zheng Jianzhi, financial consultant Gao Chengyi, and various employees from Sinotech Engineering Consultants were there to witness the event. Venerable Hsin Ting and Imperial Chemical Industries Far East representative John Chandler completed this transaction.

12/25   Clearing work commences at the construction site of the Buddha Memorial Center.

01/12 Venerable Master Hsing Yun holds a ceremony to commemorate the laying of the foundations of the Buddha Memorial Center. Guests include Venerable Hsin Ting, the representative of Supreme Patriarch of Thailand Somdet Phra Buddhachinnawong Bhiksu, Professor Suning Lukkhasatf of Mahamakut Buddhist University in Thailand, secretary of second princess Sirindhorn of Thailand, Venerable Buddharakkhita Mahanayaka Thera of Sri Lanka, Most Venerable BouKry, Supreme Patriarch of the Dharma Sect of Cambodia, Venerable Master Hyeonman of Tongdo Monastery in Korea, Venerable Master Simsan of Yilseung Monastery, Venerable Master Hyein of Yakcheon Monastery in Korea, Cardinal Paul Shan Kuo-shi of Taiwan, I-Kuan Dao Chairman Wang Kunde, the President of the Legislative Yuan Wang Jin-pyng, the Governor of Kaohsiung Yang Chiu-hsing, President of Phoenix Television Liu Changle, representative of the Fo Guang Shan's disciples Wu Poh-hsiung, and many others, totaling fifty thousand people.

2004

01/15 In celebration of the Thai Supreme Patriarch's 90th birthday, the Thai monastic orders gifted nineteen golden Buddha statues to nineteen separate Buddhist countries. The Supreme Patriarch designated Fo Guang Shan as one of the recipients. Princess Maha Chakri Sirindhorn personally oversaw the creation of the statue. Deputy Patriarch Phra Yanvarodom personally delivered it to Fo Guang Shan, where it was welcomed with a public ceremony, celebrating the friendship between southern and northern Buddhist traditions.

03/05 Vice President of the Republic of China Annette Lu visits Fo Guang Shan, attending the "Flowers and Stones Art Exhibition" held at the future location of the Buddha Memorial Center, delivering an offering of flowers to the golden Buddha statue from Thailand. In the afternoon, she met with Venerables Hsin Ting, Hui Chuan, Yung Guang, Man Qian, and Man Zhou at the Mazhu Garden.

2005

Aurora Group Chairman Chen Yung-tai and his wife Chen Pai Yuye donate one hundred and twenty-five artifacts that they've accumulated over the course of twenty years to the Buddha Memorial Center. In 2011, they would donate nine more artifacts.

2009

02/25 Fo Guang Shan's annual devotees conferences is held for the first time at the Buddha Memorial Center area.

03/20 Work on the eight pagodas begins.

09/09   Tongdo Monastery in South Korea presents a golden monastic robe to Fo Guang Shan, escorted by a hundred monastics and devotees to Taiwan. The monastics line up to greet this procession, standing in two lines from the Bodhi road all the way to the main shrine, where a celebration to welcome this gift is held. This is the culmination of the twenty-seven year long bond the two temples have formed.

10/10   Work begins on the Front Hall.

11/25   One hundred and twenty employees from the companies contracted to construct the Buddha Memorial Center make their vows and make copies of the sutra, praying for success in the project.

12/25   The Buddha Memorial Center receives permission to begin construction from the Kaohsiung County. The site is designated as five stories above ground, one story below ground, and consisting of one building populated by one family. The address is Dashu District No 1. Ling Tong Rd, No 2.

2010	

01/04   A press conference is held regarding the Buddha Memorial Center's Underground Palaces. This was held at Fo Guang Shan's Tathagarta Hall, overseen by Venerable Hui Chuan.

02/14-18   The five-day long ceremony of interment of artifacts into the Underground Palaces begins. On February 16th, the third day, Venerable Master Hsing Yun, President Ma Ying-Jeou, UN representative Roth and his wife, as well as the National Woman's League Chairperson Cecilia Koo hosted the event. Special guests for this event include Premier of the Executive Yuan Wu Dun-yih, President of the Legislative Yuan Wang Jin-pyng, Republic of China Honorary President Wu Po-hsiung Buddha's Light International Association ROC Chapter, as well as Kaohsiung County Governor Yang Chiu-Hsing.

03/01   For the purification ceremony for the foundations of the Fo Guang Big Buddha, Venerables Hsin Pei, Hui Yi, and Hui Ren led 300 monastics in chanting the Great Compassion Dharani as they sprinkled the ground with blessed Dharma water.

04/22   Led by deputy governor Ye Nanming, over a thousand monastics and devotees from Kaohsiung country visited the Buddha Memorial Center, taking a commemorative picture at the "Photo Terrace". Included in the picture is former Kaohsiung Buddhist Society Chairman and World Chinese Buddhist Sangha Congress CEO Venerable Xin Mao, Bureau of Civil Affairs Head of Religious Customs Cai Zhenkun, Yuantong Temple's Venerable Hui Zhen, Prajna Academy's Venerable Yue Ding, Chengqing Temple's Venerable Zong Dao, Xinglong Chan Temples Venerable Xin Chun, Fa Yuan Temple's Venerable Yi Ding, and Zhaoyuan Temple's Venerable Rong Cheng.

09/03   During the 2010 Fo Guang Shan Seminar for Taiwan and Foreign Disciples, Venerable Master began the "Disciple and Master Mind-to-Mind Lecture" segment at the "Photo Terrace" of the Buddha Memorial Center.

09/22   During the Mid-Autumn Festival, every member of Fo Guang Shan gathered at the Bodhi Wisdom Concourse to listen to Venerable Master Hsing Yun's instructions.

10/03   Founder of Fo Guang Shan Venerable Master Hsing Yun is invited to host the "Buddha's Light International Association 2010 General Conference and Underground Palace Artifact Internment Ceremony," along with Fo Guang Shan Religious Affairs Committee Chairperson Venerable Hsin Pei, Merit Times Publisher Venerable Hsin Ting, Venerable Hui Chi, Venerable Hui Seng, Venerable Hui Ji, Venerable Hui Ren, Venerable Hui Fu, and Venerable Hui Dao. Members of BLIA from across the globe came, numbering nearly ten-thousand as they gathered on the Bodhi Wisdom Concourse.

12/12   The Fo Guang Shan "Waterland Dharma Service" is held for the first time at the Buddha Memorial Center. The ceremony is closed at the Bodhi Wisdom Concourse.

12/27   Every monastic at Fo Guang Shan comes to the Buddha Memorial Center to clean and prepare for the Chinese New Years Lantern Festival for Peace.

2011

01/01   The Camphor Grove Tea House opens to the public.

02/02   The permanent exhibit where of Venerable Master Hsing Yun's famous One Stroke Calligraphy are put on display at the Six Perfections Pagoda. The site also introduces the "Venerable Master Hsing Yun's Public Trust Fund" to visitors.

02/02   The eighteen arhat statues are placed, including the first three female arhats in the world: Mahaprajapati, Utpalavanna, and Bhadra Kapilani Bhiksunis.

02/03-   During Fo Guang Shan's Chinese New Year Lantern Festival of Peace, the
03/04   Buddha Memorial Center transforms into a sea of flowers as every member of the temple contributed to transplanting millions of chrysanthemums, begonias, lavenders and many more. One individual commented, "Taipei may have its flower exhibits, but Fo Guang Shan has a sea of flowers" at the sight.

02/04-   The second "Underground Palace Artifact Internment Ceremony" is held at
08   the Bodhi Wisdom Concourse.

02/15 World-renowned Cirque du Soleil singer Isabelle Corradi delivers an early morning performance at the Buddha Memorial Center. Moved by the dignity of the building and the harmonious spirit of the monastic workers there, she performed the Italian pieces "Respire" and "Lona", amongst others songs.

02/24 The Venerable Master Hsing Yun guides Association for Relations Across the Taiwan Straits Chairman Chen Yunlin and his members of his Economy and Trade consultant group and Straits Exchange Foundation on a tour through the Buddha Memorial Center.

03/27 Fo Guang Shan and Buddha's Light International Association holds a major Dharma ceremony for Japan in the aftermath of the 2011 Tohoku earthquake. Venerable Hsin Pei and nine other venerable masters lead two hundred monastics and tens of thousands of lay believers in prayer.

04/04 Fo Guang Shan Anle Temple at Taitung County, Beinan Mountain donates eighty-year-old Mahogany and Camphor trees. The two trees are successfully transplanted on April 1st.

04/10 Taiwan Semiconductor Manufacturing Company Limited CEO Morris Chang and his wife Sophia Chang Shu-fen auction off her own paintings in a charity art sale, sending the donations to the Buddha Memorial Center.

04/15 The first layer of the outer shell of the Fo Guang Big Buddha is laid.

04/24 The National Palace Museum reveals the Dragon Canon, the "greatest canon produced by the Qing Empires," compiled in Tibetan by over a hundred specialists over the course of twenty-five years. President Zhao Junzhen of Long-Kuang Digital Culture Co., Ltd, the publishing company, personally travels to Fo Guang Shan to deliver the first copy. Venerable Tzu Hui, the chosen representative of Fo Guang Shan, receives the text, introducing another priceless treasure to the world.

06/01 Work begins on the Banyan Grove Tea House.

06/01 Work begins on the Fo Guang Tower.

06/11 A ceremony commemorating the laying of the first steel beams of the Fo Guang Big Buddha is held. Led by Venerable Hsin Pei, monastics and laypeople alike come to pray for the Buddha's blessing.

08/02 The four-month long "Buddha Memorial Center Employee Training Classes" begin. Nearly a hundred participants attend.

08/17   In collaboration with Fo Guang Shan, the Taiwan Bonsai Association holds the "Taiwan Bonsai Association 2011 Exhibit" at the Five Harmonies Pagoda. Bonsai artists across the country come, bringing hundreds of specimens of their works.

08/20-23   A Vegetarian Food Exhibit is held at the Buddha Memorial Center's Front Hall. The ceremony was hosted by Venerable Master Hsing Yun, Kaohsiung City deputy mayor Li Yongde, and Pingtung County deputy governor Zhong Jiabin. The following day, former vice president Annette Lu and Kaohsiung County Governor Yang Chiu-hsing visited the Vegetarian Food Exhibit. The four-day Vegetarian Food Exhibit lasted four days. 150,000 guests attended.

08/23   Fo Guang Shan celebrates the hundredth anniversary of the People's Republic of China at the Bodhi Wisdom Concourse, praying for peace. Attendees include President Ma Ying-jeou, Premier of Executive Yuan Wu Dun-Yih, President of Legislative Yuan Wang Jin-pyng, Nobel prize winner Song Kosal, founder of Fo Guang Shan Venerable Master Hsing Yun, as well as representative of every major religion. Over thirty thousand people attended, praying for love and peace on earth.

08/28   Statues of the eight patriarchs of Chinese Buddhist Schools are placed.

09/02   Work begins on the Buddha Memorial Center mountain gate.

10/08/2011 – 01/20/2012   Hundreds of artists participate in drawing the Buddha Memorial Center.

11/04-12-22   In celebration of the completion of the Buddha Memorial Center, the 2011 "International Triple Platform Full Ordination Ceremony" is begun. Five hundred monastics from America, Canada, Malaysia, Indonesia, Thailand, Sri Lanka, Taiwan, and other countries attended. Founder of Fo Guang Shan Venerable Master Hsing Yun served as the Sila Upadhyaya, Merit Times Publisher Venerable Hsin Ting served as the Precept Instructing Acaryi, abbot of Qingde Temple Venerable Hui Long served as Karma Acaryi, abbot of Fo Guang Shan Venerable Hsin Pei served as Instructing Acaryi, In addition, eminent monastics from overseas and Taiwan were invited to be Witness Acaryas, and ten acaryanis as Witnessing Acaryanis of the Bhikuni Division. Together, they served as instructors of sutras, teachings, vinaya, and liturgies, as well as witnessing monastics for all the participants.

11/22   One of the many activities held in celebration of the opening of the Buddha Memorial Center, the 2011 Beauty of the Buddha's Light Photography Contest, receives a thousand five-hundred and thirty submission from Taiwan, New Zealand, and Hong Kong. Chen Wei-sen's submission, "Quiet Contemplation", won first place. Lin Youlin and Han Shengbin's submissions "King of Beasts" and "Sacred Land" respectively won second place. Dai Zurong, Wu Zhendong, and Kang Mingya shared third place.

12/01-22   In celebration of the Buddha Memorial Center Inauguration, a nationwide alms round was conducted by the monastics in conjunction with the "Buddha's Relic Nationwide Tour – Peace for All People."

12/10   The three shrines the Avalokisesvara Shrine, the Golden Buddha Shrine, and the Jade Buddha Shrine, as well as the four permanent exhibits, the Museum of the Life of the Buddha, the Museum of Buddhist Underground Palaces, the Museum of Buddhist Festivals, and the Historical Museum of Fo Guang Shan are completed in the Main Hall.

12/25   Opening ceremony of the exhibition halls in the Main Hall of the Buddha Memorial Center.

12/26   Thousands of monastics and tens of thousands of devotees gather to welcome the Buddha's tooth relic.

12/27   Day of the Buddha Memorial Center Completion Ceremony.

12/28   Day of the Buddha Memorial Center Grand Opening Ceremony.

12/28-29   "The Biography of Buddha, Prince Siddhartha" musical performance is held in the Great Enlightenment Auditorium of the Buddha Memorial Center.

12/29   The "Million Copies of the *Heart Sutra* Joining the Dharma Body Internment Ceremony" is held at the Bodhi Wisdom Concourse.

12/30   Blessing are given for the donors for construction of the Buddha Memorial Center and Overseas and Domestic Benefactors; A Yogacara Dharma Service is held to commemorate the Completion of the Buddha Memorial Center.

12/31   In addition to the grand opening of the Buddha Memorial Center, the Buddhist Wedding Ceremony, Triple Gem Refuge and Five Precepts Ceremony, and Ten-thousand People Light-offering Ceremony are all held on this day.

2012

01/01   On the same day the Buddha's tooth relic is enshrined, the Oath Taking Ceremony for the establishment of Buddha's Light Family is held, and the International Triple Platform Full Ordination Ceremony is completed.

Special Thanks

To these photographers:

Fo Guang Shan, Buddha Memorial Center, Venerable Hui Yan:

4, 21, 24, 26, 27, 31, 32, 35, 39, 43, 45, 51, 52, 55, 57, 59, 61, 63, 64, 69, 75, 77, 81, 89, 91, 94, 95, 97, 105, 107, 114, 117, 119, 120, 122, 123 (Left), 129, 137, 145, 146 (Center), 150 (Center), 151 (Upper Right), 153, 155, 159, 163, 165, 171, 176, 177 (Lower Left), 179, 183, 189, 193, 205, 211, 219, 222, 223, 227, 232, 237, 238, 245, 246, 249, 254, 257, 265, 276, 279, 285, 288, 291, 294, 299, 306, 309, 311

Merit Times: 22

Venerable Jing Xu: 53, 185, 187

Cai Rong Feng: 8, 66, 113, 229, 316

Chen Biyun:

99, 138, 139, 141, 201 (Center Right), 221, 235, 242, 259, 260, 280, 299

Tao Fanzhen: 168, 202, 250, 272

Xiang Qiu Ping: 201 (Top, Lower Left)

Jiang Lihua: 275

Li Yunpei, Photographe indépendant:

2, 6, 28, 37, 41, 42, 47, 71, 85 (Center Right, Lower Right), 93, 101, 103, 109, 123 (Top Right), 125, 127, 133, 135, 146 (Right, Left), 147, 148, 149, 150 (Bottom, Center Top, Top Left), 151 (Top Center, Top Left), 156, 166, 172, 174, 177 (Top, Center, Lower Right), 180, 194, 195, 196, 207, 209, 213, 214, 224, 240, 263, 266, 271, 287, 302

Dreamstime.com :

Yemeky (85 Top Left), Alexei Gridenko (85 Center Left), Michael Eurek 85 (Top Right), Martha Bayona (85 Lower Left), Jessica Fitzel (201 Center Left), Ronalon thed Manera (201 Lower Right), Jinyoung Lee (313 Top Two on the Right), Vladimir Ivanov (313 Lower Right), Hans Slegers (313 Top Two on the Left), Kheng Guan Toh (313 Lower Left), Timothy Mingee (313 Top Three on the Right), Darrin Aldridge (313 Top Three on the Left), Tatiana nikolaevna Kalashnikova (313 Top Right), Samuel Wang (313 Top Left), Jianbinglee (313 Top Two in the Middle)

Glossary

Agamas: Also known as the Nikayas in the Pali Canon; they include the Long Discourses, the Middle Length Discourses, the Connected Discourses, and the Gradual Discourses of the Buddha.

Amitabha Buddha: The Buddha of boundless light and boundless life. Amitabha is one of the most popular Buddhas for devotion among Mahayana Buddhists. He presides over the Pure Land of Ultimate Bliss"

Amitabha Sutra: (Amito Jing 阿彌陀經) Sutra in which Sakyamuni Buddha describes the vows and accomplishments of Amitabha Buddha, including his creation of the Pure Land of Ultimate Bliss. The Sutra is commonly chanted and serves as the foundation of the Pure Land School

Arhat: An advanced Buddhist practitioner who has completely eliminated all afflictions and passions forever. Statues of eighteen arhats such disciples from the time of the Buddha are located at the Buddha Memorial Center.

Asoka: Asoka the Great (304-232 BCE) was a Buddhist monarch of the Mauryan Empire, and the first to unite the region we now know as India. Asoka sponsored many Buddhist missions to other countries, and is largely responsible for Buddhism spreading throughout Asia. He is considered a model for Buddhist kingship.

Aurora Group: A manufacturer of office furniture, communications, and electronics, the Aurora Group is a major brand of the Office Automation industry in Taiwan and China. The group has also made major contributions to culture and public, including donations to the Buddha Memorial Center.

Avalokitesvara Bodhisattva: The bodhisattva of compassion, whose name in Sanskrit means "Observing the sounds of the world." He is known as one of the great bodhisattvas of Mahayana Buddhism, and is very popular throughout China and East Asia.

BLIA: The Buddha's Light International Association is a lay Buddhist organization founded in 1991 by Venerable Master Hsing Yun as a way for laypeople to become involved in propagating Humanistic Buddhism. The BLIA serves a variety of social, religious, and charitable functions, and has more than 150 chapters all over the world.

BLTV: Formerly Buddha's Light Television, Beautiful Life Television is a television station founded by Venerable Master Hsing Yun to help spread the spirit of Humanistic Buddhism internationally.

Bodhgaya: Located in the modern day Indian state of Bihar, Bodhgaya is the site of the Buddha's enlightenment. Bodhgaya continues to be a major pilgrimage site for Buddhists around the world.

Bodhi: Enlightenment. In the state of enlightenment, one is awakened to the true nature of self, that is, one is enlightened to one's own Buddha nature. Such a person has already eliminated all afflictions and delusions and has achieved *prajna* wisdom.

Bodhisattva: While the term can describe a practitioner anywhere on the path to Buddhahood, it usually refers to a class of beings who stand on the very edge of full awakening, but remain in the world to help other beings become awakened.

Buddha nature: The capacity to become a Buddha that is inherent to all living beings.

Buddhahood: The attainment and expression that characterizes a Buddha. It is the goal of all beings.

Buddha's tooth relic: A relic taken from the historical Buddha's funeral pyre. Passed down by generations of Buddhists, one such relic is now housed in Taiwan at the Buddha Memorial Center.

Chan: The Chinese transliteration of the Sanskrit term *dhyana*; it refers to meditative concentration. The Chan School is one of the most important of the eight schools of Chinese Buddhism, and emphasizes mind-to-mind transmission of the teachings.

Deer Park: Located near Sarnath in India, the Deer Park is a sacred Buddhist site where the Buddha first taught the Dharma. It is also a major pilgrimage site for Buddhists around the world.

Dharma: The Buddha's teachings, as well as the truth of the universe. When capitalized, it denotes both the ultimate truth and the teachings of the Buddha. When the term appears in lowercase, it refers to anything that can be thought of, experienced, or named; this usage is close in meaning to the concept of "phenomena."

Diamond Sutra: (Jingang Jing 金剛經) Buddhist sutra in which the Venerable Subhuti asks the Buddha a series of questions on emptiness. One of the Prajnaparamita Sutras.

Faxian: A Chinese monk who traveled from China to India to acquire Buddhist texts for translation and tour sacred Buddhist sites. He later wrote a travelogue of his journey called the *Record of Buddhist Kingdoms.*

Five faculties: Five elements of personal character that are essential for spiritual development. They are faith, diligence, mindfulness, meditative concentration, and wisdom.

Five powers: Five spiritual powers that arise from developing the five faculties.

Five precepts: The most fundamental set of Buddhist precepts, or rules of moral conduct, observed by lay and monastic Buddhists alike. They are to refrain from killing, to refrain from stealing, to refrain from sexual misconduct, to refrain from lying, and to refrain from consuming intoxicants.

Flower Adornment Sutra: (*Huayan Jing* 華嚴經) One of the largest and most celebrated sutras in Mahayana Buddhism.

Flower Adornment World: The Pure Land of the Vairocana Buddha, as described in the *Flower Adornment Sutra*. Abiding in the Flower Adornment World also describes a state in which one attains knowledge and vision of how all phenomena are interconnected and dependent upon one another.

Four bases of mindfulness: The four bases of mindfulness allow us to use our mindfulness so that we do not mistake impurity for purity, suffering for happiness, impermanence for permanence, and what has no independent self for something that does. They are: 1. Mindfulness of the Body; 2. Mindfulness of Feelings; 3. Mindfulness of the Mind; and 4. Mindfulness of Phenomena.

Four bases of supernatural power: These are four subjects of concentration which serve as the basis for developing the mind: Desire, diligence, mind, and contemplation.

Four great bodhisattvas: Avalokitesvara Bodhisattva, Mañjusri Bodhisattva, Ksitigarbha Bodhisattva, and Samantabhadra Bodhisattva

Four immeasurable minds: Four immeasurable aspects of the minds of Buddhas and bodhisattvas: immeasurable kindness, immeasurable compassion, immeasurable joy, and immeasurable equanimity.

Four Noble Truths: The basic truths of Buddhism: The truth of suffering, the truth of the origin of suffering, the truth of the cessation of suffering, the truth of the path that leads to the cessation of suffering.

Four universal vows: The four universal vows are made by bodhisattvas on their path to liberate themselves and others. Even today, many Buddhist practitioners make these vows: 1) Sentient beings are limitless, I vow to liberate them. 2) Afflictions are endless, I vow to eradicate them. 3) Teachings are infinite, I vow to learn them. 4) Buddhahood is supreme, I vow to attain it.

Ganges River: The largest river in India, and of extreme religious and cultural significance to Indian religion.

Great Hakuho Temple Revival: The reconstruction of many of the buildings at the Yakushi Temple, built in the Hakuho-era style. This project was made possible thanks to the donations of over a million individuals, through their hand-copied donations of the *Heart Sutra.*

Guanyin: *See* Avalokitesvara Bodhisattva.

Heart Sutra: One of the *Prajnaparamita Sutras*, it contains a short but complete exposition of the Buddha's teaching on emptiness. It is commonly chanted by Buddhists around the world, and is also commonly transcribed as a form of practice.

Hongyi: (1880–1942) Famous master of the Nanshan Vinaya School in Chinese Buddhism. Before joining monkhood, he was a famous artist and musician in contemporary China.

Hsing Yun's Chan Talk: A series of books and articles by Venerable Master Hsing Yun which provide plain language retellings and explanations of famous Chan *gongans*, stories of the enlightened exchanges of Chan masters. The articles were later collected and illustrated as *Chan Heart, Chan Art.* Bas-relief reproductions of these illustrations, called "Chan Art and Stories," currently grace the walls of the Buddha Memorial Center.

Humanistic Buddhism: Buddhism practiced in a way that is engaged with the world and life-affirming. Major tenets include the integration of Buddhism with life and the creation of a "Pure Land on Earth." Venerable Master Hsing Yun is a proponent of Humanistic Buddhism.

Humble Table, Wise Fare: A collection of Venerable Master Hsing Yun's aphorisms modeled after the *Vegetable Root Sayings*, a 16th century collection of Hong Zicheng's morality poems.

Jetavana Grove: A monastery outside of the city of Sravasti donated to the Buddha and his sangha by the Elder Sudatta and Prince Jetakumara. The Buddha spent the rains retreat here more years than in any other monastery.

Jogye Order: Founded in 820 CE, today the Jogye Order is predominant sect of Buddhism in Korea, with over one thousand temples and nine million followers.

Ksitigarbha Bodhisattva: One of the great bodhisattvas of Mahayana Buddhism. Ksitigarbha Bodhisattva has vowed to remain in hell until all sentient beings have been released from it.

Kusinagara: The town in which the Buddha passed away into final nirvana. Today it remains a sacred pilgrimage site for Buddhists.

Lofty sentiments of Forests and Springs: (Linquan Gaozhi 林泉高致) Influential collection of 11th century pastoral poems and landscape paintings by Chinese poet and painter Guoxi.

Lotus mudra: A hand gesture which symbolizes purity and the opening of one's heart.

Lotus Sutra: (Fahua Jing 法華經): Major Mahayana sutra in which the Buddha asserts that all his previous teachings were only provisional teachings designed to lead beings to make the aspiration to become Buddhas.

Maitreya Buddha: The Buddha of the future, associated with loving-kindness. Maitreya Buddha is said to currently reside in Tusita Heaven, awaiting rebirth on earth.

Mañjusri Bodhisattva: The bodhisattva of wisdom.

Medicine Buddha: The Buddha of healing. He presides over the Eastern Pure Land.

Mudra: Mudras are gestures, primarily of the hands, that have symbolic meanings in Buddhism and Hinduism.

Nirvana: A state of perfect tranquility that is the ultimate goal of Buddhist practice. It refers to the absolute extinction of all afflictions and desires; it is the state of liberation beyond birth and death.

Nalanda: Ancient Buddhist university located near modern day Bajgir, India. Before being destroyed in the 11th century, it was the largest university in India, and became the center of Yogacara and Tantric Buddhism.

Noble Eightfold Path: The path leading to enlightenment taught by the Buddha. It includes right view, right thought, right speech, right action, right livelihood, right effort, right mindfulness, and right meditative concentration.

Non-self: A basic concept in Buddhism which asserts that all phenomena and beings in the world have no real, permanent, and substantial self. Everything arises, abides, changes, and extinguishes based on dependent origination.

One million copies of the Heart Sutra joining the Dharma Body: Campaign launched by Venerable Master Hsing Yun during the construction of the Buddha Memorial Center with the goal of having one million people transcribe the *Heart Sutra*.

One stroke calligraphy: Style of calligraphy preferred by Venerable Master Hsing Yun, in which all the characters in the piece are completed in one continuous stroke of the brush.

Palm-leaf Buddhist Sutra: An ancient and fragile form of manuscript used in South Asia since the 5th century BCE in which writing is etched upon dried palm leaves. Burmese palm-leaf manuscripts in particular are noted for their ornate layout and appearance.

Prajnaparamita Sutra: A group of Buddhist sutras including the *Heart Sutra* and *Diamond Sutra* in which the Buddha gives especially profound teachings on the nature of emptiness and existence.

Prajna Sutra: *See* Prajnaparamita Sutra

Protection for Living Beings: (Husheng Huaji 護生畫集) An album of painting drawn by famed Chinese cartoonist Feng Zikai. It was one of his most defining works, a long-term project that spanned forty-six years. The images promote the protection of sentient beings and the sanctity of life.

Pure Rules of Baizhang: (Baizhang Qinggui 百丈清規) An influential collection of early rules of discipline and decorum for Chan monasteries written by the Tang dynasty Chan Master Baizhang Huaihai.

Record on Dharma Abiding: (Fazhu Ji 法住記) Buddhist text which lists the classical eighteen arhats.

Sakyamuni Buddha: Siddhartha Gotama, the historical Buddha and founder of the religion we know today. The name "Sakyamuni" means "Sage of the Sakyans," which was the name of the Buddha's clan.

Samantabhadra Bodhisattva: One of the great bodhisattvas of Mahayana Buddhism, and one of the four most revered bodhisattvas of Chinese tradition.

Seven factors of enlightenment: The factors that lead to enlightenment: mindfulness, investigation of dharmas, diligence, joyfulness, ease of body and mind, concentration, and equanimity.

Six perfections: The six perfections are the six things that bodhisattvas seek to perfect in order to realize the bodhisattva path and become Buddhas: Giving, morality, patience, diligence, meditative concentration, and *prajna* wisdom.

Sravasti: A city in ancient India where many of the Buddha's discourses are said to have taken place.

Sutra on Cause and Effect through Three Time Periods: (Sanshi Yinguo Jing 三世因果經) Buddhist sutra which lists the various karmic effects of wholesome and unwholesome deeds. Selections from the sutra are engraved on the Benefactor's Wall at the Buddha Memorial Center.

Sutra on the Life Stories of the Buddha: (Fo Benxing Ji Jing 佛本行集經) Sutra which collects stories of the virtuous conduct of the Buddha in his previous lives. Selections from the sutra are engraved on the Benefactor's Wall at the Buddha Memorial Center.

Three Acts of Goodness Campaign: Campaign organized by Venerable Master Hsing Yun to encourage people to do good deeds, speak good words, and keep good thoughts.

Thirty-seven factors of enlightenment: A group of some of the Buddha's main teachings, organized in several lists: the four bases of mindfulness, the four right efforts, the four bases of supernatural power, the five faculties, and five powers, the seven factors of enlightenment, and the Noble Eightfold Path.

Three National Legacies: (Sanguo Yishi 三國遺事) Collection of Korean history, legends, and folktales.

Thus have I Heard: Phrase which begins the vast majority of Buddhist sutras. It signifies that the proper conditions were present for the Buddha's teaching to be given, understood, and preserved.

Dependent Origination: The Buddhist concept that all phenomena arise due to causes and conditions; thus, no phenomena possesses an independent self-nature. This concept is also referred to as interdependence. The twelve links of dependent origination are ignorance, mental formations, consciousness, name and form, the six sense organs, contact, feeling, craving, clinging, becoming, birth, and aging and death.

Ullambana Sutra: (Yulanpen Jing 盂蘭盆經) A sutra in which the Buddha instructs his disciple Maudgalyayana on how he can ease the suffering of his mother, who has been reborn in the realm of hungry ghosts.

University of the West: University founded by Venerable Master Hsing Yun in 1991 in Rosemead, California. The university offers graduate and undergraduate programs in business, English, psychology, and religious studies.

Venerable Master Hsing Yun Public Education Trust Fun: A trust fund founded by Venerable Master Hsing Yun, funded by charity auctions held for his works of one stroke calligraphy.

Vulture Peak: A hill overlooking the city of Rajagrha where the Buddha would often deliver teachings.

Water Drop teahouses: Teahouses located in Fo Guang Shan branch temples around the world. The name signifies repaying a single drop of kindness with a gushing stream of generosity.

Way: In a Buddhist context, used to refer to the path of Buddhist practice. To "attain the Way" is synonymous with enlightenment.

World Fellowship of Buddhists: An international Buddhist organization, established to help promote unity amongst Buddhists, facilitate the propagation of the Dharma, and work for the happiness, harmony, and peace of all sentient beings.

Xizhai Pure Land Poems: (Xizhai Jingtu Shi 西齋淨土詩) Collection of poems by 14th century monastic Master Fanqi Chushi which describe and celebrate the Pure Land.

Xuanzang: Prolific Chinese Buddhist translator who traveled to India to recover Buddhist sutras. The events of his pilgrimage were fictionalized into the classic Chinese novel *Journey to the West*.

Yakushi Temple: Japanese temple that was extensively damaged by a fire in 1528 CE. A campaign to restore is started in 1967, based around the transcription of the *Heart Sutra*. It inspired Fo Guang Shan's own "One Million Copies of the *Heart Sutra* Joining the Dharma Body" movement.

Yogacara Flaming Mouth Dharma Service: (Yuqie Yanko 瑜伽燄口) A Buddhist service in which gifts of food, goods, and Dharma teachings are offered to beings living in the realms of hungry ghosts and hell beings to help relieve their suffering.

Buddha Land in the Human World Donors

300-200 Copies

IBPS Hsi Lai Temple, Chung Mei Buddhist Temple, IBPS North Carolina, IBPS Toronto, 項雷、三寶弟子。

199-100 Copies

FGS Guam, Vancouver IBPS, Light of Buddha Temple, Guang Ming Temple, IBPS Holland, Shih-Hou Lin, Yueh Chin Hsu Wang, Jia Pier Wang, Yueh Chin Echo Tsai, 奧克蘭佛光寺眾信徒、羅幼水、黃少玲、吳羅錦繡。

99-50 Copies

IBPS Dallas, IBA Arizona, IBPS Paraguay, IBPS Belgium, IBPS New York, San Bo Temple, ABCS-Fremont, IBPS Sacramento, BLIA Prague, Kimberly Ann Gau, 劉美足。

49-20 Copies

IBPS Rose Hills Buddhist Columbarium, IBPS Montreal, IBPS Switzerland, Geneva Conference Center of Buddhism, BLIA-Irvine Subchapter, Griffyn Loang-En Cheng, Rebecca Chiu, Betty Husodo.
依如法師、永全法師、滿敬法師、妙地法師、妙藏法師、妙佑法師、胡順發、胡林菊、張鳳琴、葛樹華、林淑娟、吳錦鑾、黃曉君、呂秋宏、俞孟貞、馮凱、李秀。

19-10 Copies

IBPS Miami, Nan Tien Temple, Liyu Lash, Anna H. Wang, Esther Man, Louvenia Ortega, Sture Remberger, Donald Lavoie.

依勤法師、覺聖法師、覺智法師、覺凡法師、妙西法師、法良法師、林周秀子、沈周秀梅、莊謝綉卿、何秋月、李漢樞、梁沁淼、林梅燕、李梅玉、余娟妤、陳建設、蔣偉山、高瑞玉、王煊亭、黃襄宏、黃瑞菊、王小華、楊麗瓊、羅錦泉、林梅鳳、梁瑞蓉、孔繁熹、孔繁進、張合梅、莊煥章、陳玉桂、黃少芬、葉胡薇、謝珍、陳玉、段豔。

9-4 Copies

Chueh Yann Shih, Michelle Remberger, Peier Lawrence, Ken Holloway, Quang Hang, Lily Tseng, Julie Chung, Henry Hjärre, Kristina Choi, Leon Liao, Wendy Har, Karalambos Athanesiadis, Sheena Tan, Lyon Tan, Eugene Tan, Ejda Isaksson, Stefan Gagner, Benjamin Lundh, Sunny Chang, Wang Liang Wah Alan.

覺仲法師、妙度法師、心演法師、心苑法師、心嶺法師、心員法師、謝陳秀蘭、崔許輕梅、王洪麗華、歐陽王枝、歐陽滋遠、梁陳佩雲、宮下光泰、梁民里道、陳美珠、羅光国、劉真武、徐海蓁、李之英、劉綺華、吳美惠、蔡淑淑、曹笑蓮、趙玉枝、劉翠玉、沈泓安、黃淑雅、李明香、林映惜、黃亞嬌、劉秀珠、文達強、周映芬、黎曉彤、王蓓琳、王歡歡、王樂翰、余淑茶、楊昌陵、楊昌能、王文炳、吳玉燕、蕭足妹、黃秀琴、熊衛鋼、戴育仁、黃進益、蔡麗香、裴海蒂、簡婷婷、簡斌斌、何祖隆、胡安安、胡倩倩、朱美玲、韓燕梅、蘇秀珍、蘇秀愛、吳來鉋、楊志雄、林美玲、楊珮玲、邱鈺雯、蘇月梅、滕陽洋、朱賢泓、莊杏珠、鐘秀蘭、陳明正、牛淑華、田麗園、陳嵐溪、張愛萍、李夢蘭、張思超、王月嬌、陳玉秀、楊少萍、潘文卿、羅愛花、羅愛香、胡宗南、黃愛琴、

吳彩慧、吳清標、李玉針、洪綺綸、黃家昌、黃家輝、陳潔蓉、郭俊明、
杜季宣、陳志威、陳志昇、王碧君、陳語行、陳俊英、王佩玲、杜尚烈、
李惟珊、曾慶嵐、陳潔心、楊正妃、盧志森、潘建良、麥秀雲、潘慧敏、
潘慧珊、潘俊宏、史寶玉、李堅、朱蔚、朱瑩、胡捷、蕭凡、劉珍。

3 Copies

Carol Yi Yu Zhang, Tiange Fan, Rachel Xu, Helena Huang, Hwei Wen Ling,
Steve Kuo, Edward Ling, Roselynn Lee, Howard Lee, Meagan lee, Erika Lee,
Sharisse Lee, Kaitlyn Lee, Yin-Hing C. Wong, Allison Lee, Vivian Stupp,
Bryant Chandra Kwok, Nathan Chandra Kwok, Kavika Huan, Wicky.

滿弘法師、妙導法師、林陳雲香、松井桂子、周陳美惠、歐陽慧峰、
歐陽慧盈、吳有浙、林緄俊、林明湖、林季葦、林雨璇、陳巧静、
金普明、梁鈺銘、張再齡、容約源、張珊芝、符從文、葉秀亮、葉秀鳳、
葉倫煜、蘇家鋒、翁小明、許宸瑋、李偉和、戴小惠、余含章、張丙木、
吳鴻來、王安平、許珍蓉、章德新、石佩华、黃愷嘉、陳宝治、劉瓊霙、
林香玉、林慧萍、董慧君、段莘康、黃振瑋、洪佩蓮、黃裕文、黃溫仁、
李麗華、黃藤福、蔣錦霞、余妙芸、余殊萍、吳柏賢、吳佳頤、黃柏睿、
梁淑賢、梁子健、顏邑安、明義騰、明義軒、周愉絜、周愉純、熊楊艷、
熊雅慧、熊瑞陽、章译心、王亦基、張雅富、陳玲玲、陳皇絮、張樑溪、
留婉婉、徐猶正、呂德英、黃世賢、項斯中、高王蕾、林静珍、簡美玲、
江寶猜、江寶真、樊國基、樊國維、樊國銘、文國榮、文國堅、文珈欣、
鄧葵喜、詹愛琴、李天寶、康恩俊、楊宪竹、黃明達、杜偉南、史寶英、
劉瑋真、林永豐、周彥博、周佳瑩、鄧志安、章錦、章典、李琳、熊迪、
林軍、谷劍。

2-1 Copies

Huynh Steven, Huynh Michael, Vi Wong, Hannah Wong.
慧浩法師、永傑法師、永亮法師、滿蓮法師、滿灯法師、覺是法師、
妙傑法師、心因法師、如眾法師、妙曇法師、龔陳碧如、何氏玉銀、
朱蘇珊娜、簡楊麗霞、簡志達、簡鳳儀、李愛梅、陳春笑、朱八英、
夏厚祉、陳識因、楊琇雅、楊琇慈、周海燕、孔令宇、孔祥泰、吳佳芳、
莊心如、蔡培華、張錦元、黃偉中、陳彥甫、周嘉慧、周愈施、譚祖蔭、
余联明、陳瓊瑩、白昭鳳、詹絲蓉、王秀美、胡台東、宮台華、李天恩、
李旻哲、李旻原、蘇冰冰、林綾穎、吳亞則、吳宇辰、宋志炬、林錦華、
萬小平、林穎鴻、林穎涵、林擇强、林衍鋮、陳永光、陳永明、陳永興、
陳永華、陳錦雄、陳炳文、黃統義、黃美雪、羅愛民、曾寶珠、羅愛亮、
李運蓮、羅愛森、陳子蕙、薛萬發、薛彥平、石麗香、石智明、武春明、
張雪蓮、陳志祥、陳悅華、朱騫頡、朱騫進、朱冠冠、劉艳紅、董小娥、
蔣維益、程正玲、王張罔、王興隆、王秀如、王朝清、王秀純、王俊達、
彭瑞玲、盧姿伶、方美芳、孔健、李潔、龐勇、何茹、朱德。

Thank you to all who donated to help support the printing and distribution of this book.